ENGAGING ENEMIES

ENGAGING ENEMIES

Hayek and the Left

Simon Griffiths

ROWMAN & LITTLEFIELD
INTERNATIONAL
London • New York

Published by Rowman & Littlefield International, Ltd.
Unit A, Whitacre Mews, 26–34 Stannery Street, London SE11 4AB, United Kingdom
www.rowmaninternational.com

Rowman & Littlefield International, Ltd. is an affiliate of Rowman & Littlefield
4501 Forbes Boulevard, Suite 200, Lanham, Maryland 20706, USA
With additional offices in Boulder, New York, Toronto (Canada), and London (UK)
www.rowman.com

British Library Cataloguing in Publication Information Available
A catalogue record for this book is available from the British Library

ISBN: HB 978-1-78348-106-4
ISBN: PB 978-1-78348-107-1
ISBN: eB 978-1-78348-108-8

Library of Congress Cataloging-in-Publication Data

Griffiths, Simon, 1976–
Engaging enemies : Hayek and the left / Simon Griffiths.
pages cm
Includes bibliographical references and index.
ISBN 978-1-78348-106-4 (cloth : alk. paper)—ISBN 978-1-78348-107-1 (pbk. : alk. paper)—ISBN 978-1-78348-108-8 (electronic)
1. Great Britain—Economic policy—20th century. 2. Hayek, Friedrich A. von (Friedrich August), 1899–1992. 3. Socialism—Great Britain. 4. Neoliberalism—Great Britain. 5. Liberalism. I. Title.
HC256.G75 2014
330.092—dc23
2014023928

Printed in the United States of America

For Iris: something to chew on.

CONTENTS

ACKNOWLEDGEMENTS

This book would not have been completed without the support of many people. I would particularly like to thank Rodney Barker for his unfailing and good-humoured support. John Gray also provided a valuable and enthusiastic source of advice. In addition, Tony Giddens taught me a great deal whilst carrying out research for him in the early stages of this project. Matt Beech, Marc Calvini-Lefebvre, Charlie Ellis, Beth Foley, Michael Freeden, Andrew Gamble, Paul Gunn, Dan Greenwood, Kevin Hickson, Paul Kelly, Carl Levy, Raymond Plant and three anonymous referees were kind enough to comment on all or part of this project. Many insightful remarks—the significance of which was often lost on me until sometime afterwards—have also been made along the way. I would also like to thank Louise Thomas for her support. Errors and omissions remain my own.

This book was partly written whilst a Visiting Research Fellow at the Centre for Political Ideologies in Oxford, which provided a conducive environment in which to work. I would also like to acknowledge the support of the ESRC for a studentship (PTA-030-2003-00029), which made the original research on which this book is based possible. I am grateful to the publishers for permission to incorporate aspects of the following previously published material:

- 'Pluralism, Neo-liberalism and the 'All-knowing' state.' *Journal of Political Ideologies*, 16 (3), 2011. Available from: www.tandf online.com.

- 'New Labour, New Liberalism and Revisionism's Second Wave', Simon Griffiths and Kevin Hickson (eds.), *British Political Parties and Ideology After New Labour* (Basingstoke: Palgrave Macmillan, 2010).
- 'Comrade Hayek' or the revival of liberalism? Andrew Gamble's engagement with the work of Friedrich Hayek, *Journal of Political Ideologies*, 12 (2), 2007. Available from: www.tandfonline.com.
- 'Market socialism in retrospect', *Contemporary Politics*, 12 (1), March 2006. Available from: www.tandfonline.com.

1

HAYEK AND THE LEFT

A paradoxical claim?

Between the fall of the Berlin Wall and New Labour's election in the United Kingdom, the political economist Andrew Gamble wrote that 'Hayek has much to contribute to the renewal of the socialist project'.[1] Gamble's claim is surprising. Friedrich Hayek dedicated most of his long life to fighting socialism, declaring in the late 1970s that it was 'high time for us to cry from the rooftops that the intellectual foundations of socialism have all collapsed'.[2] Hayek was an important influence on the new right and on senior figures in the British Conservative Party. Margaret Thatcher praised the 'powerful critique of socialist planning and the socialist state'[3] found in his 1944 book, *The Road to Serfdom*. Waving his later tome, *The Constitution of Liberty*, published in 1960, Thatcher is said to have told an audience, '*This* is what we believe'.[4]

While Gamble's attempt to claim elements of Hayek's work for the left at the end of the twentieth century was relatively rare, it was not unique. In 1994 Hilary Wainwright, the founding editor of the radical left-wing magazine *Red Pepper*, argued that 'Reading Hayek' should 'contribute to new foundations for the left'.[5] In fact, from the late 1980s onwards several authors produced left-wing reinterpretations of Hayek's work. For some on the left, the engagement with Hayek was limited to a tentative discussion of arguments that were closely associated with him—such as his case for the market and against socialist planning. For others, the engagement involved a thorough and careful investigation of his work. In this book I focus on the work of four thinkers on the left who engaged significantly in different ways with Hayek's ideas: David Miller, Raymond Plant, Hilary Wainwright and Andrew Gamble. I look at how their different attempts to reinvent the left are influenced by that engagement.

This book is an attempt to explain the unusual engagement with Hayek, and to reflect upon its significance. I argue that what these authors were doing is worth examining for several reasons. First, the engagement provides one example of how ideologies change, and particularly the importance of enmity and context in shaping and transforming ideology. The various authors discussed here were responding in different ways to common contextual shifts: the perceived failure of the Keynesian consensus, the electoral success of Thatcherism and the collapse of 'actually existing' socialism after 1989. These events led to a period of re-evaluation on the left. The engagement with Hayek only occurred with the collapse of the relationships of enmity that dominated political thought for much of the twentieth century: the divisions between socialism and communism; planning and markets; and the Soviet Union and the United States, for example.

Second, the engagement with Hayek provides a case study that allows reflection on the fate of socialism. Did socialism survive the twentieth century? Did it collapse as Hayek claimed? Or did it transform into something else, and if so what? I argue that the authors examined in this book are part of a wider transformation of socialist thought. This has occurred as a result of a wide variety of new engagements, re-evaluations and new discoveries—the engagement with Hayek was just part of this larger story. Taken together, however, by the end of the twentieth century socialism had ceased to exist in the forms that had been dominant earlier that century, which were statist and paternalist. Socialism now largely survives as part of a hybrid ideology—its components found, for example, in liberal, pluralist or feminist varieties. In the conclusion, I reflect on the broader fate of socialism in the early twenty-first century.

Third, the debate about ideological change raises questions about historical periodization: was the engagement with Hayek part of a wider end to a long period of political thought? Was there an ideological continuity in the twentieth century that did not survive its ending? The thinkers examined in this book offer a variety of attempts to rethink the left. They reject the forms of socialism that had dominated the twentieth century. In doing so, they often draw on libertarian and anti-paternalist themes neglected within mainstream socialist thought or upon aspects of liberalism and pluralism. Often their engagement with Hayek evokes—implicitly or explicitly—debates that were prevalent in the nineteenth and early twentieth centuries. As such, the thinkers discussed here reflect a wider claim: that political thought in Britain at the end of the twentieth century had more in common with debates that had existed eighty years before than it did to discussions from the middle of the twentieth century.

Finally, the engagement with Hayek was significant because it had an influence on party politics, particularly on the 'modernization' of the Labour Party after the electoral failure of 1983 and on the later development of New Labour. The debate also raises wider questions on the role of the market for the left today. In particular, it shows how the left is vulnerable if it bases its strategy on market-led growth, something that has become far clearer since the financial crisis of 2007–2008 and the subsequent global recession.

It is this limited and surprising engagement with Hayek's work, involving only a handful of figures on the left, which provides the thread that runs through the book. Hayek was not the only thinker to undergo a radical reinterpretation at the end of the twentieth century: the British left's engagement with the ideas of the German legal theorist Carl Schmitt—a onetime Nazi—is perhaps more remarkable.[6] (I explore the rediscovery of Schmitt in more detail in the book's final chapter.) Nor was Hayek a lone voice on the right. For example, John Anderson's article, 'The Servile State', published in 1943,[7] anticipated many of the arguments found a year later in Hayek's *The Road to Serfdom*. However, although other fascinating engagements occurred at the end of the twentieth century, there is a more compelling case for examining the engagement by the left with Hayek than there is over any other figure.

First, Hayek was one of the main intellectual inspirations for the changes that occurred in Britain after 1979. His influence on Margaret Thatcher and on the wider Conservative Party has already been noted. Thatcher was explicit on Hayek's influence, arguing that her Secretary of State 'Keith Joseph gave the best political analysis of what was wrong, and what had to change. But behind him lay the wisdom of people like

Friedrich Hayek, bodies like the Institute of Economic Affairs, and a host of thinkers who had swum against the tide of collectivism which at one time threatened to sweep away our national foundations'.[8] As such, for those authors on the left seeking to understand some of the intellectual foundations of Thatcherism and her critique of socialism, Hayek provides the best starting point.

Second, Hayek was rare in the relative consistency of his beliefs throughout his long academic life and as such his work marks a relatively stable point from which to view a changing world. There were changes in emphasis and tone—but from early adulthood until his death there was remarkable steadiness. The political theorist John Gray argued that Hayek's overall consistency means that one should avoid 'periodizing his intellectual career into distinct phases'.[9] Hayek's conclusions were, from early adulthood until his death, consistently against socialism and in favour of a limited state and a free market.

In the first half of this chapter, I give a brief overview of Hayek's life and the reception his arguments received on the left up to the final decade of the twentieth century—a period when in the main part the left only discussed Hayek as a symbol of what they opposed. I then provide a brief outline of the main arguments set out in this book, introducing those thinkers on the left who engaged with Hayek in more detail towards the end of the twentieth century.

Hayek as a straw man

Hayek was eighteen at the time of the Russian Revolution, and lived long enough to see the Soviet Union disintegrate, much to his glee. Hayek was born in 1899 to a wealthy, intellectual family in Vienna. He was old enough to fight during the last months of the First World War, but the experience did not seem to affect him greatly. (He later claimed that his only lasting memory of the conflict was of trying to recapture a bucketful of eels meant for the soldiers' breakfast, which he had knocked over in a dewy field.[10]) Hayek returned to Vienna at the end of the First World War to witness a period of instability: the Austro-Hungarian Empire in which he was born collapsed; there was economic chaos marked by hyperinflation—at one stage Hayek's salary was increased two hundred times in eight months to keep up with prices[11] — and communist revolution seemed a real possibility. Béla Kun led a short-lived Soviet Government in neighbouring Hungary in 1919 and there were several revolts in Vienna. In November 1918 Hayek entered the University of Vienna. His interest was in psychology, but the war had left no one to teach it. Instead he received doctorates in law in 1921 and political science in 1923.[12] He graduated from university the possessor of 'moderate, Fabian socialist views' which were not to survive the next decade of his life.[13]

The most obvious intellectual influence on Hayek's thought in the 1920s was the Austrian economist, Ludwig von Mises (1881–1973). After Hayek's graduation, Mises gave Hayek a civil service position in the temporary government economic office.[14] At the interview Mises commented that he had not seen Hayek at any of his lectures at the University of Vienna. Hayek thought it unwise to reply that he had looked in on them, but had found Mises' views antithetical to his own mild socialism of the time.[15] It was while attending weekly discussion groups in Mises' office that Hayek encountered, and was largely converted to, Mises' critique of socialism, found in its fullest form in Mises' 1922 book, *Socialism: An Economic and Sociological Analysis.*[16]

During the 1920s Hayek became established as an economist. His work was mainly concerned with monetary theory, and between 1929 and 1931 he combined his duties as a civil servant with teaching in economics at the University of Vienna. In 1931 Hayek was invited to lecture in London by the economist Lionel Robbins (1898–1984).[17] Largely on the strength of the lectures, Robbins arranged for Hayek to be appointed Tooke Professor of Economic Science and Statistics at the London School of Economics (LSE) where he remained until 1950. It was during the 1930s that Hayek made the contributions that established his reputation as an economist. He was also to publish work that hinted at the more overtly political and philosophical approach that marked his later work, in particular, his edited collection *Collectivist Economic Planning*, published in 1935. This piece took Hayek towards much wider issues in political thought than his early narrower study of economics allowed.

Hayek became a naturalized British subject in 1938, a few weeks before German forces moved into Austria. (Hayek's British critics stressed his foreign roots, referring to him by his aristocratic Germanic name, 'Friedrich von Hayek'. In later life, particularly after being appointed a Companion of Honour in 1984, he preferred the Anglicized

'Frederick Hayek'.[18] In this book I use 'Friedrich Hayek' as an attempt at neutrality and for consistency with other thinkers.) He would most likely have stayed in London for the rest of his life had not an unpleasant divorce (after which Hayek was cut off by several close friends—including Robbins who hardly spoke to him for almost two decades) led him to take up a position at the University of Chicago. Late in his life, Hayek was to remark that the Reform Club on Pall Mall, which he would visit on the way from his home in Hampstead to LSE, was the 'only real home' he had known for years.[19]

While at LSE, Hayek became friends with John Maynard Keynes (1883–1946). Their friendship is often overlooked given the antagonism of their followers during the post-war period. Keynes' views on Hayek are summed up in a diary entry: 'Hayek has been here for the weekend,' Keynes wrote to his wife, Lydia, in March 1933. 'I sat by him in hall last night and lunched with him at Piero's today'—the Italian economist Piero Sraffa. 'We get on very well in private life. But what rubbish his theory is'.[20] When war was declared in 1939, Hayek was too recently naturalized as British to be called into government service, in contrast to most of his fellow economists. He commented afterwards that working for the government corrupted economists, and war service had won them over to planning.[21] During a stay in wartime London, Hayek joked that he jumped every time the BBC reported the number of 'Hayek-splosives' dropped by the Luftwaffe on the capital.[22] When LSE was evacuated, it was Keynes who arranged for Hayek to take up residence at King's College, Cambridge, so that he could continue his work.

Unlike Hayek's earlier work, *The Road to Serfdom*, published towards the end of the war, was an 'explicitly populist tract'.[23] It brought its author worldwide fame. Most readers probably came to know it through an abridged *Reader's Digest* version, prepared by the former American leftist, Max Eastman, of which over a million copies were distributed through the American Book of the Month Club.[24] It was even distributed in cartoon form by General Motors. Hayek's argument was that democracies risked going the same way as Nazi Germany, because their intellectuals and politicians had fallen for the idea that an economy could be centrally planned, as much of it was in the UK during the war, and that the idea would soon be put into practice in the name of post-war reconstruction. For Hayek, central planning led, via cumulative attempts to mend its inevitable failures, to 'a servile state' (the metaphor is most obviously derived from Hilaire Belloc's 1912 book of that name, although it also owes something to Herbert Spencer and Alexis de Tocqueville). Moreover, attempts at even moderate planning, such as the 'middle way' advocated at the time by the Conservative politician and later Prime Minister Harold Macmillan,[25] would set the democracies on a slippery slope that would end, just as surely, in serfdom. This explains Hayek's dedication of the book 'TO THE SOCIALISTS OF ALL PARTIES'.[26] To Hayek, the free market was not only more efficient economically, but it was also indispensable for a free society.

Hayek began *The Road to Serfdom* with the claim that 'This is a political book', and despite its apparently non-partisan dedication, its reception was shaped by party politics. In 1979, commenting on the book's publication, Hayek noted that 'Some of my more leftish acquaintances (with considerable cheek) gave me to understand that in their opinion I had ceased to be a scientist and had become a propagandist'.[27] Alvin Hansen, the American Keynesian economist, provided one example when he wrote in *The New Republic*, 'This kind of writing is not scholarship. It is seeing hobgoblins under every bed'.[28] The publication of the book, shortly before the 1945 General Election, is said to have influenced Winston Churchill's controversial election broadcast warning of the threat of a 'Gestapo' under socialism.[29] No one who had seen or heard the mild-mannered Labour leader Clement Attlee found the claim particularly convincing. (Churchill himself is—perhaps apocryphally—said to have characterized Attlee as 'a sheep in sheep's clothing'.[30]) After the broadcast, Attlee made a withering reference to Churchill's rehashing of the 'secondhand ideas of an Austrian professor Friedrich von Hayek'.[31]

'In the 1940s', wrote Samuel Brittan, 'Hayek became a hate figure to those on the political left', who overwhelmingly rejected his warnings.[32] Herman Finer described Hayek's book as the 'arsenal of the conservative counter-offensive'[33] and argued that:

> Hayek's *The Road to Serfdom* constitutes the most sinister offensive against democracy to emerge from a democratic country for many decades. In writing this answer, I am not interested in winning an argument. That is far too easy. My grave anxiety is to keep the way open for democracy to make its own free, creative choices of public

policy in the future. To build conservative barricades, altogether un-
amenable to change, as Hayek proposes, is to foment a violent explo-
sion. Hayek and his courtiers have mistaken the nature and the tem-
per of the times.[34]

Other critics were more courteous, but no less convinced of Hayek's
errors. In a second book-length response, *Freedom under Planning*,
published in 1945, Barbara Wootton reiterated the left's faith in state
planning, and attempted to show how it could be combined with a free
society. However, she did concede that successful planning depended
upon the moral decency of the planner. She argued that democratic
decentralization within a socially and economically more equal society
provided safeguards against totalitarianism: 'It is the citizens of a wisely
planned society who are least likely themselves to fall victim to the
dangers of planning . . . and it is the responsible, the alert, the active,
the informed, and the confident men and women in the street who hold
the key positions'.[35] The economist and post-war Labour minister, Evan
Durbin, described Hayek's book as 'a sincere, eloquent, and influential
work' but rejected his argument on the grounds that it gave an outdated
account of economic planning; that there is a far greater role for reason
and science in social affairs than Hayek accepted; and that he did not
establish a causal link between his historical narrative of the rise of
economic and political freedom.[36]

In the United States the book was met by 'a tumult of acclaim and
vituperation'.[37] In addition to an impassioned radio debate with Hayek
in 1945,[38] the left-wing academic Charles Merriam attacked *The Road
to Serfdom* for its misunderstanding of socialist planning; its association
of totalitarianism with the state rather than with capital; the book's
'muddled passages [which] indicate little knowledge of either the theory or the practice of administration'; and Hayek's distrust of conscious
social control.[39] Merriam concluded with a passionate defence of planning: 'For out of skilful planning will come human freedom in larger
measure, the growth of human personality, the expansion of the crea-
tive possibilities of mankind.'[40]

On the left, the exception to the outright rejection of Hayek's arguments at the time came from George Orwell. In a surprisingly sympathetic *Observer* review of the book, he noted that 'In the negative part
of Professor Hayek's thesis there is a great deal of truth'.[41] Orwell's

prognosis of the post-war situation was bleak, as his eloquent conclusion to the review showed:

> Capitalism leads to dole queues, the scramble for markets, and war. Collectivism leads to concentration camps, leader worship and war. There is no way out of this unless a planned economy can somehow be combined with the freedom of the intellect, which can only happen if the concept of right and wrong is restored to politics.[42]

Orwell remained a socialist until his death and his brief engagement with *The Road to Serfdom* perhaps tells us more about him than about Hayek. Although the review only features very briefly in Bernard Crick's biography of Orwell,[43] it is likely that Crick would have argued that it reflects his description of Orwell as a member of the 'awkward squad'—'that perennial difficult fellow who speaks unwanted home truths out of order, asks embarrassing questions' and who, among other things, 'pricks the bubbles of his own side's occasional pomposity'.[44]

Although Orwell's review was notably more conciliatory to Hayek's position, Orwell's conclusion that 'right and wrong' must be restored to politics echoes other critiques, notably that of Wootton and Keynes. Keynes made this point in a letter to Hayek, writing, 'I accuse you of perhaps confusing a little bit the moral and the material issues. Dangerous acts can be done safely in a community which thinks and feels rightly, which would be the way to hell if they were executed by those who think and feel wrongly.'[45]

What Orwell's sympathetic review does reveal is the strong left-wing libertarian streak running through his idiosyncratic version of socialism, and his scepticism about paternalist forms of socialism—a scepticism that finds echoes on the right.[46] Orwell's 'left libertarian' response to Hayek presages many of the later engagements that are examined in more detail in the main body of this book.[47]

'A prophet in the wilderness'

After the fame of *The Road to Serfdom* Hayek's reputation fell into decline, and he remained well outside the mainstream of political thought until the economic crisis of the 1970s endeared him to the opinion of formers and policymakers of the emerging new right. The year that the *Reader's Digest* circulated a condensed version of *The*

Road to Serfdom saw the landslide election in the UK of a Labour Party committed to the expansion of the peacetime state. The Conservative Party's (at times reluctant) acceptance of many of the post-war economic and welfare changes began a period of consensus between the main political parties.[48] In a highly sympathetic biography, Eamonn Butler reported that:

> Before and after the Second World War, the intellectual tide swept unceasingly in the direction of socialism. The consensus of the age was for economic planning, the setting of targets for economic growth, full employment policy, comprehensive state welfare services, and the redistribution of incomes. It was a consensus which Hayek never joined.[49]

During the 1950s and 1960s, the planned Soviet economy appeared to be doing well, and the social democracies of Western Europe, with their large and growing state sectors, prospered. For the left in Western Europe, particularly in retrospect, the three decades after the end of the Second World War marked a 'golden age'.[50]

It was during this period that Hayek, now at the University of Chicago, completed *The Constitution of Liberty*. The book, published in 1960, provided a defence of individual freedom—defined as the absence of arbitrary coercion, which it argued is needed if the social order is to develop and be sustained. Any attempt to inhibit freedom would rob society of its unique ability to allocate resources efficiently. (Throughout this book I use the terms 'freedom' and 'liberty' interchangeably.) The book contained a more detailed examination of the legal framework required to support this society than Hayek's earlier texts, and argued for the importance of the rule of law. It also examined some of the institutions which Hayek thought were necessary to build a society with the minimum of coercion, and contained a mixture of theoretical analysis and practical recommendations on planning, education, welfare, health and other policies. However, these arguments were well outside the mainstream and by 1967 the historian Eric Hobsbawm would describe Hayek as a 'prophet in the wilderness'.[51]

The Constitution of Liberty also contained an interesting postscript, 'Why I Am Not a Conservative', referring to the ideology, rather than to the British political party. Here Hayek rejected conservatism because it had no principled reason for rejecting collectivism, but could only act, in RG Collingwood's phrase, as a 'brake on the vehicle of progress', so that it has 'invariably been the fate of conservatism to be dragged along a path not of its own choosing'.[52] Instead, Hayek described himself—at least in 1960—as 'an unrepentant Old Whig'.[53]

Relating his politics to the three main political parties in the UK (which he conflated with socialism, liberalism and conservatism), Hayek noted:

> They are usually represented as different positions on a line, with the socialists [i.e., Labour] on the left, the conservatives on the right, and the liberals somewhere in the middle. Nothing could be more misleading. If we want a diagram, it would be more appropriate to arrange them in a triangle with the conservatives occupying one corner, with the socialists pulling toward the second and the liberals toward the third. But, as the socialists have for a long time been able to pull harder, the conservatives have tended to follow the socialist rather than the liberal direction.[54]

In party political terms, Hayek's alternative schema also offered his diagnosis of the errors of the post-war Conservative Party, which had accepted the expansion of the post-war peacetime state. Hayek's 'triangle' had more validity in 1960 than it did after Thatcher's arrival in office, when the Party ceased to be simply a brake on change and Labour was no longer able to pull as hard.

Hayek's work can be categorized in different ways. To critics or admirers who stress the importance of the 'spontaneous order' and the critique of rationalism in his thought, Hayek is indeed a Conservative—at least in its New Right variety. Madsen Pirie of the Adam Smith Institute explained at length 'Why FA Hayek is a Conservative' in 1987. This is partly a party political claim. Pirie wanted to strengthen the links between the Conservative Party of Margaret Thatcher and Hayek's ideas, and ensure the party did not go off track.[55] By contrast, those who have focused most of his arguments for freedom and for the market have seen him as a liberal or neo-liberal. The authors discussed in this book tend to emphasize the liberal elements of Hayek's work. Plant and Wainwright, for example, consistently describe Hayek as a neo-liberal. Indeed, his work involves concepts that would be a significant part of both liberal and conservative ideologies.

Despite entering the political wilderness in the decades after the Second World War, Hayek continued to make his case. Soon after the war ended, Hayek had rallied several thinkers sympathetic to economic liberalism to the Mont Pelerin Society, named after the site of the hotel in Switzerland chosen for the first meeting. The attendance was impressive. At the inaugural gathering, in April 1947, participants included Henry Hazlitt, Milton Friedman, John Jewkes, F. H. Knight, Ludwig von Mises, Michael Polanyi, Karl Popper and Lionel Robbins.[56] Throughout the post-war period the Society met once every year or two and indeed it continues to meet. Hayek was president from the first meeting until 1961, and remained honorary president until his death.[57]

While at LSE preparing for the first meeting of the Society in early 1947, Hayek was visited by Antony Fisher, a young former-RAF pilot. Fisher had read and been deeply impressed by the condensed version of *The Road to Serfdom*. He later recounted that his 'central question [to Hayek] was what, if anything, could he advise me to do to help get discussion and policy on the right lines'.[58] Hayek advised Fisher against taking up the political career which he was then contemplating, but instead explained his view that 'the decisive influence in the battle of ideas and policy was wielded by intellectuals whom he characterized as "second-hand dealers in ideas"' (although 'dealers in second-hand ideas' would perhaps have been a clearer description given that these were ideas that had previously been pretested to a largely academic audience, which were being repackaged and 'resold' to policymakers).[59] The advice Hayek gave, Fisher recounted, was that: 'I should join with others in forming a scholarly research organization to supply intellectuals in universities, schools, journalism and broadcasting with authoritative studies of the economic theory of markets and its application to practical affairs'.[60]

It was Hayek, therefore, who provided Fisher with the intellectual formula for the Institute of Economic Affairs (IEA), which was formally created in 1955. In the two decades after their first meeting Fisher was to become a successful entrepreneur: the first 'broiler chicken' farmer in the UK. His company Buxted Chickens was founded in 1953 and was sold by the partners in 1968 (as Allied Farm Foods) for £21 million.[61] With ample funding from Fisher, and elsewhere, the IEA continued its promotion of free market ideas through the 1950s and 1960s and was later joined by other think tanks, such as the Centre for Policy Studies and the Adam Smith Institute. As early as 1968 the distinctive combination of liberal and conservative arguments offered by the IEA and the individuals associated with it were being described as contributions to the 'new right'.[62]

Yet the thinking behind the Mont Pelerin Society and the IEA was at the margins of mainstream political debate in the immediate post-war period. As such, the award for the 1974 Nobel Prize for Economics came as a surprise to Hayek. It seemed to go against the tenor of the times—better reflected by the Swedish economist and social democratic politician Gunnar Myrdal, with whom Hayek shared the award. (Myrdal later commented that he would not have accepted it had he known he was sharing the award with Hayek.[63]) The prize was also something of a surprise because it was for economics: a discipline in which Hayek was no longer seen as a leading figure and which he had largely moved away from after the publication of *The Road to Serfdom* in 1944. Despite the surprise, the award seemed to have a rejuvenating effect upon Hayek. He had undergone a period of illness in his late sixties, but by the end of the 1970s he had produced a three-volume study, *Law, Legislation and Liberty*.[64] Hayek became increasingly active in the work of the think tanks associated with the new right. He later joked, 'Some years ago, I tried old age but discovered I didn't like it'.[65]

The ending of the long post-war decades of growth, finishing in soaring inflation, unemployment, union unrest and industrial decline, provided fertile ground for alternative ideas. Margaret Thatcher's election win in May 1979 marked an obvious end to the post-war consensus. Her governments were seen as the culmination of intellectual thinking shaped by Hayek and the right-wing think tanks, and the triumph of the new right. Thatcher claimed that she was 'a great admirer of Professor Hayek' to the House of Commons in 1981—her wider intellectual debt was mentioned at the start of this chapter.[66] The implementation of policies to bring down inflation, reduce the power of trade unions and privatize major sectors of the economy can all be justified by reference to Hayek's work. Thatcher's rhetorical link between freedom and enterprise, and her regular association of socialism and serfdom, were also most obviously derived from Hayek.

The early 1980s were a polarized time in British politics, and Hayek was seen to be at one end of that spectrum. Michael Foot, Leader of the Labour Party from 1980–1983, was excoriating about Hayek's influence, claiming that Thatcher was 'in the clutches of a mad professor'.[67] However, Labour's attempt to respond to the 'crises of the 1970s' met with electoral failure. In 1983, the most polarized UK election of the modern period, Margaret Thatcher went to the electorate on a pro-American, free market platform, while the Labour Party campaigned for renationalisation and disarmament. Thatcher won a resounding victory, which ensured a long period of Conservative dominance. In total, Labour remained out of power for almost eighteen years.

The year 1989 marked ten years since Thatcher's election. It also saw the fall of the Berlin Wall and the collapse of the Soviet Empire. Watching the events unfolding on television, an elderly Hayek would beam and comment, 'I told you so!'[68] For Hayek the fall of the Berlin Wall symbolized the triumph of individualism over collectivism. The triumph of the new right at home and the collapse of communism abroad also marked a sustained engagement with Hayek's argument by the left.

'ENGAGING' ENEMIES

The term 'engagement' needs some explanation. Several uses of the term 'engage' or its derivations provide necessary, but not sufficient, criteria to understand how the term is used in this study. A first use of the verb 'engage' means nothing more than 'to deal with especially at length',[69] and this sense certainly applies as a necessary criterion. However, while this meaning provides a useful starting point, on its own it is insufficient. The authors on the British left discussed in the following chapters were more committed to their subject than simply 'dealing with' Hayek's work.

A second, more demanding use of the verb is, 'to hold the attention of', as in the phrase 'his work *engages* her completely'.[70] (This meaning developed into the use of the term that emerged in French existential thought in the 1940s, particularly in the work of Sartre, and which, by the 1950s, was imported untranslated into English as *engagé*—that is, to be 'committed', or 'completely involved in political, moral or social questions'.[71]) This second definition is helpful in that all the thinkers examined in the central chapters of this book are committed to a serious reading of Hayek—one that engages them. This in turn implies a degree of intellectual respect. One of the most extended treatments of Hayek's thought from the left, Herman Finer's *Road to Reaction*, stands out for its hostility towards Hayek's work.[72] Finer's account (which is discussed in more detail) did not constitute an 'engagement' in the sense understood in this book. The political economist Jim Tomlinson commented, for example, that Finer's book 'cannot be said to get to serious grips with Hayek's arguments'.[73] For much of the post-war period, responses to Hayek's work from the left, when they did rarely occur, were characterized by dismissal or outright rejection. It is, therefore, a further necessary condition of 'engagement' in the sense understood here, that there is the intellectual respect that comes from taking an author's argument seriously, rather than simply as a 'straw man'—a representative of a body of thought which is discussed only to be knocked down.

A third common use of the term is military: to engage with an enemy is to 'enter into conflict' with it. All of the thinkers I examine in detail are, to some degree, in conflict with Hayek's conclusions. Perry Anderson, who coined the phrase 'a zone of engagement', is useful here. Anderson wrote that: 'The condition of a specific engagement . . . has always been respect. But I also need to feel a significant dissent'.[74] A final necessary, but not sufficient, condition, therefore, is that all the authors discussed in detail in this book at least started out occupying a position of 'significant dissent' towards Hayek's work. Once all of the necessary conditions outlined above are met, a sufficient condition for inclusion in this book is reached. The main authors discussed here, therefore, 'engage' with Hayek's work in at least three ways: they deal with his arguments at length; they are committed to a serious reading of Hayek; and, finally, they occupy a position of 'significant dissent' from him.

Rethinking Hayek

This book focuses on the engagement of the British left with Hayek by four thinkers: David Miller, Raymond Plant, Hilary Wainwright and Andrew Gamble. All of these thinkers were British and primarily contributed to debates in the UK, and all of them were primarily focused on Hayek's politics, broadly defined rather than approaching him primarily as an economist, for example. I introduce these figures below.

However, there were other contenders for detailed analysis, who have also made an important contribution to these debates. In the United States, in particular, several thinkers on the left sought to rethink Hayek around the end of the Cold War. Perhaps the best known example is the work of the American political scientist John Roemer. Roemer's influence is primarily in the United States, from where he originates and is based. He developed an argument for 'market socialism', which has similarities to that of the British political theorist David Miller, discussed in Chapter 2 (whose major statement of market socialism preceded Roemer's[75]). Roemer was explicit in his engagement with Hayek, claiming that he has found 'ways of reformulating the concept of market socialism in response to the Hayekian critique'.[76] More recently, another American scholar, Theodore Burczak, put forward an argument for socialism that was explicitly tempered by the Hayekian critique. In *Socialism After Hayek*, Burczak presented a 'socialist' argument that largely accepted Hayek's epistemological argument against traditional forms of twentieth-century socialism.[77] Burczak argued that Hayek's theory of knowledge contains similarities with recent post-modern forms of Marxism—a claim that has similarities to the rethinking of Hayek carried out by Hilary Wainwright, discussed in Chapter 5.

On the left, some groups found it easier to engage with Hayek's work than others. Economists found it easier to set aside the ideological baggage that came with Hayek, and to selectively engage with his work, than members of other disciplines.[78] For example, the Nobel Prize–winning economist Amartya Sen, who describes himself as 'someone whose economics (as well as politics) is very different from Hayek's',[79] wrote an article to mark the sixtieth anniversary of the publication of *The Road to Serfdom* in which he argued that Hayek's ideas 'remain extremely important' to this day.[80] In particular he picked out Hayek's 'insightful' argument against central planning, concluding that 'Our debt to Hayek is very substantial'.[81] However, the various contributions of left-wing economists, such as Sen, are not discussed in any detail in this book, which primarily focuses on political not economic thought.

Despite some qualifications, the engagement with Hayek was largely carried out by thinkers working in the UK, and it is the UK that is the focus of this book. Partly this is because there were strong links between Hayek, the think tanks of the new right, and the Conservative

Party of Margaret Thatcher. For most of his life Hayek was British and he spent a large portion of it working in the UK. As such, this book focuses on the engagement of the *British* left with Hayek. Although political thought is increasingly conducted across national borders (as I argue in Chapter 4), it is shaped by local context and it has a local flavour, even if many of the ingredients are imported from abroad. As the American politician Tip O'Neill commented—in a rather different sense—'all politics is local' and he is, to some degree, right.

Within the UK, two thinkers in particular could have merited greater inclusion in this book: Jim Tomlinson and Robin Blackburn. Discussing Hayek, Jim Tomlinson noted that 'the number of reasonably detailed sceptical accounts of his work are strikingly few' and that his own book-length account of Hayek's work, published in 1990, was the first by a socialist since Barbara Wootton's in 1945.[82] Tomlinson described his account not as a 'work of denigration, but of sceptical appraisal': 'It recognises the significance of Hayek's work, and recognises its attractions as a system of thought, but tries to maintain a critical distance'.[83]

To Tomlinson, the socialist's task is 'one of critically engaging with the existing intellectual traditions from a position which holds to traditional socialist objectives—egalitarianism, democracy, co-operation, fraternity'.[84] The choice of the word 'market' in the title of Tomlinson's book is partly because it is this concept which 'lies at the heart of Hayek's difference with socialism, and yet at the same time is the area where socialism seems currently most unsure of itself. . . . Hence, to focus attention on Hayek's account of the market is . . . to discuss those issues where his ideas seem currently most politically potent.'[85]

In his obituary of Hayek, Arthur Seldon, president of the Institute of Economic Affairs, noted Tomlinson's engagement with Hayek specifically:

> Hayek lived to see the criticism of his early and middle periods replaced by the respectful examination of his thinking by a wide range of academics, [including] younger academics like Jim Tomlinson whose *Hayek and the Market* (1990) identifies radical agreements, even the qualified acceptance of Adam Smith's invisible hand that leads men in the market to do good to others that was no part of their intention.[86]

However, Seldon overstated the 'radical agreements' that are found in Tomlinson's book. It is true that Tomlinson recognized the 'importance and influence' of Hayek's writing,[87] but he was quick to point out that, 'This book is written by a democratic socialist, and thus someone basically out of sympathy with Hayek's ideas'. Tomlinson's argument for a decentralized form of socialism was not built upon Hayek's thought, and he was highly critical of Hayek's overall output. Tomlinson did not go on to claim explicitly, as Gamble did, for example, that Hayek's work could contribute to a renewal of socialism. Nor did Tomlinson take up his account of Hayek in any sustained way in his other writings; as such, Tomlinson's account of Hayek is not discussed in detail.

A second British candidate for inclusion in this book was Robin Blackburn. In 1991, when Blackburn was editor of the *New Left Review*, he argued that, 'no-one pointed out that Hayek's argument from the dispersed nature of knowledge could also be deployed against a narrow capitalist entrepreneurialism by advocates of social and worker self-management.'[88] Blackburn was one of the earliest thinkers on the British left to hint that a re-evaluation of Hayek's thought could be beneficial. However, Blackburn is reluctant to develop the argument he begins above. Hayek's reputation as a polemicist for the new right is set out above and Hayek's anti-socialism became increasingly combative towards the end of his life (he was still alive at the time of Blackburn's article). Blackburn's unwillingness to carry through the self-acknowledged, explicit implications of this thinking on Hayek meant that his line of argument that the left could use Hayek's theory of knowledge (an argument set out in Chapter 4) was taken up by others, most obviously his colleague at the time at the *New Left Review*, Hilary Wainwright (who was an associate editor at the journal at the time Blackburn's article was published). Blackburn's argument is returned to in Chapter 4, but because of the limits of his engagement with Hayek's work, and Wainwright's much more extended and full embrace of Hayek's argument, it is her engagement, and not Blackburn's, which is discussed in detail in this book.

Outline of the book

The first wave in the engagement with Hayek on the British left lasted from the early 1980s to the mid-1990s. In this book it is reflected in the

work of David Miller and Raymond Plant. It was 'market socialist' in
both the specific sense that Miller develops below and in Plant's broad
sense of seeking to combine the market with socialism. The creation of
the Socialist Philosophy Group (SPG), of which both Miller and Plant
were members, set up in response to Labour's loss at the 1983 General
Election, provided an early impetus to this wave. The group was active
in the 'modernization' of the Labour Party under the leadership and
deputy leadership of Neil Kinnock and Roy Hattersley. The publication
of Alec Nove's *The Economics of Feasible Socialism*, published in 1983,
provided an important early contribution and influence to this wave.
The crest came with the SPG's text on market socialism, edited by
Estrin and Le Grand in 1989. This wave passed with the decline of
market socialism in the mid-1990s.

David Miller's understanding of 'market socialism', discussed in
Chapter 2, involves enterprises being run and owned cooperatively,
while competing in a market economy. While Miller's direct engagement with Hayek is more tentative than the other authors discussed
here, his embrace of pro-market arguments is arguably fuller. Miller's
work was specifically described as an attempt to update the 'outdated'
socialist tradition and is sometimes also presented as a form of socialist
revisionism. However, by the late 1990s Miller's market socialism
seemed too radical to attract wide support. For many on the left, market socialism was a brief stopping point as socialists moved away from
the statist traditions of the twentieth century.

Market socialists challenged older forms of socialism by arguing that
individual choice was central. This argument fitted uneasily with traditional socialist moral arguments, based on community or a critique of
'conspicuous consumption', for example, and was part of a wider rejection of the Fabian state by the end of the twentieth century. Miller,
along with several of his colleagues, also presented the argument for
combining the market with socialism as a form of 'feasible' politics,
which grated against the radical aspirations of earlier socialists. Miller's
argument for market socialism draws on elements of socialism, liberalism, pluralism, anarchism and nationalism. His arguments can be seen
as a corrosive force, wearing away the traditional barriers between the
ideological categories that had dominated the twentieth century.

Raymond Plant, whose work is examined in Chapter 3, provided one
of the fullest engagements with Hayek on the left. He carried out a

careful analysis of many of Hayek's main arguments against socialism
(which are also summarized in that chapter). While some of the early
thinkers to engage with Hayek on the left were tentative, Plant met
Hayek's arguments head-on. Plant went further than other thinkers in
explicitly accepting elements of Hayek's attack on socialism. He largely
accepted, for example, Hayek's epistemic argument that efficient planning was impossible, although he did not accept Hayek's claim that
planning led to 'serfdom'. Of all the elements of Hayek's work it is this
epistemic argument against planning that has been most attractive to
the left. All of the thinkers examined in detail in this book accept aspects of Hayek's argument in this area, and sought to claim or to re-
interpret it for use in their own thought. Plant's engagement with
Hayek's work was also based around a defence of 'positive' notions of
freedom and justice, which contrasted with those advocated by Hayek.

Plant's work demonstrates the influence of the revisionist socialism
of the 1950s and, in particular, of Anthony Crosland's separation between ends and the means used to achieve them. By focusing on debates around liberty and autonomy, Plant also owes something to the
new liberalism of the early twentieth century. As such, Plant's work
constitutes a blurring of boundaries between liberalism and socialism in
the late twentieth century. It is also a demonstration of the rediscovery
in political thought at the end of the twentieth-century debates more
common almost a century before.

As the first wave of engagement with Hayek's work began to fall, a
second wave began. It is reflected in this book in the discussions on
Hilary Wainwright and Andrew Gamble. These 'left-wing Hayekians'
were more prepared to draw on Hayek's work directly to support and
develop their own arguments. This wave began with Jim Tomlinson's
book-length riposte to Hayek in 1990, and included Robin Blackburn,
as well as Wainwright and Gamble. It peaked with the publications of
Wainwright's and Gamble's in-depth analyses of Hayek's work in the
mid-1990s. This wave of engagement still continues to some degree.[89]

While Plant and Miller presented their arguments as primarily led
by a combination of intellectual shifts (such as the rise of the new right)
and political changes (for example, the success of the Conservative Party in the 1980s), Hilary Wainwright, whom I discuss in Chapter 4,
presented her engagement with Hayek as part of a more journalistic,
sociological and psychological investigation. Her account of Hayek

came chronologically later than both Miller's and Plant's and was justified as an attempt to explain the success of parties influenced by the
new right or 'neo-liberalism', as she more often wrote, in the newly
independent countries of Eastern Europe during the early 1990s.
Wainwright's initial interest in Hayek derived from his influence upon
these parties and his attraction to their activists.

Wainwright's engagement with Hayek involved an ingenious attempt
to socialize his epistemic theory. Her argument, in sum, was that knowledge was not irremediably individual, as Hayek argued, but could be
shared imperfectly between groups and movements. Thus social movements become the key actors in Wainwright's thought. As with the
other thinkers examined in this book, Wainwright's arguments mark a
decisive break with the political thought of the twentieth century. Paral-
leling Miller, Wainwright broke with the paternalism of earlier socialism. She also largely abandoned class as a useful category, at least in any
simple economic sense, in favour of social movements. Wainwright
seemed to be comfortable with the possibility that the radical changes
that she supported might not continue to be described as 'socialist', and
her argument evokes the pluralism of the early twentieth century.

The final thinker discussed in detail in this book is Andrew Gamble,
whose work is discussed in Chapter 5. Gamble's public engagement
with Hayek did not begin until the mid-1990s—slightly later than the
other thinkers discussed here. As with those thinkers, Gamble presented his engagement as an attempt to find new foundations for socialism.
Of the thinkers examined in this book, Gamble perhaps goes furthest in
his engagement with Hayek. As with Miller and Plant, he largely accepted Hayek's epistemological argument, and he was prepared to admit the extent to which this idea challenged earlier forms of socialism.
Gamble argued, for example, that the left should claim the role of the
entrepreneur—an activity of which earlier socialists were often deeply
suspicious. He also argued that Hayek was right to point out the importance of spontaneous orders (although his view over when these orders
should be protected is much more limited than Hayek's).

In his defence of spontaneous orders, Gamble's work can also be
seen as a pluralist response to Hayek. In this respect, Gamble's argument follows that of Wainwright and Miller (although his pluralism is
more limited than Wainwright's in particular). Gamble's work is perhaps best seen as a new (or social) liberal response to Hayek's (econom-

ic or classical) liberalism. His defence of a largely positive form of liberty in response to Hayek's critique shifted the debate away from socialism as it was understood for much of the twentieth century and generated a pluralist and left-liberal argument in its place.

In the final chapter, I return to the questions set out at the very start of this introduction and examine the fate of socialism at the end of the twentieth century, the ending of a unique historical period, the nature of enmity and ideological change, and the significance of the engagement with Hayek for the modernization of the Labour Party and for contemporary party politics.

2

THE RISE AND FALL OF
MARKET SOCIALISM

'**S**ocialism', wrote Hayek, is in its methods concerned with 'the abolition of private enterprise, of private ownership of the means of production, and the creation of a system of "planned economy" in which the
entrepreneur working for profit is replaced by a central planning
body'.[1] Hayek's description, written in 1944, was largely uncontrover-
sial. The connection between socialism and central economic planning
was loosely accepted (with a few notable exceptions) by left and right
for much of the next fifty years: the left was generally in favour of state
planning, the right was in favour of the market.

The attempt to combine markets with socialism, therefore, marked a
radical break with the politics of the past. The idea gained its most
explicit support with the revival of 'market socialism'—a theory that,
narrowly defined, sought to combine social ownership of the means of
production with the extensive use of market mechanisms in the economy. By the mid-1990s 'market socialism' was widely discussed in academia and in think tanks on the left of British politics. Yet, since the early
years of the twenty-first century the term has rarely been heard. This
chapter offers an account of the rise and fall of the 'market socialism' in
the UK during the final decade of the twentieth century.[2]

I examine market socialism through focusing on the work of one of
its principle advocates: David Miller—for most of his career Professor
of Political Theory at Nuffield College, Oxford. From the mid-1970s
until the mid-1990s Miller carefully constructed and sustained a case

for market socialism, through a series of academic publications and through his participation in groups associated with the Labour Party. In contrast to the later discussions of Hayek's work examined in this book, Miller's engagement is limited and tentative given the central role that the market plays in his work. Yet Miller is included for detailed discussion because he does explicitly recognize the role of Hayek as one of the main exponents of pro-market policies and because his engagement with these pro-market arguments pre-dates that of most other left-wing thinkers.

For some critics, markets and socialism are simply incompatible. This raises questions about the broad approach taken to ideology, and ideological change taken in this book, which I turn to below. In the second section I move to a discussion of the shifting historical context behind the rise of market socialism in the late 1980s. Third, I examine the concept of market socialism itself in more detail, focusing on Miller's arguments. The final section compares market socialism with more mainstream forms of twentieth-century socialist thought. I conclude by discussing the decline of market socialism, and argue that, through its adoption of the market and its jettisoning of statist forms of socialism, its significance lies in its challenge to the conventional categorization of political thought into socialist, liberal and conservative—a categorization which had dominated the twentieth century.

IDEOLOGIES: ESSENTIALIST MODELS AND DECENTRED ACCOUNTS

Miller argued in 1989 that 'It is quite possible to be for markets and against capitalism'.[3] Some critics of market socialism began with the view that markets and socialism are essentially incompatible: the essence of socialism is its opposition to the market. For these critics, the term 'market socialism' has been dismissed as an oxymoron.[4] In an early article, David Miller wrote, 'I do not believe that essentialist definitions of socialism are particularly helpful. Socialists are committed to the abolition of capitalism, but beyond that minimal commitment socialism stands for a diverse bundle of aspirations and ideals, together with institutional proposals intended to realise those aspirations and ideals'.[5] Even Miller's 'minimal commitment' is contestable. It reflects his understanding of the essence of socialism at that time, and claims a greater commitment for socialists than many have themselves made. The debate about whether socialism and the market are compatible raises wider questions about the approach taken to ideology in this book.

John Stuart Mill once wrote that, 'One of the mistakes oftenest committed, and which are the sources of the greatest practical errors in human affairs, is that of supposing that the same name always stands for the same aggregation of ideas'.[6] Indeed, the practice of presenting political ideologies, such as socialism or liberalism, as possessing fixed and unchanging cores is common (particularly in introductory courses to political thought). Hobhouse's book, *Liberalism*, provides an example of the attempt to cut through the peripheral arguments and search for the 'essentials' of an ideology.[7] To critics of 'essentialism' like Greenleaf, Hobhouse's 'exercise is a sort of Platonic attempt to transcend the contingency and vagaries of the world'[8] and the attempt to define ideologies through their essential components is 'the depiction of caricature rather than a satisfactory characterization of the ideology in question'.[9] Simple essentialism creates ideological distortion; it presents ideology as ahistorical and non-contingent, and provides no account of ideological change.

At the other pole from essentialist models of political thought are various 'decentred' accounts. The second volume of Greenleaf's series on *The British Political Tradition* is perhaps the best known example of this approach.[10] Rather than summarising the core elements of a political tradition, Greenleaf looked to its edges:

> Instead of nuclear designation, therefore, it is necessary to establish the character of an ideology by, first, admitting the inevitability of diversity and change and then, secondly, by delimiting this variety through observation of the extreme and opposing manifestations between which the point of view appears to be confirmed. An ideology is identified by describing the cardinal antithesis of the political disposition it reveals.[11]

An example of this approach can be seen in Greenleaf's account of the British pluralist-socialist, Harold Laski, who is briefly discussed in Chapter 4. Greenleaf wrote that the limits of British socialism

> seem to be set by the two rather distinct, and ultimately contrasting, motives or goals. . . . These poles of endeavour, potentially so anti-thetical, are (on the one hand) organization and efficiency, and (on the other) liberty, fulfilment, and moral regeneration. . . . This is especially the case so far as one major question (perhaps *the* major question) of political thought is concerned: that is, the attitude to be adopted to the state and its proper role and purpose. [12]

However, Greenleaf's approach can create a misleading impression of the argument he is examining. While recognizing the overlapping and changing character of ideologies, Greenleaf does not so much offer a 'decentred' interpretation of political themes, as an entirely hollowed out one. In characterizing political ideologies by describing their extremes, Greenleaf missed much that goes on in the centre. His description of socialism, for instance, focused excessively on its libertarian and collectivist extremes (which constitute only one of several possible axes).

A more recent anti-essentialist approach is found in the work of Mark Bevir. Bevir attacked what he calls a 'reified model of ideology', by which he means the method of turning 'a contingent and changing product of human activity into a fixed entity, defined by an enduring core of fixed values'. [13] To Bevir the underlying methodological problem with this approach is that it gets the causal explanation between ideologies (such as socialism or liberalism) and individual cases (such as Miller's engagement with Hayek) the wrong way round. For Bevir, reified approaches generally begin with a decision over the content of an ideology and a view as to which are its dominant strands. Reification occurs in this method because there are no adequate *prior* criteria with which to decide what does and does not belong in each ideology. The historian uses previously constructed abstract models, and then classifies particular cases by their similarity to those models. Priority is thus given to the abstract models in locating particular cases rather than the other way around: 'The models effectively act as prior, given, objects in terms of which to understand particular cases'. [14] For Bevir, ideologies are 'webs of interconnected beliefs or concepts mapping on to a perceived reality at various points'. [15] Bevir argued that ideological change can occur at any level, from policy to principles:

[N]o concept can stand on its own, so the content of any concept depends on those around it and the initial change will cause further changes throughout the ideology. Like a stone dropped in a pond, the initial change will send out ripples disrupting other parts of the ideology. [16]

To Bevir, the role of the historian of political thought is a limited one: it is not the job of the historian to identify ideational similarities to reified ideologies, [17] but merely to 'trace historical connections back through the immediate influences on the case we are explaining'. [18] This seems to be an unnecessarily narrow definition.

The approach to ideology pursued here seeks to find a middle way between 'essentialist' and 'decentred' models. A basis for this model can be found in a concession that Bevir makes when he asks why so many thinkers are drawn towards 'reified' models of ideology. A possible explanation he suggests, 'would be that we simply have to abstract from particular thinkers if we are ever to identify pattern, and so ideologies'. [19] Bevir concedes that there are 'necessary tasks of generalisation and abstraction' [20] and even that his own 'decentred model of ideology does not preclude classification in terms of ideational similarities'. [21] In conceding that abstraction and generalization are 'necessary tasks', Bevir reopens the door to the kind of approaches to ideology that he is dismissing.

Bevir's concession is significant: if ideological discussion rests, as he now accepts, on abstraction and generalization from particular cases then this readmits the possibility of arguing that some ideas are at or near the centre of particular ideologies. If from reading the work of numerous political thinkers, certain ideas are repeatedly central to their argument, then those arguments can be grouped with others of ideational similarity as socialist, conservative, or whatever else. Bevir and Greenleaf are both sceptical of the use of abstraction and generalization. To Greenleaf it provides nothing more than a 'caricature' of an ideology. Yet a better metaphor would be drawing a map—sometimes abstraction and generalization are useful tasks which enable us to better understand where we are. (The redrawing of 'ideological maps' is one way to look at the discussion on the fate of socialism in the final chapter of this book.)

Given Bevir's concession that ideological discussion rests on abstraction and generalization from particular cases, the difference between decentred approaches and, what he describes as, 'sophisticated reified models' becomes one of emphasis rather than significant difference. An example of a sophisticated reified approach, according to Bevir, was put forward by Michael Freeden (to whom the approach taken to ideology in this book is greatly indebted). Freeden argues that ideologies are composed of both core concepts and peripheral components (the latter are often 'specific ideas of policy proposals rather than fully fledged concepts').[22]

The use of ideology in this book differs slightly from Freeden's. First, Freeden presents a 'conceptual' approach to ideology, whereas a broader approach is taken here. As Barker has argued '"Concept" suggests something precise, even academic, but lacking the penumbra of politics, rhetoric, policy, . . . aversions and aspirations'.[23] Second, rather than accept Freeden's stark contrast between the core and the periphery, one could argue that some values, beliefs, aspirations and so on, will be closer to the centre of ideological webs and may even stay there for sustained periods. The contrast between core and periphery is relative, rather than absolute.

Ideologies, as the term is used in this book, are composed of concepts, values, aspirations and even aversions, which can shift around and change the shape of the ideological web over the years, perhaps becoming increasingly peripheral. As they move from the centre to the outer areas of the web they pull other values with them, changing the overall shape of the web. (The pun that, 'Socialism was once defined as a great spider with a little Webb at its centre' seems apt here,[24] given the centrality of Sidney Webb's Fabian views to socialism for much of the twentieth century.) Eventually the configuration of ideas that make up an ideological web may change its shape to such an extent, or the links to other webs will be so strong, that it no longer makes sense to classify it as being a conservative, socialist or whatever else. In some circumstances a part of the web may break as values and concepts lose their connections with one another. In such cases the ideology can disappear, almost overnight. For some commentators, including Hayek, this disappearance is what happened to socialism at the end of the twentieth century. In this book I use the wider engagement with Hayek by the left as a way of examining how ideologies change.

I return to debates about ideology later in this chapter, but first I look at the role of contextual change on Miller's engagement with Hayek and on wider pro-market arguments.

CONTEXTUAL CHANGE AND INTELLECTUAL ENGAGEMENT

Miller dates his engagement with pro-market argument to the mid-1970s. At the time, he was unusual for a writer who saw himself on the left for adopting concepts normally associated with the right:

> I began [he wrote] in the 1970s with fairly ill-defined socialist beliefs that seemed naturally to entail an antipathy to markets as a means of economic co-ordination, a point of view which is I suppose fairly common. I was shaken out of it by encountering, in the middle part of that decade, various libertarian writings that set out polemically, but still powerfully the arguments in favour of markets. These arguments left me with two basic convictions. One was that the libertarian position in itself—the belief in a minimal state and economic laissez faire—was ill founded and untenable. The other was that the pro-market arguments found in libertarian writings were none the less strong in themselves and deserve to convince socialists. [25]

It took a series of important contextual shifts to force market socialism onto the agenda, including the perceived failure of statist forms of socialism and Keynesian techniques, and the revival of the new right.

The failures of statist socialism

The revival of market socialism was, in part, a response to the increasingly widespread perception on the left that statist forms of socialism had failed. Miller argued that socialism needed to cast itself free from its association with state planning and the unattractive form of statism that emerged in Eastern Europe.[26] Many other thinkers on the left made the same argument around this time. Writing in Saul Estrin and Julian Le Grand's book on market socialism, Estrin and David Winter stated explicitly that the case for market socialism rested on more than just the attractiveness of arguments in favour of markets; it also rested on the failure of the principle alternative: central planning.[27]

To Miller, there were several reasons for the failure of central planning. The arguments he sets out owe much to Hayek and the new right, introduced in the previous chapter. The first of Miller's arguments was over the ineffectiveness of statist socialism. Miller argued that 'planned production is unable to respond as quickly and flexibly to consumers' preferences as a market', creating problems in the day-to-day production of consumer goods for state socialist systems. This argument was unusual on the left, because it involved placing value on the consumer demands that drive a market system. As I argue later in this chapter, and in Chapter 6, there is a significant tradition on the left that is deeply sceptical about consumerism, from which Miller distances himself.

Miller's second argument was that 'central planning negates democracy' through the creation of a large professional bureaucracy in which power gravitates to those with specialist knowledge. Again, this breaks with the arguments of those post-war socialists who assumed the benevolence of the bureaucratic class—as an argument it shares more with Hayek than with Barbara Wootton's argument that there could be *Freedom under Planning*, providing there were strong democratic safeguards.

Third, Miller argued that 'central planning severely restricts the scope for workers' self-management' as decisions over production of goods and services are transferred to a central authority. By the late 1980s this concern was more commonly associated with the right than the left (although democratic, anti-centralizing arguments provide an undercurrent in left-wing argument which runs through the works of William Morris, G. D. H. Cole and the guild socialists, to the post-war new left and beyond).

Finally, Miller argued that in any state socialist system 'freedom to change employment will be circumscribed' as workers' choices are limited to those jobs that planners make available (although in practice under capitalism this choice is often limited).[28] Again, Miller breaks with mainstream socialism through implying new job-creating enterprises can be created—an anti-statist, pro-enterprise approach to job creation that remains more common on the right than the left.

The failings of a planned economy in the Soviet Union marked the end of the major non-capitalist alternative. The USSR had acted as a guiding star for the British left in the middle decades of the twentieth century from which they were able to find their own, often very different, positions. For example, while in the 1930s and 1940s, George Orwell's socialism was, at least in part, an argument against the totalitarianism of the USSR, Sidney and Beatrice Webbs' socialism was increasingly based on respect for its orderliness. (The Webbs' book *Soviet Communism: a new civilization* tellingly dropped the question mark from its subtitle by the second edition.[29]) However, despite their contrasting views on socialism, both Orwell and the Webbs defined their positions in relation to the Soviet Union. After the fall of the Berlin Wall, Miller and other market socialists no longer had the example of 'actually existing socialism' in the USSR to guide them and offer an alternative (for better or worse) for their own re-examination of political first principles. By the 1990s, the polar relationships of enmity that had defined the twentieth century—the Soviet Union versus the United States, left versus right, state versus market, socialism versus capitalism—began to break down. Political thought was freed from many of the relationships that helped to define it during the twentieth century.

The limits of Keynesian solutions

Miller was also candid in his rejection of Keynesianism as a successful means to a socialist society. There are several elements to this. Writing in 1989, he argued, first: 'it is no longer clear that Keynesian methods can be used in the desired manner to secure full employment'. This is in stark contrast to post-war socialists, such as Anthony Crosland, who had argued—at least in his earlier writings—that Keynesian economic management would ensure, if not socialism, at least growth and full employment.[30]

Second, Miller noted that 'there is substantial evidence that the impact of fiscal measures on the overall distribution on income and wealth has so far been quite limited'. In evidence he cited research which showed that in 1985 the top 10 percent of British households enjoyed post-tax incomes some ten times greater than those in the bottom 10 percent.[31] This critique is something that many post-war socialists would largely accept. Crosland, for example, argued that 'by 1951 Britain had, in all the essentials, ceased to be a capitalist country'. Instead he described it as 'statist'.[32] To Crosland, this should not be enough for socialists. He argued that 'Statism cured the worst social evils of the previous society, but its achievement was a negative one, confined to the elimination of abuses. It remains to create the new society'.[33]

Last, Miller argued that the welfare state, although successful as a means of tackling poverty, 'has been far less successful as a vehicle for overall equality [because] freely provided services . . . may be used more effectively by those who are already better off to an extent that eliminates . . . the progressive element in their funding through income tax'.[34] This argument had continued relevance in debates over New Labour's 'choice' agenda for public services a decade later.[35] Julian Le Grand, who co-edited a collection on market socialism in 1989 (which includes a contribution from Miller), went on to advise Tony Blair's government on health reform. Noting the relative failure of 'universal' provision to provide for those who are worst off, Le Grand argued that giving patients greater choice over their health care in a quasi-market system, free at the point of use, would benefit those at the bottom.[36] By contrast, sceptics expressed concern that those with greater social, economic, cultural or symbolic capital are able to take advantage of choices in a way that others are not.[37] Although Miller's argument touches on these issues, he never explicitly examines the sociological challenges surrounding the ability to choose that follow from the pro-market argument.

Related to limits of Keynesian social democracy, at least in the mind of Miller and other market socialists, was the party political failure for the British Labour Party. The Labour Party lost four consecutive General Elections after 1979 and was out of office for almost eighteen years. In their collection on market socialism,[38] Estrin and Le Grand described how their book originated as a specific response to Labour's loss of the 1983 General Election when the Fabian Society called together a group of sympathetic academics to describe what had 'gone wrong'. It was agreed that the group would meet on a regular basis under the name of the 'Socialist Philosophy Group' to begin 'rethinking and reconstructing' socialist ideas.[39] (Raymond Plant's involvement in the Socialist Philosophy Group was discussed in the previous chapter.) At the first meeting of the group, David Miller presented a paper on market socialism, discussions of which formed the basis for several subsequent meetings. For the left by the 1980s, neither Soviet socialism nor Keynesian social democracy appeared to be able to provide any kind of guidance.

Political theory and the rise of the new right

If Miller, and other market socialists, were responding to what they saw as the multi-levelled failure of statist forms of socialism, they also wrote in a changing intellectual environment. In particular Miller's account of market socialism was a response to two overlapping intellectual shifts that gathered momentum in political thought from the 1970s onwards: the resurgence of political theory, and the emergence of various 'libertarian' or pro-market arguments which came together under the heading of the 'New Right'.

'The resurgence of political theory' changed the way in which academic political debate was conducted, especially in the Anglophone countries.[40] In particular, the publication of John Rawls' *A Theory of Justice* in 1971 focused debate on normative political liberalism.[41] Writers at the centre of this resurgence, like Rawls and Robert Nozick,[42] provided an account of justice which was compatible with market institutions. (Miller even argues that Rawls and Nozick tried to forestall criticism from socialists in their different ways by arguing that 'fundamental socialist values can be realized through a suitably ordered market': for Rawls a market society in which his two principles of justice are operational could meet many socialist aspirations; for Nozick socialist values such as workers' control and freedom from alienation could be achieved by voluntary means in a market system.[43]) To Miller, this resurgence 'prompts a reexamination of socialist attitudes towards the market'.[44]

The rise of various, sustained, libertarian arguments grouped together under the heading of the 'New Right'[45] also changed the political environment. Miller took this challenge seriously, arguing in 1989 that:

> The cause of the libertarian Right . . . has been aided by such works of undoubted intellectual power as Nozick's *Anarchy, State and Utopia*, Hayek's *Law, Legislation and Liberty*, and Oakeshott's, *On Human Conduct*, all published within a short space of time in the middle 1970s. Even if one is critical of the positions taken in these books, there is no escaping the fact that they do advance arguments of a

suitably basic kind for a libertarian position in politics. They need to
be taken seriously as political theory. [46]

An admission of this kind was rare on the British left for much of the
post-war period, when its members were intellectually secure enough
to dismiss the challenges of Hayek and others as out of touch with the
time. In claiming that libertarian argument needed to be taken seriously, Miller demonstrated the extent to which a re-examination of first
principles was occurring for socialists by the final decade of the twentieth century.

The result of the shifts discussed in the previous sections—the limits
of statist forms of socialism, the resurgence of political theory and the
rise of the New Right—shook the foundations of socialism, as it had
been understood for much of the previous century. As Estrin and Le
Grand wrote in their collection on market socialism: 'What was needed
was nothing less than a rethink of socialism: a re-evaluation of its basic
tenets and a reconstruction of its philosophical and economic foundations.'[47] The 'revival' of market socialism, which is examined below, can
only be understood against this changing context and was one attempt
among many to revive the British left by the last decades of the twentieth century.

THE REVIVAL OF MARKET SOCIALISM

The origins of the market socialist revival of the late 1980s and early
1990s are found in earlier debates. For much of the twentieth century
these debates occurred outside of the mainstream British political tradition. In this section I briefly discuss earlier iterations of the concept,
before examining David Miller's engagement with pro-market arguments in more detail.

Earlier accounts of market socialism

'Market socialism'—or concepts very close to it—underwent several
revivals from the late nineteenth century onwards. However, it was only
ever a minor part of socialist thought in the UK. It is possible to identify
four broad recurrences of interest.[48] In the nineteenth century, John

Stuart Mill proposed an early form of what John Gray described as market socialism.[49] Mill's proposals were based on ownership and control of firms by workers and on a wider redistribution of income and wealth in society.[50]

A second, more significant wave was associated with the economist Oskar Lange in the 1930s. Lange's work produced a revival of market socialism following the 'Calculation Debate', which dealt with the question of whether successful economic planning was possible without the knowledge transmitted by market pricing that allowed for the rational calculation of costs.[51] (The 'Calculation Debate', and Hayek's involvement in it, was discussed in Chapter 1.) Lange's market socialism contained a much greater role for the state than envisaged by later market socialists, such as Miller, with a Central Planning Board still setting prices for capital goods and productive resources outside of labour and the state still possessing exclusive control of firms.

The third wave of market socialism was developed in Yugoslavia after the Second World War under Josip Tito, as part of a wider break with Stalin's Soviet Union. Yugoslav market socialism involved large-scale economic decentralization to workers' collectives that produced, bought or sold most capital goods and owned the residual net profits which they then allocated between wages and investment.[52] Several other East European states also made moves away from more dirigiste forms of socialism to incorporate the market in various degrees during the post-war period. The term is now often used to describe the marketization of the Chinese economy initiated by Deng Xiaoping after 1978.[53]

It is the fourth wave of market socialism that provides the focus for this chapter. It was found in the theoretical expositions put forward by several thinkers in Britain and the United States in the decades after the collapse of communism in Eastern Europe. There are several, often quite different, variations of this argument. Important contributions were made by Joseph Carens, Alec Nove, Christopher Pierson and John Roemer.[54] As Miller and Estrin pointed out, perhaps the only 'community of view' among those describing themselves as market socialists was the shared belief that 'markets are not automatically to be identified with capitalist markets'.[55]

Miller's market socialism

David Miller provided perhaps the most sustained and best developed account of market socialism during this last revival.[56] He argued that the case for the market is compelling. First, he claimed that the market has epistemological advantages over rival systems. Miller sums up his acceptance of the epistemological argument concisely:

> Markets serve simultaneously as information systems and as incentive systems. The price mechanism signals to the suppliers of goods what the relative demand is for different product lines, while at the same time giving them an incentive, in the form of potentially increased profits, to switch into lines where demand is currently high in relation to supply.[57]

The argument that markets act as both information and incentive systems approximating supply with demand was most often associated with the right. This epistemological argument for the market is set out in length in Chapter 4. Below, in the section on 'the significance of the revival' market socialism, I argue that the consequences of such an argument make it difficult to incorporate unproblematically into the wider socialist tradition.

Second, Miller argued that markets provide a structure within which free choices can be made. Freedom, Miller claimed, had returned to prominence on the left,[58] and—unlike some earlier socialists—he places this value at the core of his ideology. Miller is explicit that 'Freedom is valuable precisely because of the possibility that people may make radically different choices about how they want to live their lives'.[59] Markets allow several liberties that planned systems do not. They allow freedom of choice over purchases—dinner jackets or denim, opera or pop; the market allows people to 'define their own social identities. . . . Nobody wants to have to justify choices of this kind to some public agency.'[60] Markets also provide freedom over when and where to work (although often within extremely circumscribed parameters). This is an argument most famously made by Hayek in *The Road to Serfdom*, rather than on the left. Finally, markets allow freedom of expression through providing resources to propagate views counter to that of the state. (There is a tension here with left-wing 'political economy' views of the media which argue that freedom of expression is often stifled in a capitalist market society.[61]) Miller's claim that markets are linked to freedom of expression is also found in Hayek's *The Road to Serfdom*, which cites Trotsky on this point: 'In a country where the sole employer is the State, opposition means death by slow starvation. The old principle: who does not work shall not eat, has been replaced by a new one: who does not obey shall not eat.'[62]

Third, Miller argued that markets are closely associated with democracy. In particular, Miller notes that the market economy allows industrial forms of democracy in a way that a state-run economy does not, because members of each enterprise in a market have substantial autonomy to control their work environment. For example, they have a say in what, how much, where, how and when goods are produced. In a planned economy, on the other hand, targets are given from above by an elite group of bureaucrats.

For Miller market socialism is an attempt to come to terms with the defects found in the statist models and to take advantage of the benefits of the market. Miller lays out his model of market socialism in some detail. The 'key idea is that the market mechanisation is retained as a means of providing most goods and services, while ownership is socialised'.[63] Social ownership is to be contrasted with both state ownership and private ownership—both of which can be described as forms of 'exclusive ownership'. Social ownership aims at large-scale ownership in common—as exemplified in the cooperative. In his book *Market, State and Community*, Miller provides a concise sketch of his model of market socialism:

> [A]ll productive enterprises are constituted as workers' co-operatives. Leasing their operating capital from an outside investment agency. Each enterprise makes its own decisions about products, methods of production, prices etc., and competes for custom in the market. Net profits form a pool out of which incomes are paid. Each enterprise is democratically controlled by those who work for it, and among the issues they must decide is how to distribute income within the co-operative.[64]

Miller's market socialism had two egalitarian elements. First, under market socialism income differentials would be reduced to a fraction of what they were under capitalism.[65] Miller is keen to stress that the first element does not depend on the idea of equal allocation, an idea which, he argues, is unpopular. Miller's theory of distributive justice is largely based on desert, which he argues is mirrored in popular understandings of the concept. (This marks an obvious break with needs-based conceptions, such as those derived from Marxism.) If a just system is one which rewards according to desert, then there is a degree of inequality admitted under market socialism, which is, for Miller, compatible with justice. Primary income is determined largely by the market, but Miller argues the market must be framed in such as way as to ensure that incomes bear a close relation to effort and ability, and therefore, Miller claims, income differentials will be far narrower under market socialism.

The second egalitarian element in Miller's market socialism is that it would provide income supplements, in cash or kind, to those in need based on need. Miller wanted a shift from the current system, where welfare is often presented as a kind of 'collective charity', to a socialist conception where welfare is a right, owed as a matter of distributive justice and claimed free from stigma. A practical condition of the shift towards welfare rights, Miller argues, is a 'strengthening of communal ties'.[66] The importance Miller places in community, which he often associates with nationalism, challenges more internationalist forms of socialism, as I argue in the next section.

THE SIGNIFICANCE OF THE REVIVAL

How should this revival of market socialism be judged against the wider political landscape? At the outside, there seem to be two possible interpretations. First, 1990s market socialism could be seen as merely part of 'the revisionary socialist project'—as Miller suggested at some points in his work.[67] In the UK this tradition stretches back to Anthony Crosland and perhaps further.[68] Revisionism was, above all else, a criticism of the effectiveness or necessity of traditional economic socialism as a means of running a successful economy. (Social democratic revisionism is discussed in more detail in Chapter 3 on Raymond Plant.)

A second view interprets market socialism as something more radical, an argument alien to the socialist tradition. Under this interpretation market socialism involves a post-Hayekian suspicion that there is no defensible basis for publicly articulated and applied collective values.

At some points this seems closer to Miller's argument. Market socialism is presented as a 'radical redefinition of the meaning of socialism' and an 'alternative' to other forms of socialism which are 'outdated'.[69]

I examine how Miller's market socialism fits with the broader traditions of British political thought in the twentieth century, by looking at some of the major discontinuities between market socialism and the more statist forms of socialism that dominated the twentieth century. In particular, I focus on how Miller's arguments for the market rely on themes either submerged by mainstream twentieth-century socialism or found as part of non-socialist traditions. I begin with an account of freedom in market socialism and how it contrasts with many earlier socialist accounts.

Freedom in the market

Miller's account of freedom challenges older socialist traditions. It is explicitly the freedom of a market society: 'Individual freedom is enshrined in consumer choice, and in workers' rights to move in and out of enterprises'.[70] At his most candid Miller admitted how radically the acceptance of market freedoms affects the socialist argument. At one point Miller identified 'two strands in the socialist critique of capitalism'.[71] The first element of this critique focused on the 'distributive inadequacies of capitalism'. The argument was that capitalism distributes resources, freedom and power in a way that is grossly unfair. (This argument is found in Marx's theory of exploitation—the claim that under capitalism the surplus value created by the labour of the worker is systematically expropriated by the capitalists.) This critique led to an argument for distributive justice in most socialist thought. The second element of the socialist critique of capitalism concerns the 'quality of life' in capitalist society. This is a broad critique which includes the accusation that capitalism produces for profit and not for use and therefore fails to provide people with what they really need, that capitalism stifles creativity and that it fosters competitive, rather than co-operative human relations. (This line of argument is found in Marx's theory of alienation.) Together, Miller argued, these claims 'add up to the thesis that capitalism does not and cannot provide the good life for man'. He continued:

No matter how radically resources are redistributed, activity in a market must be governed by instrumental rationality, people must behave non-tuistically (that is, each must aim to maximise his holdings, regardless of the welfare of his partners in exchange), and so forth. The 'quality of life' critique seems therefore inevitably to point beyond markets. [72]

Miller's acceptance of the market, and with it the freedoms necessary to drive a market society, led him to conclude that:

if we want a feasible form of socialism, it seems that we have to accept a major role for markets, and that to that extent, we must abandon the 'quality of life' critique . . . [which] requires us to judge some modes of human life as better than others, regardless of the preferences the people actually display. [73]

This acceptance among market socialists of other individuals' choices, no matter how quirky, foolish or acquisitive they may seem—both for normative reasons and because individual choice is required for markets to work—is also part of an often submerged rejection of paternalism in left-wing thought: the idea that people should make their own choices and that it is not the job of the authorities to tell them what to do. This discovery—or rediscovery—of libertarianism on the left is discussed in more detail in the final chapter of this book.

The return of radical pluralism

Miller's market socialism marks an acceptance that the state is not morally or economically sovereign. He describes both his system and its justifying theory as 'radically pluralistic'. [74] If mainstream socialism in the twentieth century was statist, there is a strong strand in socialist thought which advocates pluralism and cooperation largely in terms of the 'quality of life' critique of socialism that Miller claims to have rejected: the argument that working together is morally desirable in its own right. This claim links Miller's arguments for cooperatives and also allows parallels with both the English political pluralism of the early twentieth century—most notably the guild socialism of G. D. H. Cole—and the socialist pluralism of Harold Laski. A parallel attempt to revive pluralism on the left was made by Paul Hirst, who explicitly linked his argument for pluralism at the end of the twentieth century with the arguments of earlier twentieth-century pluralist thinkers.[75] This is a move made by several thinkers discussed in this book and is part of a wider rediscovery of pluralism on the British left at the end of the twentieth century,[76] which is discussed in more detail in Chapter 4. The argument for workers' control also provided Miller's market socialism with a radicalism, and a transformative aspiration to go beyond capitalism, seldom found in contemporary left-wing debate. Miller's market socialism is often presented as part of a move to a 'feasible' form of socialism, but by the standards of the late 1990s it appeared radical, as the wider left narrowed its aspirations.

Miller's argument for workers' control within the cooperative also straddles other political traditions. The non-statist pluralism that is a part of Miller's market socialism was found in the nineteenth and twentieth centuries among anarchist thinkers, particularly in the mutualism of Pierre-Joseph Proudhon, on whom Miller has written. His early work reflected this interest in the communitarian-anarchists of the nineteenth century.[77] However, scepticism about the state has also been an undercurrent in socialist thought, from Joseph Lane and William Morris in the late nineteenth century to the socialist revisionism of Anthony Crosland in the post-war period. (These anti-paternalist precursors to Miller are discussed in more detail in Chapter 6.) Crosland in particular on the British left registered this scepticism about the state—cautioning his fellow socialists that they 'should not forget that they have anarchist blood in their veins'.[78]

Markets and community

Miller's views on the market also challenge some traditional socialist conceptions of community. Hilary Wainwright, whose work is examined in Chapter 4, argued that Miller equated anti-market socialism with a 'primitive communalism' desired on purely moral grounds, citing Miller's comment that those who support the anti-market tradition in socialism remain 'romantically attached to a pre-industrial vision of community'.[79] For Miller, she argued, such commitments among today's socialists are an unscrutinized legacy of nineteenth-century utopianism. Wainwright's interpretation of Miller's argument allows parallels between his thought and that of Friedrich Hayek, who dismissed socialism as an atavistic desire for a sense of community that was lost with the evolution of the market.[80]

However, Miller's actual account of community is more nuanced than Wainwright admits. His writing contains similarities with writers on nationhood, such as Linda Colley and Andrew Pilkington.[81] Miller notes the importance of enemies in the construction of communal identity, arguing that the stronger the loyalty one has to a community the stronger the animosity seems to be to those outside it. Thus socialists face a trade-off between small, intense communities which relate to each other in non-socialist (rivalrous or hostile) ways or more inclusive communities in which the socialist elements, such as solidarity and simplicity of relationship, are diluted. (A similar argument made a more recent appearance through the controversy sparked by an article in the magazine *Prospect*, in which the then editor David Goodhart argued that there was a trade-off between ethnic diversity and a strong welfare state.[82])

Miller was also critical of the view held by many socialists that communal relationships must, in some way, be unitary. He traced this view to the argument of German Romantics and cited the concern of Raymond Plant, whose work is examined in the next chapter, that their view of community 'involved some notion of the whole man, in which men were to be met by other men in the totality of their social roles and not in a fragmented or segmental way'.[83] Miller argued that Marx, Morris or Kropotkin would not have accepted the argument of the German Romantics either, for it leaves no room for the development of individuality. For Miller, the goal of these thinkers was to 'reconcile individual self-development with communal solidarity, not to extinguish the former in the name of the latter'.[84] Yet in arguing for the market, which necessarily involves partial relationships as people relate to one another as buyers and sellers of goods, Miller has tipped the balance further away from community and towards the individual than did the nineteenth-century thinkers upon whom he draws to support his argument.

Miller's work on community involves a further break with older socialist accounts of the concept. For Miller, community is crucial in the constitution of one's sense of personal identity and in making possible the distributive arrangements that socialists support, and he argues that this sense of community can be derived from nationality.[85] As Miller admits, his 'rescue operation on behalf of nationality'[86] contrasts with earlier forms of socialism, which had, in theory if not in practice, been overwhelmingly hostile to the idea of nationhood, which was associated with aggressive forms of nationalism. (Although there are notable left nationalists; for example, George Orwell and Robert Blatchford both drew on nationalism as a source of support for their socialist arguments in the first half of the twentieth century.[87])

Miller, and other writers on the left by the 1980s, also deprioritized another form of community in their analysis: class. This partly needs to be understood as a reflection of socio-economic change. In the last decades of the twentieth century the decline of manufacturing industry in Britain led to a decline in 'class' as a unifying category for the left. The decline of class identity[88] led to the collapse of the main condition that thinkers on the left had relied upon to make socialism coherent. (The same changes also led to the decline of the tory tradition within conservatism.)[89] As class-based politics declined, the politics of identity increasingly took their place. A good summary of these changes is found in the work of Raymond Plant (whose work is discussed in Chapter 3), when he wrote in 1989 that:

> These values within the Labour movement are not theoretical but are rooted in working-class experience, in the solidarity of the neighbourhood, the workplace and the union. But with the numerical decline of such communities, and the consequent decline in such values, we seem to be entering what *Marxism Today* has called New Times in which individualistic values have displaced those of the community. There is a dire need on the left to accommodate to this change, of which free markets seem to be the best institutional embodiment.[90]

In accepting the market, socialists and social democrats have accepted a mechanism that allows the expression of identity politics, but also a mechanism that undermines the homogeneity of the working-class communities the left has relied upon for its electoral support.

Miller and Plant, in particular, explicitly recognized that the value of solidarity is undermined for socialists and social democrats by this 'new individualism'. Miller argued that there was a historical tension in socialism between a modernizing commitment to industrial society and a nostalgic attachment to pre-industrial forms of community. This attachment paved the way for the later identification of socialism with state planning. Socialists must face this tension and 'discard components of the tradition which closer analysis reveals to be untenable'.[91] Plant explicitly sought to develop a left-wing argument that accepted the increasing diversity, both in terms of community and individuality, of British society in the late twentieth century. The British left in the last decades of the twentieth century was more individualistic than the forms of socialism and social democracy that dominated the twentieth century.

Market socialism is often presented as a form of socialist revisionism. Yet the central position it grants to market freedoms (and the acceptance of the results of those freedoms), its pluralism, its challenge to traditional socialist understandings of community and its explicit search for feasibility mean that it largely lies outside those forms of socialism—including revisionism—that dominated the twentieth century.

CONCLUSIONS: MARKET SOCIALISM IN RETROSPECT

If market socialism was in vogue from the late 1980s to the mid-1990s it is no longer in fashion. In retrospect, the attempt of David Miller and other market socialists to provide a popular alternative to statist socialism failed. As Miller would write in 1997, 'market socialism, once thought to be a rather timid idea, is now regarded by many on the left as dangerously radical'.[92] After regularly returning to the issue of market socialism for much of the two decades from the mid-1970s, the interest of Miller (and many of the other main advocates of market socialism) has waned. The graph on the next page (Figure 2.1) gives some indication of how the term has also fell out of academic debate after the mid-1990s.[93]

Several reasons can be suggested for the decline of market socialism. In the UK, market socialism failed to attract support on the left, while appearing too radical for those in the centre. In the early 1990s the left-wing thinker GA Cohen dismissed market socialism as an example of 'Adaptive Preference Formation', by which he meant a 'process in which, irrationally, a person comes to prefer A to B just because he believes A is available and B is not'. To Cohen, and other critics, 'market socialism is at best second-best'. Cohen, for example, argued that market socialism is inadequate from a socialist point of view because it

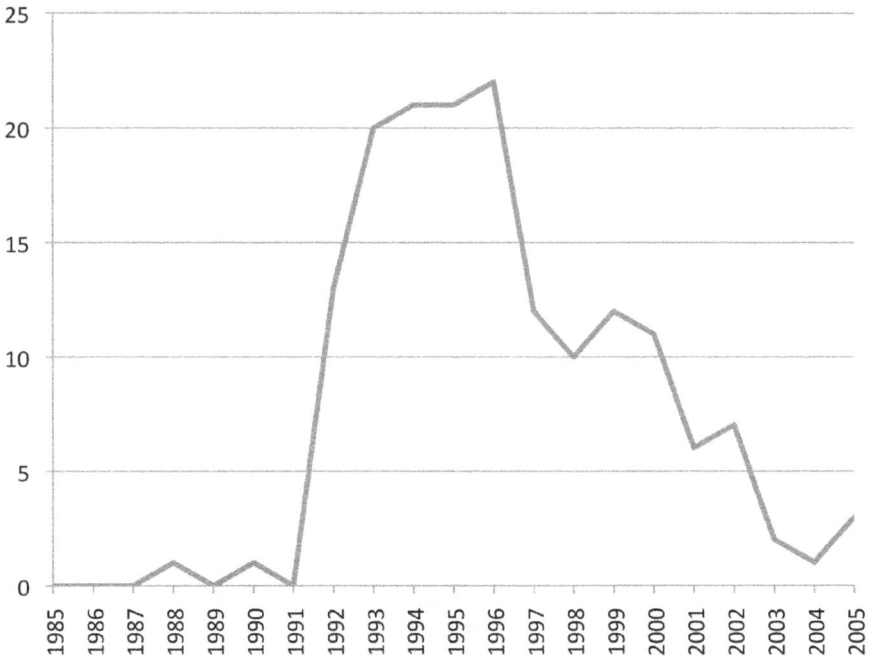

Figure 2.1.   Academic publications on 'market socialism'

fails socialism's egalitarian distributive principles, offering higher rewards to those that happen to be talented in the creation of productive
cooperatives.[94] If market socialism fails the distributive aims of some of
the left, others would reject it on the basis of Miller's admission that it
fails the quality of life criterion on earlier socialists. As Miller admitted:
'[I]f we want a feasible form of socialism, it seems that we have to
accept a major role for markets, and that to that extent, we must abandon the "quality of life" critique' associated with Marx's critique of
alienation.[95]

By contrast, for those in the centre, by the 1990s market socialism
appeared too radical. Whilst from the left Cohen accused those who
supported the doctrine as accepting it just because 'the grass looks
greener on this side of the fence'; for people near the centre market
socialism did not appear to be on 'this side of the fence' at all, but many
miles distant. The distance between the vision for the Labour Party laid
out in Estrin and Le Grand's *Market Socialism*,[96] written for the party

as a specific response to the 1983 election defeat, and the policies of New Labour in office after 1997 make the radical nature of market socialism particularly clear. Market socialism offered a second best: too utopian for critics near the political centre, but an uninspiring second best for many on the left.

There were other reasons for market socialism's rapid disappearance. The violent collapse of the Yugoslavian model of market socialism, discussed above, during a series of conflicts and independence struggles in the early 1990s, meant that the main 'actually existing' source of inspiration for market socialists catastrophically and quickly disappeared.

Finally, market socialism, less than two decades after its heyday in the UK, seems curiously parochial and outdated in its concerns. Miller's discussion of the market is largely national in its scope. Contemporary discussion of the market, especially since the rise of debates about globalization in the late 1990s, tends to view the market as global (or at least regional) rather than national in scope.[97] Writing before the contemporary globalization debate got under way in full force, Miller never fully faces the question of how market socialism can be attained when the powers of the state are circumscribed by globalization—especially as market socialism has only ever received limited popular support. By the late 1990s much of the debate on the centre and left had been refocused onto questions of how to manage globalization.[98]

For much of the twentieth century the traditions which dominated political discussion in the UK—socialism, conservatism, and, to a lesser extent, liberalism—were relatively stable. The dominance of this taxonomy was challenged at various times—notably by feminism at various points in the century, and by the New Right from the late 1960s. By the end of the twentieth century this taxonomy was less clear. Market socialism is not alone in challenging the old categorization; but it was a notably corrosive force in breaking down the old structures, in particular the separation between socialism and liberalism.

Market socialism is no longer a significant part of the political landscape. If it acted as a corrosive force in breaking down the old barriers between socialism and other ideologies, it also burned itself out. In seeking to provide a self-described *socialist* argument for the market, the concept clung to the categories it was itself helping to destroy. The political theorist Michael Freeden has described this as the 'perimeter problem of market socialism'.[99] Market socialism does not fit easily into the socialist tradition: its acceptance of the market, not just for reasons of efficiency (a value for which even the Fabian socialists would have felt some affinity), but often for reasons related to individual freedom, contained ramifications that challenged some of the central themes of earlier socialism. Miller's model of market socialism, through supporting freedom of choice within a market system, broke with the paternalist strand found in Fabian socialism. The concept also broke with mainstream twentieth-century socialism through its non-statist pluralism, its rejection of a strong conception of community and its focus on providing a 'feasible' alternative.

In the UK, by the end of the 1990s the forms of socialism (and conservatism) that had dominated the twentieth century no longer played a significant role in political debate. Contemporary political discussion takes place within a less clearly mapped political terrain, in which ideas that were often a neglected part of the major political traditions of the twentieth century are being rediscovered and reused in the construction of new arguments—for the most part free from those traditions in which they had been previously located. By the end of the twentieth century 'feasible socialism' began to appear more like social liberalism, and liberalism—divided into its social and economic sides— was increasingly dominant. The rise and fall of market socialism provides a case study of the much wider collapse in traditional political traditions that structured politics during the twentieth century. These are themes I examine in more detail in the final chapter.

3

REVISIONISM REVISED

The journalist John Willman wrote in 1993 that Raymond Plant 'was unusual among politically committed thinkers in his willingness to engage with contrary points of view. Lord Plant's distinctive contribution to thinking on the left has been to grapple with the intellectual challenge of the new right'.[1] Plant's contribution to political studies in the UK has been significant, both through his political philosophy and his wider involvement in political life. His active role in the Labour Party is greater than that of any of the other thinkers examined in detail in this book. He was made a life peer in 1992, and sits on the Labour benches. In this role he has been a party Spokesman in the Lords on Home Affairs from 1992 to 1996 and has also spoken for the party on constitutional and welfare issues. He has sat on a variety of groups which helped to shape contemporary British politics. He chaired the Labour Party Commission on Electoral Systems between 1991 and 1993, and the Fabian Society Commission on Taxation and Citizenship between 1999 and 2000. He was also a columnist for *The Times* newspaper between 1986 and 1988.

In many respects the responses made by Plant to the contextual changes of the late twentieth century paralleled those of David Miller. Particularly significant in shaping the thought of both thinkers was the Labour Party's loss of the 1983 General Election, which was seen as symptomatic both of its wider intellectual failings and of the successes of the new right. Like Miller, Plant was heavily involved in the creation

of the Socialist Philosophy Group (SPG), which was set up to rethink
and reconstruct socialist ideas after the 1983 defeat.[2]

In contrast to Miller, Plant was far more willing to tackle the arguments of Hayek and the new right directly. Much of Plant's earlier
work, including his doctoral thesis, had been on Hegel and on issues of
community,[3] and his earlier work demonstrated a familiarity with Hegelian and new liberalism[4]—a category to which Plant's arguments are
close, as I go on to argue.

Much of Plant's work during the 1970s was in the tradition of revisionist socialism. He was concerned with the inequalities of power and
status that arose in the practical workings of the welfare state.[5] His
examination of the right and wrongs of selling blood,[6] for example,
deals with the same concerns and themes as Richard Titmuss's classic
text, *The Gift Relationship*.[7] Plant's work at this time also examined
questions over the limits of the market (as Titmuss's work had done)
and therefore can be seen as a prelude to his fuller engagement with
pro-market arguments during the 1980s and 1990s.

From tentative debates about the limits of the market in the 1970s,
the electoral success of the Conservative Government under Thatcher
during the 1980s led Plant to an early and much fuller engagement with
pro-market arguments. Plant's 1984 Fabian pamphlet, *Equality, Markets and the State*,[8] was an explicit attempt to claim freedom for the
left. The centrality of freedom in Plant's argument places it very close to
Miller's (examined in the previous chapter). As such the argument in
Equality, Markets and the State marked an important break with older
left-wing arguments. (Plant's argument in this pamphlet was developed
in several publications during the 1980s and 1990s and is discussed in
more detail below.)

As the political journalist John Lloyd commented, the arguments in
favour of freedom made by members of the SPG were 'conducted
necessarily on the terrain chosen by the right since for a long time the
left disdained the fight, saying it was a phoney'.[9] By the 1980s the
electoral success of the Conservative Party meant that this fight could
be disdained no more. Plant's argument was particularly influential on
key figures within the leadership of the Labour Party. Bryan Gould,
onetime Shadow Treasury Spokesman, drew on them in his book *Socialism and Freedom*.[10] The then Deputy Leader of the party, Roy

Hattersley, also acknowledged Plant's pamphlet (and wider support) in his book, *Choose Freedom: The future for democratic socialism*.[11]

In this chapter, I begin with a discussion of those arguments Plant identifies as crucial in Hayek's account: his argument against end states, his procedural account of justice and his negative view of liberty. I also set out Plant's response to Hayek, including his case for making the *value* of freedom more equal. I then argue that Plant's engagement with Hayek allows him to make an argument that is well outside mainstream socialism thought, as it was understood in the twentieth century, but which straddles the new liberalism of the early twentieth century, and the revisionist social democracy of the early post-war period.

PLANT'S ENGAGEMENT WITH HAYEK

Plant argued that: 'Hayek's writings pose the most coherent contemporary challenge to socialism. The failure to respond adequately to the questions he posed and the agenda he set is one of the main reasons for socialism's intellectual decline'.[12] It is significant that Plant, a socialist, bothered to write a commentary in *The Times* for Hayek's ninetieth birthday, and a demonstration of Plant's 'willingness to engage with contrary points of view' noted in the quote that begins this chapter. His claim that Hayek's challenge 'is one of the main reasons for socialism's intellectual decline' shows the importance which Plant places in his engagement with Hayek's work.

Hayek features in many of Plant's works, but the most detailed engagements begin in the late 1980s, notably with two book chapters, 'Socialism, Markets and End States',[13] and 'Hayek on Social Justice: A Critique',[14] and in his book, *Modern Political Thought*,[15] which reasserted and clarified many of the arguments concerning Hayek, presented piecemeal elsewhere in Plant's work. Plant returned to the arguments of Hayek and neoliberalism in more detail in an extended examination of *The Neo-liberal State*, published in 2010, which grew out of a series of lectures on the issue. (It is a demonstration of Plant's influence in party politics that part of the book grew out of work with leading Labour politicians Gordon Brown and Ed Balls.[16]) However, it is the earlier presentation of Plant's engagement with Hayek that I focus on

here, written in part as a response to the electoral struggles of the
Labour Party and the success of Thatcherism.

One of Plant's 1989 chapters on Hayek appeared in Julian Le Grand
and Saul Estrin's book, *Market Socialism*[17]—the popularity of which
was discussed in some detail in the previous chapter. Plant never em-
braced market socialism as fully as other contributors to the book, and
his thought is not best classified as narrowly market socialist. Plant's
contribution to the Estrin and Le Grand book was not so much an
argument specifically for market socialism, as Miller's was, for example,
but an examination of the more general question of whether market-
based views can be reconciled with 'accepted socialist values'.[18]

Plant, as a philosopher of Hegel, in the main engages with Hayek's
political theory.[19] He regards Hayek's arguments against social justice
as central. Other thinkers studied in this book have focused on Hayek's
political economy. Plant's account of Hayek's argument against central
planning is largely presented in terms of its imposition of values, not its
epistemological difficulties. His writings on Hayek's epistemological account are characterized best as concession rather than engagement.
Plant summarized Hayek's epistemic challenge to socialists thus: '[The
central planner] may have better computers and better techniques of
co-ordination, but this fragmented knowledge, crucial to effective action, cannot be put into propositional form for planning purposes. The
market, rather than the state and the central plan, is able to use this
dispersed knowledge and will yield more efficient outcomes'.[20]

The social democrats of the 1980s and beyond have conceded significant ground to this argument. Plant has commented that Hayek's epistemology seems to be 'in the right neck of the woods'.[21] Plant's acceptance of the limits of state planning is more profound than that of post-
war social democratic revisionists, such as Anthony Crosland. Crosland
argued that calls for further nationalization mistook ends, such as equality, with means; Plant by contrast explicitly accepted Hayek's epistemological case that nationalization would lead to economic inefficiencies.
This concedes significant ground to the right and marks a departure
from earlier Fabian socialist thinkers, who presented an argument for
state planning in terms of its efficiencies over market-based approaches.
Plant leaves it for others to launch more detailed engagements with the
Hayekian critique of central planning. The thoroughgoing engagement
with Hayek's epistemology is set aside for later writers on the left; in

particular Hilary Wainwright, whose work and engagement with Hayek's epistemological arguments are examined in the next chapter.

Unlike other commentators discussed in this book, Plant's work is already the subject of an extended study. Even more to the point, he is the subject of an extended analysis that compares his work in detail with that of Hayek. João Carlos Espada's 1996 book, *Social Citizenship Rights: A Critique of F.A. Hayek and Raymond Plant*, is an examination of the views of Hayek and Plant on 'welfare' or 'social citizenship rights'.[22] The first part of the book focuses on Hayek—a sceptic over the existence of this type of right. In the second part of the book Hayek's rejection of welfare rights is contrasted with Plant's argument for them. In the foreword to Espada's book, the sociologist Ralf Dahrendorf (who supervised the doctoral thesis from which the book emerged) wrote: 'The author did not find it easy to identify one person to make the opposing case, a Hayek of the Left (if that is not too absurd an idea). Raymond Plant . . . was eventually singled out'.[23]

The description of Plant as a 'Hayek of the Left' is slightly misleading. Hayek's work was notable—at least after the publication of *The Road to Serfdom* in 1944—for its polemical quality and its lack of engagement with the arguments of his opponents (as I argued in Chapter 1). Plant is quite the opposite. His work engages seriously and respectfully with an alternative point of view. Yet Hayek was crucial to Plant. As Espada noted, 'Raymond Plant's reflection has been developed in a critical dialogue with the thought of Friedrich A. Hayek'.[24]

Espada's summary and collation of the main arguments and their tensions are useful and I occasionally draw upon his work in this chapter. However, his approach to Hayek and Plant is very different from my own. Espada's work is a piece of political philosophy in which the two thinkers are used as a springboard from which to launch a normative analysis of social rights (which Espada does in Part Three of his book). This book, by contrast, is largely a contribution to the recent history of thought. Espada's book is also a piece of political philosophy which focuses fairly exclusively on one aspect of Hayek's and Plant's argument: the concept of social rights. (There is no discussion in Espada's book of Plant's thoughts on Hayek's epistemic argument, for example.) In addition, although Espada engages seriously with both thinkers, he sets Hayek and Plant up as polar opposites because of their opposing views on social rights. The political categories, of which their work is selected as an exemplar—described by Espada as neo-liberalism and socialism—are seen as largely static and opposed. By contrast this book is interested in the changing nature of political discourses, and it is the messier middle area of partial agreement, not polarity, which is used to highlight these changes. It is to Plant's 'critical dialogue' with Hayek that I now turn.

Social justice and end states

One important area of debate between Hayek and Plant was over the claim that socialism attempted to 'impose' particular end states on the wider polity, particularly forms of equality. Hayek's argument against end-state conceptions of social justice is that there is the intractable problem of trying to provide a justification for the nature of that end state. The most important target of Hayek's argument was the socialist view of justice, which was characterized as 'distributive' or 'social'.

First, neo-liberals called into question the criteria used to define social justice.[25] There are many possibilities: Plant listed 'desert, merit, need, entitlement, etc.'. Socialists, Plant argued, 'will want to place need at the centre of moral concern, even if they find a role for some of the other criteria too'.[26] (Marx's rallying cry 'From each according to his ability, to each according to his needs!'[27] is perhaps the best-known example of this type of argument.) However, placing 'need' as central raises various questions, which would appear to have intractable answers: why prioritize need over other values? What does need consist of? How does one decide the weight given to need, compared to other values, such as merit, in the theory of social justice?

Second, even if we could decide what bundle of resources was required to meet each and every person's needs, Hayek argued, neither needs nor merits are commensurable. When two needs conflict, there is no higher principle to which one can appeal to resolve the dilemma. The same problems apply when we come to rank different conceptions of merit against one another. For many neo-liberals dilemmas of the kind raised above can never be solved by rational argument. Hayek, with many of the Chicago and Austrian School thinkers, argued that values are irreducibly subjective and attitudinal. Alongside this claim, Hayek also made a complementary sociological argument against end-state values. Society, he argued, is now so morally diverse in character, that the kind of consensus needed to support socialist end states could never be achieved. The philosophical argument regarding value pluralism has undergone a revival in recent years, for example, in John Gray's reinterpretation of Berlin's 'agonistic pluralism'.[28]

The third line taken by Hayek is sociological. It is the argument that society is now so morally diverse in character, that the kind of consensus needed to support socialist end states could never be achieved. The only way to achieve socialist end states, and Gray summarized Hayek's point usefully here, would be through 'the political conquest of state power and the subjugation of rival value systems'.[29] Part of the case for the market, as it is presented by some on the left, rests on its ability to provide for individual preferences; this leaves some thinkers associated with the new right asking why the market socialist's argument does not extend to individual *moral* preferences concerning the end-state principles of the society that the individual would like to live in. 'All of this', Plant concluded, 'adds up to a formidable critique of traditional forms of socialism and demands a response'.[30]

These claims would mean that the only way to achieve socialist end states, would be, in John Gray's words, through 'the political conquest of state power and the subjugation of rival value systems'.[31] By contrast, in a market, we do not pursue any set of philosophically unjustifiable ends; instead we are presented with a procedural system for following our own good in our own way. 'All of this', Plant concluded, 'adds up to a formidable critique of traditional forms of socialism and demands a response'.[32]

Plant largely accepted the sociological assessment of value pluralism, and this view has an important affect on his work. An example of how the increase in value pluralism in society affected Plant's political outlook can be found in his report on electoral reform, which he carried out for the Labour Party.[33] The issue of electoral reform was deeply divisive within the party. Neil Kinnock (who was Party Leader from 1983 to 1992) was largely in favour of a move towards some form of proportional representation, while Roy Hattersley, the Deputy Leader, was vehemently opposed to it. The suggestion that Plant should chair the committee came originally from Hattersley,[34] who had found discussions with Plant helpful in writing his *Choose Freedom*.[35] Hattersley's work contained many ideational similarities to Plant's own. On the left of British politics, the call for constitutional and electoral reform gathered momentum during the 1980s. This is reflected in the work of several of the thinkers discussed in this book, particularly Hilary Wainwright—the subject of Chapter 4. Support for electoral reform was galvanized by the pressure group Charter 88.[36] It is ironic, therefore, that for all the passion over the issue elsewhere on the left, Plant's original 'unique selling proposition as chairman [of the report], however, was that he had given no great thought to electoral reform before and could thus be presented as having an open mind'.[37]

The 'Plant Report', published in 1993, caused some controversy by calling for the replacement of the British first-past-the-post electoral system. Plant was described as 'an unlikely harbinger of political revolution'[38] and it was suggested that the author 'appears to have launched an upheaval that could alter the UK political landscape irreversibly'.[39] Plant's reasons for advocating electoral change were largely based on a sociological assessment of value pluralism. He argued that the social conditions which produced two largely class-based political parties have now disappeared and that in a more pluralistic society a voting system is needed which is not designed simply to award complete victory to the party with the highest number of seats.[40]

Procedural justice

A second area of debate between Hayek and Plant was over the claim that justice is 'procedural'. Socialists, Plant noted, have invariably argued that justice is a matter of end states. By contrast, neo-liberals have tended to argue for 'procedural' justice.[41] Hayek's argument for the market, for example, does not support any particular end state. Justice is conduct that avoids interfering in individual's liberty, property or contractual rights in the market; it is not a matter of achieving an end state. Unintentional action, argued Hayek and others, could not result in injustice. To say hurricane damage is unjust, for example, would be a literal 'nonsense'. Injustice could not result from the outcomes of uncoerced market transactions because they were unintentional. The market, notes Plant quoting Fred Hirsch, is 'in principle unprincipled'.[42]

Plant noted that it is possible to combine ethical views about what the end state should be with procedural arguments. This is what happened in practice during the post-war period of 'consensus'. Here the market is allowed to operate within a certain framework, and the government intervenes through provision of welfare to secure certain outcomes (such as meeting need) when they are not provided. However, Plant noted that there were limits to how much the left could achieve through this approach. The collapse of the Keynesian consensus from the mid-1970s onwards, with rising unemployment and inflation and stalling growth, made these limits even clearer.

If the collapse of the post-war consensus created deep practical problems for the left's attempt to run together end states with procedural justice, Plant argued that neo-liberals' theoretical distinction between procedural and end states also raises important challenges for socialists. Socialists must dispute the procedural view of justice put forward by Hayek and other defenders of the free market that injustice occurs only as a result of *intentional* action.

Plant presents both logical and intuitive arguments against Hayek's procedural conception of justice.[43] Under the logical argument, Plant noted, socialists could argue that we are not just responsible for our *intended* actions, but also the *foreseeable* results of our actions, so that these too become a matter of justice. When Hayek offered his argument he did so in relation to individuals—the shipper, estate agent or arbitrageur raised in the example above—yet socialists had tended to present their arguments in relation to groups: class being the most obvious example. To Plant, although the outcomes of many millions of market transactions may well be *unintended*, as they are *foreseeable* they do become a matter of justice.[44] If there is a class of people who will enter the market and, although it is intended by no one, will foreseeably get less from it, this is a matter of justice.

This claim avoids a problem suffered by Hayek's procedural understanding of the concept. If one accepts his view that injustice can only be caused intentionally 'there would constantly be a strong incentive continually to narrow down the characterization of intention so that it does not include the foreseeable consequences of action'.[45] To Plant, the consequence of this widening of the scope of justice is that 'those who support the market do bear responsibility for the least well off',[46] because this group does foreseeably end up with less after entering the market.

A second argument against Hayek's procedural conception of justice is derived from what Plant sees as our intuitive understanding of the term. Plant noted that 'we could argue against Hayek at this point that justice and injustice is not only a matter of how a particular outcome came about or arose but is rather a matter of our response to that outcome'.[47] Plant gives a hypothetical example. He sees a frail and elderly person fall after a gust of wind, knock themselves out, and end up facedown in a gutter full of water. He could save that person's life at no great personal cost. The issues of justice here, he suggests, are not just how the person came to be there, but his *response* to the outcome—it would be an injustice to walk on by.[48] Intuitively, justice concerns our *response* to outcomes, not just whether we intend them to occur. An extension of this is that justice demands responsibility in citizens. This is redolent of new liberal thinkers almost a century before as well as New Labour's link of rights with responsibilities.

Plant opens himself up to difficulties when the principle is introduced to the real world. He accepts this in an account of his thoughts on a service at Winchester Cathedral, written over Christmas 1989 and published in *The Times*.[49] The practical difficulty that Plant's conception of justice raises is that if justice is a matter of our response to outcomes (not just whether they were intended), then how do we chose which outcomes we should respond to? Plant quoted *The Book of Common Prayer*, in which we are bade to confess that 'We have left undone those things which we ought to have done'. 'This', he writes, 'has always worried me. . . . There are an indefinitely large number of things which I have not done. Which among them ought I to have done?' or, in philosophical terms, an indefinitely large number of outcomes to which one has not responded. This in turn raises questions of knowledge, ignorance and justice. Plant wrote:

> Am I responsible for all the harm which my inaction rather than action could have prevented? If such harm is a foreseeable consequence of my failure to act, can I limit my moral responsibility by putting myself in a position in which I am unaware of the consequences of that failure to act? To limit my moral responsibility I should not read or watch television reports of drought and disaster. I should not look at charity advertisements. Such ignorance would make for moral bliss, a limited moral responsibility, following from limited knowledge of the world and my capacity to act in it. Does watching the news or buying newspapers widen our circle of moral duty?[50]

Plant ended his article here, and the problems of overextending our conception of morality and justice were not fully answered.

Negative liberty

A third area of debate between Hayek and Plant was over the claim that liberty is negative. A parallel philosophical challenge to socialists from neo-liberals occurs when it comes to defining freedom. The neo-liberal's view of freedom tends to be negative—it is defined as the *absence* of intentional coercion.[51] Here negative liberty is contrasted with the positive freedom of being able to *do* or *be* something.[52] For neo-liberals there is a categorical distinction between freedom and ability.[53] If they were not distinct, then, it is argued, any kind of inability would be an unfreedom—Plant uses the case of a man's inability to bear a child as an example. For neo-liberals, this negative understanding of liberty is then applied to the market. The market is not coercive because it lacks agency and therefore intentionality. If a lack of money prevents me from having tea at the Ritz, it is not a lack of freedom; it is a lack of ability to pay—I am no less free.

Plant attacked Hayek's negative conception of freedom, arguing that the neo-liberal gives no account of why freedom is valuable to us.[54] A point Hayek seems unconcerned with. At several stages in his work Plant stresses—in an unfashionably un-postmodern manner—that we are beings of a particular type that value freedom.[55] Sometimes this argument is expressed in more straightforward terms. In his 1984 pamphlet *Equality, Markets and the State*, Plant argued, 'In order to live a purposive life shaped by my own values and not those of others I need opportunities and resources to choose my own way of life and values'. As well as negative protection from coercion, we need positive economic and social resources.[56]

Elsewhere the argument is presented philosophically. In 1980 Plant asked, '[A]re there any basic human ends that are wanted by all persons, with basic needs being the necessary means for the pursuit and realisation of those ends'? He continued, if there are 'such ends generating such basic needs' then, following Rawls, they could be described as 'primary goods which could be the basic concern of social policy'.[57] He argued that every moral code, whether personal or shared, relies on people having certain moral capacities which allow them to pursue the moral goals enshrined in that code. Plant's argument bears similarities to that of those liberals whose central concern has been individual autonomy. The canonical figure in this tradition is J. S. Mill, with Joseph Raz, among others, providing an important modern expression.[58] Thus, the capacity to act as a moral agent becomes the basic human end which generates basic human needs. As Plant wrote, 'There are some conditions necessary for doing anything at all. . . . No matter what morality one adopts, these conditions will be necessary for carrying it out'.[59] These basic human needs, he argued, following the work of the philosopher Alan Gewirth, are 'survival' and 'autonomy' (understood as the freedom to act morally).[60]

Plant gave a positive account of positive freedom or autonomy. To live a meaningful life as 'purposive creatures'[61] he claims we need both negative protection from arbitrary constraint *and* a bundle of resources and skills. On its own, however, this is an argument that would support at its most generous a residualist welfare system: all must have a basic bundle of resources in order to live autonomous lives. The argument for basic needs as a necessity to living autonomous lives undersubscribes any distinctly left-wing argument. In the next section I examine the relation between equality and freedom (qua autonomy) in Plant's work.

Plant is arguing that for freedom to be valuable to us it must be 'effective'. Hayek's attempt to define freedom negatively is rejected in favour of a positive view of liberty, which is a heritage that stretches in the British tradition back to proto-new liberals such as J. S. Mill and T. H. Green in the late nineteenth century. It is this new liberal strand—in the British context—by which Plant is influenced.

Plant and the equal value of freedom

Plant's defence of social democracy builds on his engagement with Hayek's work and provides and account of equality that avoids the Hayekian charge that it is simply an imposition of end states. Plant argues that a just, social democratic will be in some form a more equal one. Equality is the value that divides right from left. In short, as the Italian philosopher Norberto Bobbio commented, 'the left is egalitarian and the right is inegalitarian'.[62] Yet, the question that follows from this is always, in Amartya Sen's phrase, 'Equality of What?'[63] Plant largely accepted the neo-liberal criticism of equality of outcome, yet he still argues that equality is important.

Neo-liberals are comfortable with forms of argument based around equality of opportunity, rather than outcome. Yet Plant (like Crosland before him), rejects this form of equality as insufficient for several reasons. First he argued it failed to take into account the moral arbitrariness of genetic endowment.[64] Second, he noted that there were limits to what can be achieved with the attempt to equalize starting positions—particularly because any radical action in this direction will lead to considerable intervention within the family.[65] Third, he argued that equality of opportunity 'takes the existing structure of equality for granted and is concerned about recruitment to it'.[66]

Plant's own conception of equality emerges out of a simultaneous critique of both equality of outcome and equality of opportunity. A first step he takes is to re-examine why equality is important. It is important, he argues, because it is a means of securing other values. For example, the left tended to argue that a more equal society would be more peaceful, crime-free, comradely, and so on. To Plant, equality is valuable because it is a method of securing greater *freedom*.

In the previous section, Plant gave an account of positive freedom or autonomy. His argument is supplemented by a further egalitarian step. He moves from a defence of the provision of basic needs in order to achieve autonomy, to an argument for their more equal distribution, so that *liberty is of roughly equal value to all people*. Plant gave several reasons for the equalization of the value of freedom, but one in particular is derived straight from his engagement with Hayek's work. Plant turned Hayek's argument that there are many conceptions of the good and that we cannot prioritize any one conception, on its head:

> If this is accepted, then it could be argued that no individual merits more or less in the distribution of those basic resources which are necessary to enter the market of a fair basis and thus those resources should be distributed as equally as possible because, if the neo-liberal is correct, there is no other criterion which would not involve weighing up incommensurable merits and deserts.[67]

Plant's account of equality is based on an argument for liberty. As such, it avoids the neo-liberal criticism that socialists are attempting to impose one particular set of values on all. Instead it frames the social democratic argument in terms of making the value of freedom equal. In doing so, Plant uses many of the neo-liberals' own arguments around the importance of freedom. Despite the equalitarian argument, Plant accepts various inequalities. He accepted, for example, that there could be a 'rent of ability' on grounds of efficiency, which would be set at the amount of legitimate inequality that citizens should accept if they want 'to mobilize skills which otherwise would no longer be mobilized and without which we should be worse off'.[68] The difficulty often raised with Rawlsian-like difference principles like this by those on the left concerns the question, how much equality do they actually allow?[69] If the trickle down of market economics really is of 'greatest benefit of the least advantaged' then Rawlsians should accept that system.[70] While Rawls, arguably, did not answer this question, Plant adds a *presumption of equality* which turns this question on its head. His question would be how much *in*equality do we allow? Equality is the basic rule, and the burden of proof lies in departures from it.[71]

SOCIALIST REVISIONISM, NEW LIBERALISM AND NEW LABOUR

In his autobiography the philosopher Karl Popper, a friend and contemporary of Hayek, wrote: 'If there could be such a thing as socialism combined with individual liberty, I would be a socialist still. For nothing could be better than living a modest, simple and free life in an egalitarian society. It took some time before I recognized this as no more than a beautiful dream'.[72] The attempt to combine the values of equality and individual liberty has been the project of a significant, but often neglected, strand in left-wing thought. The work of Plant and other second-wave revisionists is one version of this project. Plant's engagement with neo-liberals in the 1980s married the egalitarianism of social democracy with the liberal basis of new liberalism.

Two waves of revisionism

Plant's work is one of the most significant contributions to 'second wave' social democratic revisionism. He knew the earlier revisionist Anthony Crosland personally and admits that Crosland made a great impact upon him. Plant discusses Crosland's work at several points.[73] Plant comes from Grimsby where Crosland's parliamentary seat was and even sought selection there after Crosland's death in 1977. Discussing his academic development Plant admitted to 'a bit of hero worship' towards Crosland and to being 'fascinated by this . . . heavyweight, intellectual'. Looking back at his earlier work, Plant commented that 'I was interested in revitalising social democratic thought, [developing] a new form of revisionism in the same way as Crosland'.[74]

The first wave, in the 1950s, is associated with Roy Jenkins, Denis Healey, Hugh Gaitskell and Anthony Crosland, among others.[75] It emerged as a social democratic response to the left. The Labour government that lost office in the general election of 1951 had been composed of a variety of fellow travellers who until the 1950s had found themselves on same track but with little agreement about their final destination. The electoral loss of 1951 further opened up disagreements about ends of social democracy that had previously rarely been explicit among the Labour leadership.[76] Perhaps the most significant area of debate was over the economy. On the left, followers of Aneurin Bevan pushed for further nationalization.[77] By contrast, revisionists such as Crosland rejected greater nationalization as a confusion of ends and means. Nationalization is not an end of social democracy, and it was debatable for revisionists whether it would lead to greater equality of the kind socialists would want.

During the 1950s Crosland had written confidently that the state was increasingly able to control the economy, that there had been a shift of power from management to labour, that private industry was becoming humanized and that the Labour Government's extension of the welfare state and introduction of Keynesian economics promised economic growth and full employment. By the mid-1970s the confidence that these problems were on their way to being solved appeared 'complacent' as even Crosland noted.[78] Much of the impetus for second-wave revisionism must be seen against the collapse of the post-war consensus.

While the first wave of revisionism was a response to the left, the second emerged in the context of the rise of a neo-liberal or New Right and its influence within the Conservative Party. The first wave of post-war social democratic revisionists paid little attention to the right. Its enemies were abstinent Fabian planners or radical socialists. Crosland, for example, only mentioned Hayek once in *The Future of Socialism*, and then to reject his argument as 'unplausible (*sic*) enough . . . in a British context, even when it was first advanced [and now] . . . thoroughly discredited.'[79] The electoral success of Conservative proponents of neo-liberalism led to a period of re-evaluation on the left. Raymond Plant, for example, became involved in the creation of the Socialist Philosophy Group, which was explicitly set up to rethink and reconstruct socialist ideas after the 1983 General Election defeat[80] and give those ideas a 'public philosophy'—what in contemporary terms might be called a narrative—which the group felt that Thatcher's government was beginning to achieve.[81] This group was one part of a much wider re-evaluation of the left in the UK and wider world that occurred during the 1980s and 1990s. The second wave of social democratic revisionism, of which Plant was a major part, was, therefore, largely a response to the right.

The assertion that there were 'two waves' of revisionist thought can be contested. There are similarities with the debate within feminism over the common account of two waves. As Dale Spender implied in her 1983 book *There's Always Been a Woman's Movement in this Century*,[82] descriptions of 'waves' neglect the activity of those authors writing between the peaks of activity. It is undoubtedly true that there were significant writers working in the revisionist tradition between, say, Crosland in the 1950s and Plant in the 1980s, including J. P. Mackintosh and Evan Luard.[83] However, the argument that there were waves of activity in this area does not deny this. There is water under the trough of a wave as there is at the peak, but the total amount of activity rises and falls.

New Liberalism and New Labour

Plant is also candid about the new liberal aspect of his thought. He has commented modestly that 'I suppose in a way, if there's anyone who I would now see as being a kind of model for my life it's been somebody like [the proto-new liberal, T. H.] Green [although] I'm not conceited enough to think I'm in the same league'.[84] Plant would not demure from the label 'new liberal' as a description for his own thought, commenting 'I mean I call myself a social democrat but new liberal wouldn't stick in my throat—so long as you didn't mean neo-liberal'.[85]

(New liberalism is also explored in Chapter 5.) To Plant, writing in *The Times* in 1990, there were considerable parallels between his own political debate with the neo-liberals and those between classical and new liberals earlier in the century: 'I have commented before in these columns about the resemblance between contemporary political debates and those which took place within Liberalism at the end of the last century'.[86]

Plant's ability to combine the liberal and social democratic traditions in part comes from his intellectual approach. Many political thinkers on the left drew on an account of politics and ideology which derived from Marxism, in which arguments were seen as deriving from and serving the interests of the class location of those who advanced them. The response of socialists writing in the Marxist tradition to arguments from Hayek, Jewkes, Oakeshott and so on, in favour of private property or the market, had been to criticize the interests that those arguments were taken to promote and the values and aspirations for which they were instrumental. If this view of political argument is held, it is difficult to give an argument for the market serious attention in its own right or to 'engage' with it. Plant's understanding of political argument is well outside Marxist tradition. It depends on a worldview in which, although political thinking may interact with other forms of social life, it is neither dependent upon, nor merely derived from, them. Plant's background owes more to Hegelian Idealism than the Marxist materialism of some of his colleagues.

There has always been an overlap between socialist revisionism and new liberalism, but Plant operates in the hinterland between the two ideologies. An important strand of Crosland's work rejected Fabianism and drew on a more liberal heritage. For example, Crosland entitled a much-read section in *The Future of Socialism*, published in 1956, 'Liberty and Gaiety in Private Life; the Need for a Reaction against the Fabian Tradition'.[87] The first wave of revisionism provided a libertarian correction to Fabianism. Similarly, in an early response to Hayek, the post-war Labour Minister Evan Durbin wrote that 'Most of us are socialist in our economics because we are "liberal" in our philosophy'.[88]

For much of the twentieth century the difference between socialism and liberalism was over means—a definition that Hayek largely accepted. His identification of socialism largely with its economic means was common. Socialism, as I argued above, was largely focused on planning. This identification was increasingly questioned, in particular after the work of Crosland and the other post-war revisionists. Once the orthodox, economic means to socialism are rejected, the closeness between left-liberalism and democratic socialism is apparent. As Michael Freeden has noted of the work of Plant:

> Whether this is left-liberalism masquerading as democratic socialism depends entirely on where one wishes to draw the boundary line between the two; indeed, on whether they can be separated by so crude a device as a line. [89]

The claims for a revival of the turn-of-the-twentieth-century liberalism in political thought are found throughout this book. To some thinkers the ideologies of the twentieth century marked nothing more than a bloody detour before the rediscovery of a path which was embarked upon a century before. [90] I take this argument up again in Chapter 5, in my discussion of Andrew Gamble, whose work, like Plant's, also contains many similarities with the liberalism of an earlier age.

There has been a considerable amount of discussion over New Labour's heritage: the influence of Thatcherism, new liberalism or revisionism, for example. [91] Perhaps what is most striking about Plant's thought from the mid-1980s is its prescience about elements of New Labour. Julian Le Grand has argued that the Socialist Philosophy Group, of which Plant was a key part, 'In many ways . . . was a kind of precursor of New Labour.' [92] Writing in 1984, Plant argued that 'egalitarian policies should always be designed to secure and promote the greatest amount of freedom possible within the institutions which it endorses'. [93] His example of school freedom of subject and specialism anticipates the introduction of specialist schools under New Labour. Similarly, his claim that 'freedom in the field of social policy suggests services in cash rather than in kind to give those in receipt of the services the widest discretion to spend their money in their own way and to avoid as far as possible the dependency and paternalism which might come from the provision of services in kind' presages exactly the arguments made around the introduction of Individual Budgets in social care twenty years later (as does his argument for social workers close to the user to make choices, rather than the state, where the user is unable). [94] The links between the engagement with Hayek and New Labour are discussed further in the final chapter.

CONCLUSIONS: A LIBERALIZATION OF SOCIALISM

Plant's engagement with Hayek's work can be seen as a limited tactical retreat for socialists. Plant concedes some ground but then seeks to bolster the defences around other arguments. By accepting a large part of Hayek's argument regarding the problems of prioritizing different versions of the good life, while twisting that argument's conclusion to favour equality, Plant provided a basis for a left-wing theory that allowed for markets while avoiding some of the shots fired by Hayekians at more traditional forms of socialism.

Plant's attempt to provide a version of socialism that largely accepted Hayek's attack on end states was important: it showed again a re-discovered respect among both revisionist and market socialists for individual freedoms (though freedom that was not defined in a solely negative way). Plant attempted to offer a version of socialism that placed freedom as central and so aimed to minimize its interference with individuals' ends. Plant's socialism values equality, but as a means to achieve greater freedom, rather than as an end in itself.

In redefining socialism thus, Plant developed the arguments of Crosland, who argued for a broadening of the conception of equality among socialists from equality of outcome to equality of status and privilege and evoked the new liberal arguments of the early twentieth century. In accepting this broadened conception of equality, Plant's thought constitutes a significant liberalization of socialist thought, alien to many older forms of socialism.

4

SOCIAL MOVEMENTS AND PLURALISM

'A new kind of knowledge'

Since the early 1990s the left-wing journalist, academic and campaign-er Hilary Wainwright has provided an explicit and extended attempt to claim aspects of the thought of Friedrich Hayek for the left. Wainwright is perhaps best known now as the founding editor of *Red Pepper*—the 'independent magazine of the green and radical left'—but she has been academically active since the late 1970s. Wainwright is not alone on the left in pursuing an interest in Hayek, as this book shows. However, as a journalist as well as an academic, Wainwright arguably has influence on a wider (and different) public than the other thinkers discussed here. Her interest in Hayek as a 'libertarian' thinker—and her attempt to explain his popularity and reclaim this libertarian tradition for the left— also goes beyond most of the other thinkers mentioned above.

In the first section of this chapter I look at what it took for Wain-wright to discover Hayek as a source of intellectual inspiration for the left: Wainwright's engagement with Hayek's work can initially be seen as an attempt to understand the popularity of neo-liberalism in post-Soviet Eastern Europe during the early 1990s. The second section of this chapter examines Hayek's epistemology and Wainwright's 'social-ised' version of it. In the final section, I look at the wider significance of Wainwright's thought. I argue that her engagement with Hayek led her to rediscover a form of political pluralism, which had not been an im-portant theme in left-wing thought in Britain since the first decades of the last century. However, Wainwright's argument raises many of the same questions that faced earlier pluralists but remained unresolved with the waning of pluralism and the rise of statist forms of social democracy in the middle decade of the twentieth century.

Preludes to Wainwright's engagement

In 1991, between the revolutions in Eastern Europe and the dissolution of the Soviet Union, the left-wing British sociologist Robin Blackburn wrote: 'So far as I am aware no-one pointed out that Hayek's argument from the dispersed nature of knowledge could also be deployed against a narrow capitalist entrepreneurialism by advocates of social and worker self-management'.[1] (Hayek's epistemological argument is set out below.) Blackburn was one of the earliest thinkers on the British left to note *explicitly* that a re-evaluation of Hayek's thought could contribute towards rejuvenating what he describes as 'socialism after the crash' of the collapsing Berlin Wall. Blackburn's left-wing credentials are clear— a self-described leftist, a frequent and long-term contributor to the *New Left Review*, and its editor at the time the article was published. His article hints at an earlier period of engagement between left and right, before the polarization of politics during the middle decades of the twentieth century. His article attempts to reconstruct 'a subterranean dialogue in which arguments [are] passed from Bakunin to Kautsky, or from Trotsky to Hayek'.[2]

In support of Blackburn's argument, Hayek's earlier writings do provide some evidence of the greater engagement between elements of the left and right during the interwar years. Hayek's earlier work was more prepared to deal in detail with arguments of his opponents than anything written during his later career. For example, he concluded his article, 'The Use of Knowledge in Society',[3] with a claim that there is an area of agreement between left and right over the role of the price mechanism:

> When we find Leon Trotsky arguing that 'economic accounting is unthinkable without market relations'; when Professor Oscar Lange[4] promises Professor von Mises a statue in the marble halls of a future Central Planning Board; and when Professor Abba P. Lerner rediscovers Adam Smith and emphasizes that the essential utility of the

price system consists in inducing the individual, while seeking his own interest, to do what is in the general interest, the differences can indeed no longer be ascribed to a political prejudice. The remaining dissent seems clearly to be due to purely intellectual, and more particularly methodological, differences.[5]

Similarly, the book Hayek edited towards the end of the 'calculation debate' over how prices were set in a planned economy, *Collectivist Economic Planning*, published in 1935, contains contributions on common questions from all sides of the debate—from the Italian socialist economist Enrico Barone, to the anti-socialist thinker Ludwig von Mises (an important early influence on Hayek, as I noted in the introduction). The tone is friendlier, and the extent of detailed engagement with those of opposing views is higher in Hayek's writings before the Second World War than after.

If there was greater engagement between elements of the left and right between the wars, it was not to last. As Blackburn wrote, 'The calculation debate petered out in the forties without achieving resolution. The critical points made by each side were, perhaps, stronger than their arguments for the economic systems they themselves favoured'.[6] Blackburn noted that '[t]he syndicalist strain within socialism was particularly weak in the forties, and belief in the big battalions particularly strong'.[7] In the post-war years the planned Soviet economy appeared stronger than its capitalist rival, and in Britain the post-war nationalizations seemed to have been largely successful. Until the collapse of the Soviet empire the Cold War dichotomized political thinking and, literally and metaphorically, erected political and ideological barriers to engagement between left and right.

Despite Blackburn's claims, it may be the case that the extent to which there was an engagement between left and right in the years before the calculation debate is easy to exaggerate. After noting Mises's arguments against socialism as a 'exclusive action of the government', Blackburn conceded that '[m]ost on the left chose to ignore this critique, pointing to the palpable evidence of capitalist failure and apparent Soviet success'.[8]

Blackburn was reluctant to develop the argument he began above (that Hayek's arguments concerning the epistemological limits of planning could be used in support of the left) or to credit Hayek with much originality. This reluctance to take his engagement with Hayek further means that parallels can be drawn with the work of Miller, discussed in Chapter 2. While Blackburn argued that the left pre-empted much of Hayek's work, Miller presented pro-market arguments most obviously associated with Hayek without often admitting their heritage. Blackburn wrote, for example, that Hayek's argument based on the limits of knowledge 'parallels' earlier work from Leon Trotsky[9] or is a more strongly formulated version of that put forward by the Polish socialist Abba Lerner.[10]

One could say that a problem with Blackburn's attempt to recover the left's early discussions of the epistemological problems of central planning is that they were never in the mainstream of its thought. Hayek was not misguided in his belief that socialism was largely about economic planning—as I discussed in Chapter 2 and elsewhere. This was the dominant strand of British socialism for most of the twentieth century. Blackburn's skillful reconstruction of a 'subterranean dialogue' over the limits of epistemology sometimes seems composed of carefully selected and positioned quotations, pasted together to form an argument which has little resemblance to the meaning of the original pieces from which they are cut. Blackburn did not admit how deeply buried these arguments were in the century's socialist traditions. Blackburn's reluctance to carry through his thinking on Hayek meant that it was Wainwright, who was also involved with *New Left Review* as an associate editor, who took up his challenge—in most detail in her 1994 book, *Arguments for a New Left*.[11]

The libertarian impulse in Eastern Europe

Hilary Wainwright writes that reading Hayek made her 'conscious of a dimension of the left movements in which I had been active' and should contribute to new foundations for the left (as quoted at the start of this book).[12] Wainwright's claim that Hayek can help to provide foundations for what she still described as 'a new left' would have been a shock to both Hayek and the older representatives of that tradition, such as E. P. Thompson and Raymond Williams, who would both have disagreed vehemently that Hayek's legacy was something for which to fight.

If Blackburn's tentative suggestion about the possible implications of Hayek's work for the left was a precursor to Wainwright's arguments, then the success of 'neo-liberalism', as she describes Hayek's thought, in post-Soviet Eastern Europe provided the immediate historical context. By the mid-1990s Wainwright presented her engagement with Hayek as an attempt to explain the popular success of parties inspired by neo-liberalism in what had been the Eastern bloc after 1989. She began her book *Arguments for a New Left* in 'the autumn of 1989' as a direct response to the collapse of the Soviet bloc.

Wainwright was initially optimistic that the revolutions of 1989 could lead to a new form of socialism. This view was shared by many on the left. Tony Wright, who was later elected a Labour MP, wrote:

> I remember meeting with a young Hungarian academic, just at the moment that these momentous changes were in motion, in which my enthusiastic suggestion that here was the opening towards the socialist 'third way' (I remember waving a copy of Alex Nove's *Feasible Socialism* at this point) was met by the sharp message that I could forget all about that kind of thing. Socialism in Western Europe might be in trouble but there was no rescuing cavalry coming over the hill from the east.[13]

Despite these initial hopes for many on the Western left, the revolutions of 1989 tended to usher in governments of the right. More recently, Johanna Bockman has written of her experience as an exchange student in Hungary in 1988 and her discovery of the academic popularity of neoclassical economics in the Easter bloc, which she sees as providing the roots of later neo-liberalism.[14] Wainwright's 1994 book, which includes her fullest early engagement with Hayek, is a response to the successes of the right, and more specifically the success of parties influenced by neo-liberalism in Eastern Europe. As such, *Arguments for a New Left* was an attempt to explain the popularity of neo-liberalism for the people of Eastern Europe after 1989. Wainwright recounts her surprise at meeting students who had protested in Prague during the uprising of 1989 for the first time and finding that it was the 'moral and philosophical notions of neo-liberalism, above all its challenge to the all-knowing state and party, which attracted them'.[15]

Wainwright's work in the 1990s is best understood as an attempt to explain and counter the popularity of the right in Eastern Europe after 1989. She turned to Hayek, as 'the main guru of neo-liberalism', to 'comprehend how its appeal in Central and Eastern Europe could be answered'.[16] Although Wainwright's conclusions differ greatly from

Hayek's, the extent to which her work is both an 'appreciation and [a] critique of Hayek's theory of knowledge'[17] is a surprise. She wrote that:

> Reading Hayek's early work on the economic uses of knowledge produced an eerie sense of recognition. Here was this arch right-winger, guru of General Pinochet's Chile and spiritual tutor to Margaret Thatcher, writing about knowledge in ways which I had come across already amongst radical shop stewards, in the consciousness-raising groups of early women's liberation movement and amongst critical socialist philosophers. Here was this right-wing philosopher giving credence to tacit skills and capabilities ignored by conventional philosophers.[18]

The extent to which Wainwright engaged with Hayek's arguments provided an example of a new fluidity in political thought—of the melting of the post-war allegiances and enmities that was beginning to occur by the start of the 1990s.[19]

AGAINST THE 'ALL-KNOWING' STATE

Since the early 1990s Wainwright has sought to retain what she sees as the insights in Hayek's thought: his account of the 'tacit skills and capabilities ignored by conventional philosophers'. In order to achieve this, Wainwright builds on Hayek's epistemic argument against planning.

Knowledge and planning

To Hayek, attempts at economic planning are epistemologically flawed—they misunderstand the nature of knowledge. Hayek's argument was more sophisticated than many earlier conservative arguments about the limits of human reason. His epistemic argument against socialism, as he defined it, is that it misunderstands the nature of knowledge itself. His argument is that the 'kind' of knowledge needed to plan an economy centrally does not exist in the form that a planner would need it.

Hayek's account of knowledge, the political philosopher John Gray argued, is his 'greatest contribution to political thought'.[20] At one level, Hayek is arguing that central planning is impossible to achieve successfully because our knowledge is limited. The number of calculations needed to supply the demands or needs of every person living in a socialist economy is beyond our capabilities. Dobb pointed out that the second Soviet Five Year Plan mentioned only three hundred specific products, while the plan of 1960 had to deal with 15,000 products, produced by 200,000 enterprises.[21] The number of calculations needed to match supply with demand increases exponentially with the complexity of the society.

If this was Hayek's argument, then one could easily object that the problem could soon be solved. Technology has made socialist economic planning possible. The science writer Ray Kurzweil claimed that the twenty-first century will see the emergence of machines more 'intelligent' than their creators. By 2019, it has been predicted, a $1,000 home computer will match the processing power of the human brain, about 20 million billion calculations per second.[22] This is a processing power many times that of the supercomputers used by the Soviet Ministries in the decades before the collapse of the USSR. If complexity is the only calculation problem, one could argue that technological advance could be used to the benefit of a planned economy: Silicon Valley could be the saviour of state socialism. However, Hayek's epistemic argument against socialism, as he defined it, is not just that its attempts will be contingently unsatisfactory, based on the limits of human knowledge when he was writing, but that it radically mis-describes the nature of knowledge itself.

In making his epistemic argument Hayek drew a contrast between two approaches to political economy. Central planning is defined as the 'direction of the whole economy according to one unified plan'; whereas competition is defined as 'decentralization between many separate persons'.[23] Hayek then argued that which 'of these systems is likely to be more efficient depends mainly on the question under which of them we can expect the fuller use will be made of the existing knowledge'.[24]

This contrast led Hayek to argue that there are 'different kinds of knowledge' and to develop a contrast between 'scientific'[25]—also described as 'theoretical' or 'technical'[26]—knowledge and the knowledge of the particular circumstances of time and place. In 1948 Hayek was able to write that:

Today it is almost heresy to suggest that scientific knowledge is not the sum of all knowledge. But a little reflection will show that there is beyond question a body of very important but unorganised knowledge which cannot possibly be called scientific in the sense of knowledge of general rules: the knowledge of the particular circumstances of time and place. It is with respect to this that practically every individual had some advantage over all others because he possesses unique information of which beneficial use might be made.[27]

Socialism, therefore, is an attempt to use knowledge in a way that it cannot efficiently be used. Most knowledge cannot be collected centrally in the way that the socialist planners believe that it can; it exists in people's heads at particular times and in particular places. Hayek's examples of this knowledge are revealing in the type of economic order he envisaged:

The shipper who earns his living from using otherwise empty or half-filled journeys of tramp steamers, or the estate agent whose whole knowledge is almost exclusively one of temporary opportunities, or the *arbitrageur* who gains from local differences of commodity prices—are all performing eminently useful functions based on special knowledge of circumstances of the fleeting moment not known to others.[28]

Influenced in his early work by Ernest Mach, Hayek argued that knowledge is composed of sense-data unique to each individual; in his later work Hayek incorporated 'tacit knowledge' from the Hungarian-born polymath, Michael Polanyi, into his definition. If we now return to Hayek's question, laid out above, over which economic system is likely to be the most efficient, we are closer to his answer:

[T]he ultimate decisions must be left to the people who are familiar with these circumstances, who know directly of the relevant changes and of the resources immediately available to meet them. We cannot expect that this problem will be solved by first communicating all this knowledge to a central board which, after integrating all knowledge, issues its orders. We must solve it by some form of decentralization.[29]

This still leaves Hayek with the problem of how one could communicate to 'the man on the spot' such further information as he needed to fit his decisions into the whole pattern of changes of the larger economic system.[30] The answer is found in the price system of the market—'a mechanism for communicating information'.[31] It is, to Hayek, this 'marvel'[32] upon which we have been able to 'develop that division of labour on which our civilisation is based'.[33] So, to Hayek, the social order arises as a 'spontaneous' by-product of the interactions of many individuals acting within a market system upon information given to them in the price mechanism.

In later work, Hayek developed the role of the state in this system. It should be limited, he argued, to protecting this spontaneous order. With this in mind Hayek advocated an upper house composed of 'men and women elected at a relatively mature age for fairly long periods, such as fifteen years' to prevent them from succumbing to the short-termism of the electorate.[34] A more frequently elected lower house would have limited powers to raise tax for basic infrastructure and social services.

From tacit to social knowledge

Although she strongly rejected Hayek's right-wing conclusions, Wainwright accepted a large part of this epistemological argument against central planning. She argued that by prying open what Andrew Gamble would later describe as the 'ideological closures' in Hayek's work,[35] Hayek's argument could be reworked to form an epistemological foundation for the existing practices of many social movements and provide a new foundation for the left.

To Wainwright, the conclusions that Hayek drew from this argument were the result of a flawed individualism. She argues that Hayek treats knowledge as 'an individual attribute, rather than as a social product'.[36] The individualism of Hayek's theory of knowledge is summed up, for her, in Hayek's comment that, 'all man's mind can effectively comprehend are the facts of the narrow circle of which he is the centre'.[37] The examples of economic knowledge which Hayek gave—quoted above—seem to confirm his individualist assumption: the shipper, estate agent and arbitrageur are all examples of individuals working alone to use their personal knowledge of the market. To Wainwright, this statement was significant, not because it implied that there were limits to reason (an implication she accepts), but because it excluded the possibility 'of social action to share information and extend the knowledge of individuals through associating for that purpose'.[38] To Wainwright, knowledge is best understood, therefore, not as an individual attribute, but as a 'social product':

> If knowledge is understood as a social product, the foundation of Hayek's case for the free market begins to crumble. For if knowledge is a social product then it can be socially transformed though people taking action—co-operating, sharing, combining knowledge—to overcome the limits on the knowledge that they individually possess.[39]

Wainwright gave various examples of how knowledge is a social product. A first illustration concerned a 'central economic networking institution'—part of the Japanese Ministry of Information and Technology—which shared information on technological development and international markets among the economic elite. These networks of knowledge sharing, Wainwright argued in 1994, have been successful for the wider Japanese economy. (Two decades of Japanese economic problems since Wainwright wrote might lead to a different example being used today.)

A second quite different example of how knowledge can be shared involved the state textile cooperatives of Modena, where a centre had been set up to gather information about the international market and share it among all those cooperatives affiliated with it. To Wainwright, this cooperation demonstrated a way of using knowledge that was not individualist, in the sense that Hayek thought it must be, but did not rely upon what Wainwright saw as the traditional socialist assumptions of an 'all-knowing state'[40] either: 'There is no presumption to be all knowing. But there is a determination to share and combine the insights of individual experiences, in order to meet shared goals'.[41]

Indeed, the actual practice of economic decision making under capitalism also seems to involve the attempt to gather information that is imperfectly articulated and of fleeting relevance. The sharing of information needed to make economic choices among the board of major corporations, for example, seems to be far from Hayek's ideal of the individual ship owner, estate agent or arbitrageur.[42] Outside of a few cases of individual decision-making entrepreneurs, capitalism works through groups doing the best they can with the information available to them at the time.

The belief that knowledge is a social product, rather than an individual attribute, leads Wainwright to call for 'the democratization of knowledge'[43] and to reject other understandings of it. On the one hand, she rejects what she describes as the scientism or positivism of Fabianism and Leninism—the 'powerful fantasy at the back of many a socialist mind' of the omniscient state[44]—while on the other, she rejects Hayek's 'dogmatic assumption that this knowledge is constitutionally and irredeemably individual'.[45] To Wainwright, recognition of the social character of knowledge implies that people can, through social cooperation, increase their understanding of the social consequences of their actions, even though they can never know these consequences in every detail for certain. Wainwright has argued for a middle way between, as she sees it, a socialist state that assumes no significant limits of knowledge, and hence its ability to plan for certain outcomes, and a Hayekian account in which knowledge is held by individuals and where society emerges as the 'haphazard outcome of individual activity'.

Wainwright's middle way implies that actors can purposefully influence society with some knowledge of the likely outcome, albeit limited. Any particular arrangement, for example, the organization of a market, thus becomes not the 'haphazard outcome' of individual actions that Wainwright dismissed in Hayek's work, but an outcome whose relation to the intentions of the human actors involved must be open to empirical inquiry. To Wainwright, recognizing that knowledge has a social character, means that humans can achieve a 'more or less intended outcome' dependent on how comprehensive their understanding of the actors involved and the extent of their power to act.[46] So Wainwright reestablished the connection between 'human intention and social outcome', which she believed was missing in Hayek's work, but recognized the limits of human intention, arguing that, 'social evolution is the outcome of attempts by people rationally, if never perfectly rationally, to construct/design social projects which are then the subject of trial and error'.[47]

For Wainwright, with this understanding of the scope of knowledge, we are not led to Hayek's free market conclusions. Instead, 'we move the private market from the realm of the sacred—God's finger, as the

Czech economist describes popular conceptions of the market—to the profane: particular historically shaped and historically transformable institutions' created by human intention capturing what limited knowledge is available.[48]

From social knowledge to social movements

When Wainwright sets her engagement with Hayek aside to examine the wider consequences of her account of knowledge, she tends to shift her argument from the economic (the Japanese Ministry of Information and Technology and the Modena textile cooperatives introduced above) to the social. She argued that:

> social movement activists, in much of their more innovative practice, have pioneered an approach to knowledge which, like Hayek, appreciates its practical and tacit aspects but, unlike Hayek, treats these and its theoretical aspects as social products. The democratisation of knowledge runs through their methods.[49]

For Wainwright, it is the individuals within social movements who hold information, which they share imperfectly among themselves, about the conditions they experience. It is this knowledge that was neglected by the post-war socialist planners:

> The consequences [of this neglect] are visible in the often well-intentioned legacy that post-war social democratic governments left to those who grew up during the post-war boom and since; a legacy for which these latter generations have appeared at times rudely ungrateful: university campuses on bleak parklands miles from city life, designed with little practical knowledge of students' needs and desires; medical training and hospital organizations developed with little knowledge of the particular concerns of women; transport systems worked out as if children did not exist; employment legislation passed as if the passing was enough, and the implementation could be left to the courts, without thought that the knowledge of the workers affected should be built in; investment grants made to keep jobs in a poor region, without consideration given to the inside knowledge needed to monitor their use.[50]

Wainwright's claim that it is 'social activists' who can share knowledge raises questions. The examples she gives above are not what one would generally consider forms of social activism. The users of a particular transport system, the students of a particular university, and so on, do not necessarily look like social movement activists. Instead their knowledge seems to be something rather more immediate, contingent, local and particular. They are citizens for whom public services are not working (a theme Wainwright develops in some of her later work[51]). Citizens' abilities as individuals to organize themselves—as disgruntled users of top-down services—in order to share their knowledge does happen in many cases, but it is likely to be rather more problematic than the ability of activists already cooperating with one another in close networks or organizations. The movement from social knowledge to social movements is not as straightforward as Wainwright implies, as several commentators noted.

The challenges of institutionalising social movements

There have been several critical responses to Wainwright's engagement with neo-liberalism. First, critics have claimed that she 'overestimates the potential of social movements in civil society' and that it is unclear 'that social movements are flourishing'.[52] For Wainwright, it is social activists, embedded in social movements, who have the knowledge to advance left of centre ends. If participation in social movements is limited, then it becomes unclear how the whole scheme gets off the ground in the first place. Underlying Wainwright's argument is the presumption that social movements in Britain are thriving, leading Tony Wright to make the jibe that 'her world is peopled entirely by "movements", "networks", and "activists" '.[53]

Second, it is claimed Wainwright understates the role of elites in social movements. The journalist Paul Anderson criticized Wainwright's rejection of the knowledge of the expert in favour of the knowledge of the participant, writing that for 'most of the social movement networks that have survived over a long period. . . . Power is concentrated in the hands of paid professionals who make their primary task persuading legislators'.[54] To Anderson, as social movements grow and establish themselves, the expert is reinstated in the guise of the paid lobbyist, trade union negotiator, fund-raiser, lawyer and so on. This constitutes a threat to Wainwright's view, which is centred on 'breaking the "expert" monopoly on knowledge' and calling for its democratization.

Third, critics have pointed out that many social movements are not 'progressive'. Anderson writes that, 'Some of the most effective organisations in British civil society today are, moreover, deeply reactionary: the groups pressing for Islamicist schools, racist tenants' associations and so on.'[55] Wainwright is an optimist about the progressive outlook of citizens. She takes as a starting point a definition of democracy from Tom Paine's *Rights of Man*, which talks of a 'mass of sense' lying dormant in all people.[56] Yet, tacit 'knowledge' is subjective and is not always of the kind of which Wainwright would approve. It is not just found in the kind of examples which Wainwright gives—'the women's movement, radical trade unionism and the environmental movement'— it is also possessed by many other groups, from the Countryside Alliance to racist groups. Supporters of the British National Party, for example, claim to possess tacit 'knowledge' about immigrants, knowledge that is, as Wainwright says, 'by its nature fragmentary, rooted in intuitions, emotions as well as ideas, in the things people do rather than only those they wrote down'.[57] 'Knowledge' shared by some groups is conservative and sceptical of difference. Although Wainwright is pessimistic about the knowledge of the expert, she is sanguine about the 'knowledge' of groups and has no mechanism for weeding out 'good' knowledge from 'bad'.

Fourth, critics have argued that there are problems linking social movements with parties or government. Anderson argues:

> The problem is that one person's empowering, enabling network is another's self-interested, self-perpetuating, unaccountable clique. If the state is opened up to the myriad organisations of civil society, who represents all those people who do not belong to such organisations—and how does the state resolve competing claims?[58]

Wainwright was vague when it came to the details of the link between parties and groups, although she did call for 'political parties of a new kind'.[59] She noted that 'non-state forms of public action need a supportive and independent relationship to political power if they are to be effective agents of economic and social change'.[60] In the mid-1990s Wainwright suggested that these new parties included the German Greens, the Danish Socialist People's Party and the Dutch green left.

By the 2000s the focus had shifted to Lulu's Workers' Party in Brazil and particularly Brazilian experiments in participatory budgeting, such as that tried in Porto Alegre.[61] These parties provided 'a means by which the practical knowledge shared and accumulated by people to define and find a solution to their needs' can influence 'the exercise of political power'.[62] To Wainwright, Britain provided an isolated exception to this kind of national organization. No major party has arisen influenced by post-war social movements, and she argued that the Labour Party has remained impervious to movement politics—although it could be argued that the Bennite left constituted a possible exception in the 1980s attracting wide support from a variety of worker, peace, green and women's movements. (I discuss how these 'fragments' fit into Wainwright's thought below, in the section 'From class to movements'.)

These critical responses raise several questions for Wainwright: which groups should the new type of party be trying to attract, or should the state be granting rights to? What rights are conferred on those who are not members of social movements?[63] These questions have been raised before, in challenge to the political pluralism of the early twentieth century.

SOCIAL MOVEMENTS AND THE REVIVAL OF PLURALISM

Wainwright's engagement with Hayek reflects wider scepticism about the benevolence of the state and an account of groups that was both part of, and drew upon, a move away from straight-forward class-based analyses at the close of the twentieth century. An obvious parallel with Wainwright's argument is Paul Hirst's case for associational democracy, which explicitly sought to revive the English pluralism of the early twentieth century. In this section I place Wainwright's work in wider context and draw historical parallels with earlier pluralist thinkers.

Rethinking the 'all-knowing' state

In the main, the British left in the twentieth century was statist. For Wainwright, and many others, it was dominated by a Fabian social democratic strand which stressed organization and efficiency.[64] When it came to questions over state power, British social democracy was optimistic, especially after 1945 when the election of a majority Labour government created the possibility of 'a People's State'. 'In consequence of their friendly attitude towards the state', Barker concluded, 'socialists have tended to have little to say about its reformation'.[65] Wainwright's work is part of a wider break on the left with this statist tradition at the end of the twentieth century. In an article written to defend the constitutional pressure group Charter 88, she argued that the dominance of Fabianism in the British left has 'tethered' labour and socialism to the state,[66] and wrote that 'the instruments of the benevolent state have been tried and found wanting'.[67] Wainwright was explicit in berating earlier socialists for failing to provide an adequate non-statist theoretical response to Hayek. She targeted Barbara Wootton[68] and, 'more indirectly', Anthony Crosland as 'the last sustained responses to Hayek's neo-liberalism'.[69] To Wainwright, these authors are irremediably statist: they require 'us to place undue faith in the benevolent expertise and good judgement of people like themselves'.[70] (Wootton's response to Hayek was discussed in Chapter 1.) On several occasions Wainwright cited the Fabian Beatrice Webb's remark that 'the average sensual man can describe his problem but is unable to prescribe a solution'.[71] Webb's comment is representative of a paternalist—or even 'Tory'[72]—element in British socialism. It was Douglas Jay who stated Fabianism's paternalist strand most bluntly when he wrote that 'in the case of nutrition and health, just as in the case of education, the gentleman in Whitehall really does know better what is good for people than the people know themselves'.[73] This paternalism corresponded to a dominant view of the state—and its administrators—as benevolent.

Hayek's thought includes an anti-paternalistic, libertarian strand. It is this strand, Wainwright believed, that partly accounted for the popularity of Hayek in the newly open Eastern Europe[74]—a contrast to the heavy paternal hand of the Soviet state. Wainwright also saw herself as a libertarian, although a libertarian of the left. Explaining the idea behind the choice of name for a new political magazine, *Red Pepper*, which was launched in 1994, Wainwright wrote that the original *Red Pepper* had been an anti-bureaucratic, satirical, socialist Russian magazine which closed in 1926. The new *Red Pepper* would aim to revive its tradition: 'Our aim is to develop its libertarianism, satire and commitment—unashamedly left, but dissenting, open and democratic'.[75] It was this link between libertarians within very different ideologies that produced 'an eerie sense of recognition' and led Wainwright to write about Hayek. (In some ways Wainwright's scepticism about the socialist state echoes that of George Orwell, whose review of Hayek's *The Road to Serfdom* was discussed in Chapter 1.) Hayek was popular in Eastern Europe as a libertarian and iconoclast, in much the same way that libertarians of the left had become poster-figures for the 1968 generation.

From class to movements

Wainwright's view of class differs from that which was dominant during the middle years of the twentieth century. By viewing social movements as the key actors, Wainwright made, in Wood's phrase, a 'retreat from class'—at least in its simplest form.[76] More specifically, she distanced herself from a narrow economic understanding of class. In its place she presented an argument that reflected the increasingly pluralistic society of late twentieth- and early twenty-first-century Britain and the rise of identity politics. Yet Wainwright's retreat from simple conceptions of class pre-dated her engagement with Hayek. As far back as 1979, in a book co-written with Sheila Rowbotham and Lynne Segal, Wainwright had argued that the increasingly organized 'fragments'—'gays, blacks and youth',[77] but particularly the women's movement—were connected, though at a distance, to a narrow economic understanding of class disadvantage based solely on economics:

> There might be some logic in this if all the inequalities and sources of exploitation and oppression which the women's movement, the trade union movement, the black movement, etc., are up against were separate, unconnected to each other. If workers were simply up against bosses, women up against the sexual division of labour and sexist culture, blacks against racial repression and discrimination, with no significant connection between these forms of oppression, no state power linking and overseeing the institutions concerned, then strong independent movements would be enough. But it is precisely the connections between these sources of oppression, both through the state and through the organization of production and culture, which makes such a piecemeal solution impossible.[78]

The groups Wainwright mentioned were to be described, in the context of the 'new urban left' of the mid-1980s, as a 'rainbow coalition'. In a rainbow the colours seem distinct, but are all caused by the sun's refraction through water. Similarly, as Barker noted, to Wainwright and the other authors of *Beyond the Fragments,* 'Class remained the comprehensive category' that inspired the various movements.[79] As such, class held the various groups together and provided a narrative which placed the work of Wainwright and others on the 'new urban left' of the 1980s in the modernist and socialist camp, although their conception of class was both subjectively felt and fragmented, rather than objective and monolithic, as it had traditionally been perceived on the left.

By the time she wrote *Arguments for a New Left* in the early 1990s Wainwright had moved further from class as an explanatory tool, focusing more fully on 'movements'. Indeed both *Arguments for a New Left,* published in 1994, and *Reclaim the State,* published in 2003, end with a directory of campaigns, networks and newsletters. Wainwright's focus on movements caused much chagrin for those on the more traditional left. Sheila Cohen, for example, argued that Wainwright's approach 'totally overlooks the issue of how the workers' independent class interests . . . shape forms of organisation and resistance which have less to do with "radicalism" than with an incipient—and in this case transitional—socialism' and criticized Wainwright for her 'free floating radicalism'.[80] From a different political angle, John Gray raised some related questions: once class no longer binds the various social movements together, what are the 'coherence conditions' that hold a society together? Is the state reduced to a battleground for competing social movements?[81]

Post-socialism?

There is continuity in Wainwright's thought with the submerged socialist tradition concerned with liberty, fulfilment and moral regeneration. However, one can ask whether the term 'socialism' remains suitable to describe an analysis largely stripped of the traditional understanding of class and of central planning. As other thinkers examined in this book have shown, Wainwright's flight from central planning is part of a much larger move: she is just one swallow in a summer, and by no means the first.

By the 1990s, the future of 'socialism' became uncertain against historical shifts that meant that the right, electorally and intellectually, was dominant and Eastern bloc socialism had collapsed. Once the Union of Soviet *Socialist* Republics was gone, the idea of 'socialism' appeared less certain and was uttered with decreasing assuredness.

Reticence about the use of the term 'socialism' is a feature of Wainwright's work; her words are those of a doctor who cannot promise a healthy future to a patient. Anticipating the arrival of the 'new kinds of institutions' that she advocated, Wainwright wrote, 'Whether the result will always and everywhere be called "socialism" is an open question'.[82] Wainwright's work is open to the possibility that the left she advocated is unknown (and for epistemic reasons is partly unknowable) and that it may not be known as socialist. She quoted William Morris in *The Dream of John Ball*, who wrote that 'if the folk . . . have tried many roads towards freedom, and found that they led nowhither, then they shall try another'[83] and argues that, 'This book [*Arguments for a New Left*] has explored the ways in which there is a left influenced by different movements which *did*, in a variety of ways, anticipate that existing roads "went nowhither", and *did* begin to map out alternatives.'[84]

Wainwright's journey is in many ways a journey into the unknown, both logically, as a result of her epistemological argument, and historically, because it is with a note of uncertainty that she ends. Surveying the world around her and seeing unemployment, international instability and 'poverty caused by international finance', Wainwright concluded: 'In these circumstances it is not utopian to explore new roads to freedom, and to pick up maps which have not yet been completed'. If it is uncertain that 'socialism' is on the map Wainwright uses. Conservatism seems to have undergone a similar fate, although—as I argue in Chapter 5—in Britain, conservatism, at least in name, remains more of a term in contemporary debate than socialism through the survival of the Conservative Party.[85] To Wainwright, the use of the term 'left' seems more clearly defined as a wider and more embracing category. I return to these questions in the concluding chapter.

Reviving pluralism

Wainwright's argument can be placed in a wider ideological context by drawing on the work of others 'rethinking the state' at this time. By the last decade of the twentieth century several older political themes were making a comeback and had become established at the margins of a political landscape increasingly dominated by elements of the liberal tradition. Wainwright's work, which involves a rejection of a paternalist state and a move from an obvious class analysis to a variety of radical social movements, has several similarities with the wider revival of the English political pluralism of the early twentieth century, notably the guild socialism of G. D. H. Cole and the socialist pluralism of Harold Laski.[86]

Most explicit in his revival of the pluralist tradition was Paul Hirst. In 1989 he wrote that there was a need 'to put an important body of work back on the political agenda': English pluralism.[87] The links between Wainwright and the early pluralists became clearer in Hirst's definition of this pluralism. It was, he noted, 'a critique of state structure and of the basis of the authority of the state. The English pluralists challenged the theory of unlimited state sovereignty and of a unitary centralized state embodying such sovereign power in a hierarchy of authority'.[88]

Hirst found in the works of the early twentieth-century English pluralists similar themes to those that emerged in the above account of Wainwright's work. He wrote:

> Central to pluralism were the belief in the vitality and the legitimacy of self-governing associations as means of organizing social life and the belief that political representation must respect the principle of function, recognizing associations like trade unions, churches, and voluntary bodies. In the pluralist scheme it is such associations that perform the basic task of social life. Pluralism is strongly anti-statist in its basic principles. Respect for the autonomy of associations freely formed of citizens and the principle of functional representation both involve a limitation and not an enhancement of state power.[89]

Wainwright would supplement the account of 'associations like trade unions, churches, and voluntary bodies' that were the concern of the earlier English pluralists, with, among others, movements for racial and sexual equality, for disabled people, cooperative movements or those of and for the unemployed.

By the 1990s, pluralist arguments, which had seemed largely forgotten in the middle of the century, were increasingly remembered. Hirst attempted to repackage the English pluralism of the first decades of the twentieth century in a contemporary guise as 'associational democracy'.[90] He argued that pluralism had failed in the middle part of the century 'because it could not compete in given political conditions with collectivism and centralism'.[91] The wedding of social democrats and socialists to the benevolent state had seemed apposite when it created the possibility of the reforms of the 1945 government. It was the use of the same strong state in the last two decades of that century to enact a programme that owed a great deal to neo-liberalism, which largely brought about the divorce of the left from the state and the revival of pluralism.

Although pluralism appeared to be in decline in Britain by the middle decades of the twentieth century, variations on the theme were influential upon Wainwright. Rainer Eisfeld traced the re-emergence of the argument in Continental Europe:

> Laski's death in 1950 seemed to mark 'the exhaustion of a hope and a temper' . . . for more than a decade. In the late 1960s, however, socialist pluralism was rediscovered by Euro-communist parties (particularly the PCI [Italian Communist Party]), by dissenters from the ranks of their more orthodox sister organizations, by Yugoslav and Czechoslovakian communists. During the short-lived Czechoslovakian 'reform communist' experiment of 1968, workers' councils, political, producers' and consumers' associations were projected as 'multiple autonomous subjects' of the economic and political process.[92]

Thus Wainwright's pluralism was filtered through the protests of May 1968 and the Czech dissidents who created Charter 77, which argued against centralized control. The pluralism of both Wainwright and Hirst met again in their joint involvement in the creation of Charter 88, and its commitment to formally limit the power of the state through a written constitution.

Wainwright's engagement with Hayek appears to be part of a larger shift towards a revival of pluralism at the end of the twentieth century. Grahl wrote of

> an increasingly prevalent view on the Left that voluntary association within civil society . . . is to become itself a terrain of social transformation, while state action, although it will often remain necessary, becomes a secondary aspect of the advance and one which is continually dependent on civil society as its support.[93]

Yet, as Barker has argued, there is a 'pluralism of British pluralism'.[94]
Cécile Laborde presented a classification of the early twentieth-century
political pluralists that helps situate Wainwright's thought.[95] She divided pluralist thinkers according to their views on social regulation and
on the role of the state. Laborde classified pluralist thinkers' accounts of
social regulation as organic or contractual. Organic thinkers, she
argued, 'were scornful of any attempt to explain associations primarily
through individual wills and interests. Groups, in their view, emerged
naturally out of social life and could not be reduced to their individual
components.' By contrast, contractual thinkers were self-proclaimed socialists, 'stressing the role of grassroots groups, notably trade unions—to
inject socialism with a voluntarist, participatory, libertarian, sometimes
openly anarchist spirit. Their pluralism was a celebration of individualism within socialism'.

On the role of the state, Laborde classified pluralist thinkers as being
in favour of co-ordination or integration. She argued that 'the co-ordinating state both neglected overall discussions of the political community and reduced the state to a minimal role'. By contrast, proponents of
an integrative state were 'concerned to solve the problem of overall
societal regulation and ensure the achievement of basic common purposes by the state'. They sought to escape the Hegelian and Rous-
seau–inspired theory of the state but never rejected 'the need for *a*
state'.

These two distinctions allow pluralist thought to be presented in a
four box taxonomy (depicted in Figure 4.1). Laborde describes the
classification as made up of: organic integrators (who in practice have
tended to be 'corporate pluralists' such as Léon Duguit); organic-coor-
dinators (who include 'Whig pluralists' like J. N. Figgis); contractual
coordinators (such as 'anarchist pluralists' like Édouard Berth and Max-
ime Leroy); and contractual-integrators (who have tended to be socialist pluralists, such as the later Harold Laski and G. D. H. Cole).

A more accurate classification of Wainwright's pluralism would
seemingly place her in this last group: *contractual-integrators*. Her view
of associations is largely contractual. They tend to be social movements
to which membership is voluntarist (although these movements are
often based on identity, such as sexuality, ethnicity or gender, which is
less open to choice). It seems also that at times, while holding to a
contractual account of social movements, Wainwright wavers between a

Coordinating state

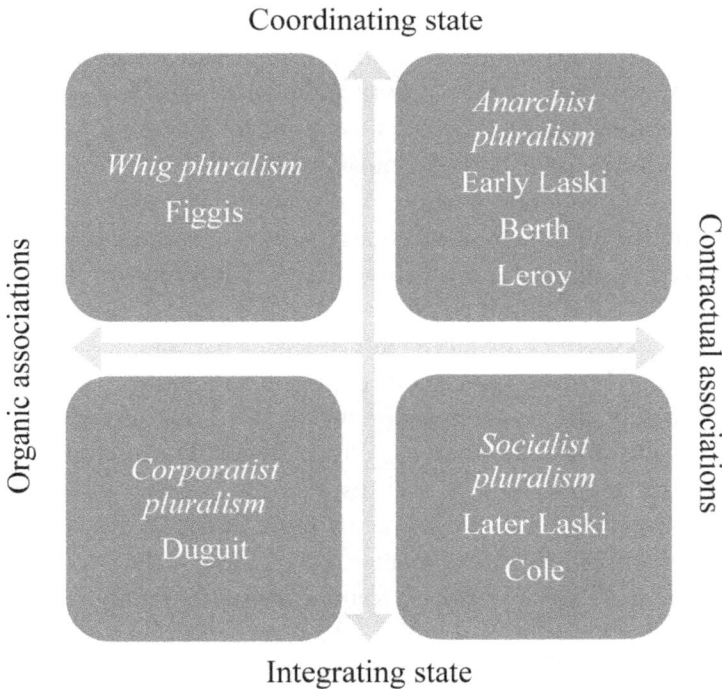

Figure 4.1.   Classifying pluralist thought

co-ordinating and an integrating view of social regulation. When she raises this issue, she appears sympathetic to Diane Elson's account of a 'socialised market', based on co-operative planning between autonomous enterprises. Here Wainwright's argument meets up again with that of Robin Blackburn, discussed above, who is also sympathetic to Elson's model.[96] The argument for a 'socialised market' grants the state a substantial role in promoting equality between the various associations.

Globalization and British political thought

Wainwright's career is also interesting because it provides an example of the wider globalization of political thinking in the late twentieth century. Commenting on post-war socialist revisionism, the former Labour politician Denis MacShane wrote that, 'In the 1950s, British Labour did not need to learn from abroad. One of the oddest absences from [Crosland's] *The Future of Socialism* is any discussion of what is happening in other countries. Island Britain still existed alone unto itself.'[97] By the end of the century political debate was decreasingly contained within national borders, or even by reactions to capitalism and communism as it was during the Cold War.[98] As the scope of political debate widened geographically, so the content changed. One element of this 'widening' was a change to what socialists' thought could be achieved by the state at a national level. Globalization, it was often argued, limited the state's power and, as a corollary to this, diminished the radical hopes of many on the left.[99] This is part of a move towards a more 'feasible' form of socialism discussed in Chapter 6.

The work of the thinkers examined in this book provides a useful illustration of the globalization of political issues. During the 1970s and 1980s Hilary Wainwright, as well as Andrew Gamble whose work is discussed in Chapter 5, wrote about issues that, in the main, were parochially British: the Conservative Party, British decline, Thatcherism, the Labour Party and British feminism and trade union disputes.

By the 1990s, as the Cold War structuring of political thought collapsed and both Gamble and Wainwright broadened their horizons, Wainwright's most detailed accommodation, set out in *Arguments for a New Left*, with Hayek can be read as an attempt to explain the electoral success of parties influenced by the new right for Eastern Europe. Gamble in the 1990s was concerned with, among other things, debates about 'regionalism' in the world order.[100]

By the start of the new century the debates that the two thinkers were engaged in had broadened geographically still farther. In 2003 Wainwright published a book—still drawing on Hayek—that can be read as an attempt to provide a theoretical basis for the anti-globalization movement and contained case studies 'from Beswick to Brazil'.[101] Gamble was by now concerned to argue against the 'Endism' associated with, among others, the American thinker Francis Fukuyama and with the relationship between Europe and the United States.[102] David Miller takes this expansion of the spatial scope of his argument farthest. He moves from a concern with debates around the modernization of the Labour Party in the 1980s to a global concern with 'justice for Earthlings' by 2013![103]

By the end of the period examined, the question can be asked whether it makes sense to talk of a distinctly British left at all. The debates that occur in Britain may have a local flavour, but that flavour is just one of a more global set of ingredients now constituting political debate in the UK.

CONCLUSIONS: THE REDISCOVERY OF POLITICAL PLURALISM

Wainwright's engagement with Hayek pushed her in the direction of an account of knowledge as social. However, in conceptualizing knowledge in this way she evoked a pluralist tradition very different to Hayek's own. The Hayekian foundation of Wainwright's argument is ironic given that Hayek had specifically rejected pluralism (in the form of syndicalism) in his edited collection *Collectivist Economic Planning* in 1935. Yet Wainwright was not alone on the left in the final years of the twentieth century in rediscovering pluralism. By the late 1980s and early 1990s many left of centre thinkers presented arguments that were sceptical about the power of the central state, and which supported the devolution of power, not to the individual (as Hayek argued), but to a variety of groups within society.

Wainwright's engagement with Hayek is part of a wider pluralist response to the shifts in British political thought around end of the twentieth century. Motivated by the success of libertarians of the right in newly opened Eastern Europe, Wainwright found some common ground with them. Like Hayek, Wainwright rejected the 'all-knowing' paternalist state of mainstream socialism, with its reliance on the knowledge of benevolent experts. Unlike Hayek, she argued that knowledge could be shared within a plurality of social movements, which become the main instruments of change. Wainwright's epistemological engagement with Hayek led to an argument for social movement politics, which allows one to draw parallels with both the English political pluralists of the first decades of the twentieth century and with her contemporaries, notably Paul Hirst. As such, Wainwright's radical, movement-based, participatory politics is one example of a wider revival of pluralism since the final years of the twentieth century.

5

THE REVIVAL OF LIBERALISM

'Comrade Hayek' or 'Citizen Gamble'?

Throughout his career, Andrew Gamble—whose quote on the role that Hayek could play in renewing socialism began this book—would have described himself, and been seen by others, as on the left of British politics. His academic work began in the early 1970s with a series of articles in the Marxist tradition, and by the mid-1990s he was a key figure behind the idea of stake-holding, which became associated with New Labour. Gamble remains in close contact with several senior figures in the Labour Party and for many years jointly edited *The Political Quarterly* with the Labour MP, Tony Wright. Given this background, Gamble's comments during the 1990s that Hayek could be a source of inspiration for socialists, or his tongue-in-cheek account of 'Comrade Hayek' in the monthly magazine *Prospect*,[1] seem a remarkable departure, which is explored in more detail in this chapter.

I argue that Gamble's journey from Marxism to the market provides a particularly illuminating case study of the way in which the wider political landscape changed in the late twentieth century. The first section of this chapter contains a discussion of Gamble's early work and examines the contextual changes that shifted him and others away from a broadly Marxist position in the mid-1970s. As such, Gamble's work provides an interesting case study of the way in which contexts help to shape intellectual and ideological change, and reflects the wider ending of a particular period of ideological thought. In the second section I

examine Gamble's engagement with Hayek's work, particularly in the
mid-1990s. The third section reconstructs Gamble's account and compares his position with mainstream forms of twentieth-century socialism
in the UK. The final section of this chapter examines the limits of
Gamble's engagement with Hayek and his defence of a position which
has many similarities to the new liberalism of the early twentieth century—a position that was influential on the development of New Labour,
and particularly their attitude to the market, in the mid-1990s.

THE 1970s AND 1980s: CRISIS, LANDSLIDE AND HEGEMONY

The historian Eric Hobsbawm identified a 'short twentieth century' that
ran from 1914 to 1991. Hobsbawm's assertion sparked a wider debate
over the extent to which the collapse of the Soviet Union marked an
end, not just to a distinct historical period but of a unique intellectual
one as well. Gamble's early academic work came during the final years
of a period of extraordinary economic growth in the West. Hobsbawm
described the middle period of the short twentieth century, the years
from 1947 to 1973, as 'the golden age' of peace and economic growth,
and this framework is helpful in understanding the shifts in Gamble's
thought after the mid-1970s. Gamble's first full-length academic book,
From Alienation to Surplus Value, written with Paul Walton in 1972,
was completed before the end of the 'golden age'. It was the culmination of a string of articles written as a result of an engagement in debates in Marxism.[2] The central argument of *From Alienation to Surplus
Value* was that 'Marx's theory of capital accumulation, based on his
labour theory of value . . . is still the only theory which provides a
completely consistent account of the genesis and reproduction of capitalism'.[3] Given the context of the 'golden age', and the rising living
standards of the working class in the West, Gamble and Walton avoid
discussion of the immiseration of the proletariat and make 'no pro-
nouncements about the likelihood of revolution'.[4] The book was
awarded the *Deutscher Prize*, given annually for a work that 'exem-
plifies the best and most innovative new writing in or about the Marxist
tradition'. The recipients of the prize are invited to deliver the annual

Deutscher Memorial Lecture, which Gamble did, with his co-writer, in 1973.[5]

By the time Gamble and Walton had developed the content of the Deutscher lecture into a full-length book, which appeared in 1976, the long post-war boom in the West was ending. As Hobsbawm wrote, 'the golden age' was over and 'the landslide' had begun. Writing in 1994, Hobsbawm described the 'landslide' years pessimistically, as a time of 'decomposition, uncertainty and crisis'.[6] Gamble's assessment of the new context during the early years of the 'landslide' supports this interpretation. It is reflected in the title of his book, *Capitalism in Crisis*, again co-authored with Paul Walton. The authors noted that:

> the scale and the seriousness of the crisis cannot be doubted. Since 1945 governments have generally set themselves four basic economic objectives—full employment, economic growth, a balance or surplus on foreign-trade payments and price stability. It was common to fail to achieve one out of the four in any one year, but it is now common to achieve none.[7]

The 'crisis' of the mid-1970s resulted in the centrist thinking—offered by the right of the Labour Party and the left of the Conservative Party—appearing obsolete. The confidence of Labour in the revisionist socialism of the 1950s now seemed 'complacent', as even its advocates noted.[8] During the 1950s, Anthony Crosland (whose work was introduced in Chapter 3) had written that the state dominated the economy, that there had been a shift of power from management to labour, that private industry was becoming humanized and that the Labour Government's extension of the welfare state and introduction of Keynesian economics promised economic growth and full employment.[9] Capitalism, red in tooth and claw, had not been abolished, but it had been tamed. Furthermore, leading figures of the Conservative Party, at least in parliament, largely accepted the 1945 'settlement'. The end of the post-war economic boom destroyed the revisionists' complacency. As Gamble noted at the end of the 1970s, 'We are living through a crisis that should never have happened, the crisis that Keynesian techniques and social democratic policies and institutions were supposed to have banished for ever'.[10]

By the mid-1970s the centrist path appeared un-navigable. Political debate in the UK seemed to have reached a T-junction, offering the choice to turn right or left. Gamble's writing provides an example of this interpretation. He argued in 1976 that, 'The impasse of the mixed economy is such that mere patching is no longer enough. On the left, as well as on the right, solutions for breaking out of the impasse have emerged'.[11] A turn to the right, he argued, would continue the direction taken by Heath in the early years of his Government. In the Conservative Party, Gamble associated this path with Enoch Powell—in some ways an ideological precursor to Thatcher. It would mean an end of 'interventionist' government and the abandonment of the full employment commitment. At the time, Gamble argued that a turn to the right was less likely than a turn to the left. He wrote that 'unemployment in the low millions' is 'hardly compatible with regular elections, because it promises the kind of social upheavals that many countries faced in the 1930s. Hence it could only be maintained in practice if the political market were closed down, an authoritarian regime established, and trade unions effectively suppressed'.[12] Looking back, Gamble and Walton were wrong in their prediction: the unthinkable largely happened. The Conservative Government elected in 1979 held power for over seventeen years and largely followed the first strategy that Gamble identified, turning to the right, but managing to combine the suppression of trade union power and rising unemployment with regular elections.

During the years Thatcher was Prime Minister, Gamble became an established political commentator whose work often displayed a fascination with the politics of what Crosland described in 1962 as *The Conservative Enemy*.[13] Gamble's article, 'The Free Economy and the Strong State'[14] published in *The Socialist Register* (and substantially developed and updated some years later into a book of the same name) became one of the most influential accounts of 'Thatcherism'.[15] The decision to focus on an analysis of the politics of the right is unusual for a writer on the left, but the article had its roots in another of Gamble's early books, *The Conservative Nation*, published in 1974, a study of the opinion of the Conservative Party during the post-war period. By 1988, still relying on a terminology derived from Marxist thought, Gamble was arguing that the crisis of the mid-1970s was the result of the breakdown of one 'hegemonic project', while Thatcherism should be interpreted as creation of a new one.

'TWO SIDES TO HAYEK'

Given this background, Gamble's discovery of Hayek as a source of support for socialism is part of long political journey. In this section I begin by examining Gamble's intellectual discovery of Hayek in the mid-1990s, before exploring some of the contextual changes that provided the conditions under which this engagement could take place.

Gamble's intellectual discovery of Hayek

Gamble's early engagement with Hayek is limited, despite writing as early as 1979 that Hayek's 'writings repay careful study'.[16] It is notable, for example, that there is only passing mention of Hayek in Gamble's 1981 textbook, *Introduction to Modern Social and Political Thought*. Before the mid-1990s, where Gamble does discuss Hayek, it was as a thoughtful contributor to the new right, not for any insights with wider applicability. This approach to Hayek was taken, for example, in Gamble's brief book review of Hayek's *Collected Works* in 1992, which showed a scholarly familiarity with Hayek's arguments but no significant engagement with their content. Gamble suggested, for example, that the addition of previously unpublished and little known pieces in the *Collected Works* 'will be of considerable interest to all students of Hayek and twentieth-century liberalism', but he did not write, or even imply, that they will be of interest to wider groups.[17] By the mid-1990s, however, Gamble's view of Hayek's wider significance had begun to change.

It was in a 1995 review that Gamble first argued that there were 'two sides to Hayek'. It was in his review of this book that Gamble noted that 'Hayek's reputation as a political theorist has often been hard to separate from his reputation as an ideologue'.[18] There is a Jekyll and Hyde quality to Hayek: a consequence of this, Gamble argued, was that Hayek was generally only studied by his ideological sympathizers (those who were happy with Hyde as well as Jekyll): 'His critics have not thought it necessary to study him in detail'.[19] Gamble claims that it is Hayek's reputation as a social scientist, not as an ideologue, that will be remembered. Given Hayek's influence on Thatcherism and the new right, and his often polemical approach, this is a brave prediction. Gamble developed the concept of 'ideological closure', a concept with some previous use in the study of literature but not in the social sciences. [20] To Gamble, Hayek 'failed to develop many of his insights because of the ideological closures he imposed on his work'. [21]

Once Gamble established a second side to Hayek, one that even Hayek himself never fully developed due to the closures that he imposed on his own work, then Gamble's engagement with the author begins. Gamble now describes Hayek as a 'thinker of extraordinary range and subtlety . . . whose best work raises questions and identifies problems which are immensely fertile'. [22] By the time Gamble published his full account of Hayek's work, *Hayek: the iron cage of liberty*, in 1996, he was arguing that 'Hayek turns out to have been more right than wrong'. [23]

'New Times': Context and intellectual change

What did it take for Gamble to start writing about Hayek? Four events stand out in particular; combined, these provided the conditions for a reconstitution of the political landscape in the UK. The first event challenged the understanding of what it is to be a socialist (a label which Gamble, and most of the other thinkers on the left who undertook an engagement with Hayek's work, would at one time—if not still—have accepted); the other events involved a change in the status of the enemy. An engagement with Hayek's work was one response to these changing conditions at the end of the twentieth century.

First, the collapse of Soviet communism and with it the end of the Cold War shook the political landscape. The division of the world between communism and capitalism shaped the political thought of the short twentieth century. The intellectual historian Perry Anderson has written that: 'Polemical zeal can produce an [*sic*] fixation on the other side, or sides, of purely hostile intent. The Cold War was full of that kind of literature, as ephemeral as it was instrumental'. [24]

The collapse of the USSR after the revolution of 1989 led to a crisis in socialist thought, even for those who had never supported Soviet communism. The ending of the most obvious manifestation of the 'long ideological conflict' in which Hayek had been engaged did not just mean the collapse of the statist communism but the space that it generated for non-capitalist alternatives. The collapse of communism led many on the left to rethink their positions. The end of the Cold War generated a less constrained political dialogue than that which had existed for much of the previous century.

The second contextual change was the rise of a popular new right,
intellectually and electorally (upon which Gamble became a key commentator). This shifted the grounds of debate in the UK, and elsewhere. The hopes for radical change, which many socialists held as a
response to the 'crisis' of the 1970s, were dashed, and aggressive rightwing arguments were increasingly voiced as the solution. These arguments had an important influence on the Conservative Government
elected in 1979.

A third important change was the Conservative Party's decline from
around 1990. The first left-wing riposte aimed specifically at Hayek—
that of Jim Tomlinson—did not come until 1990, after the unpopular
introduction of the 'poll tax' and the year Margaret Thatcher resigned
as Prime Minister. (Tomlinson is discussed briefly in Chapter 1.) Gamble's re-evaluation of Hayek did not come until even later in the
decade, by which time the Conservative Party was in 'crisis'—'in office,
but not in power' as the Conservative's resigning Chancellor, Norman
Lamont, memorably put it.[25] By 1995, Gamble could ask whether the
Conservative Party had reached 'the end of an era' as the 'pillars of
Conservative hegemony' that had existed since the late Victorian era
collapsed.[26] The impending electoral defeat of the Conservative 'enemy' (which eventually occurred with the general election of 1997) made
an engagement with the works of one of their intellectual supporters
possible on a more equal basis. Engagement with an intellectual adversary seems easier if they are also bowed, and a charge of capitulation
can be avoided.

Ideas and institutions are mutually supportive. This is a relationship
which Rodney Barker elegantly described as Constantine, after the Emperor whose conversion to Christianity leant support to, and in turn
supported, the Roman Empire.[27] A prime example of the Constantine
Relationship was the survival in the UK of the ideological description
'conservative' through the institution of the Conservative Party. A less
elegant metaphor for describing this relationship between institutions
and ideas would be to refer to their 'stickiness'.[28] Hayek's ideas cohered, first, around various right-wing think tanks and then around
increasingly powerful groups within the Conservative Party. The electoral decline of the Conservatives after 1990 acted as a solvent, freeing

Hayek's ideas for more general use. It was only after this date that the left began to work with them.

Fourth, Hayek's death, in 1992, was perhaps significant. Hayek became less willing to engage with the arguments of his rivals in his final years, and more acerbic in his condemnation of socialism. One can compare Hayek's harsh assessment of socialism in his last major book, *The Fatal Conceit: The errors of socialism*, published in 1988, when he was writing as intellectual hero for many on the new right, with the relatively open engagement in his early work. Along with others, such as Wainwright, whose work is discussed in the Chapter 4, Gamble's engagement with Hayek's work did not begin in full until after Hayek's death. An early example came, for instance, in Gamble's review of Birner and Zijp's collection, *Hayek, Co-ordination and Evolution: His legacy in philosophy, politics, economics and the history of ideas*, written (as the title suggests) to debate Hayek's legacy and published two years after Hayek's death. An engagement with an intellectual enemy—such as Hayek—is easier once one is dealing with a body of work, rather than an individual still wishing to 'shout from the rooftops' that socialism is dead.

During the short twentieth-century, thinkers, ideas and institutions would often cohere, as I argued above. The changing contexts outlined in this section 'unstuck' many of these connections and allowed former enemies to be drawn on as a source of support. Political thought became freer in its influences and dialogues. The engagement of the left with Hayek is perhaps the prime example of this, although there are several other important (and equally unlikely) examples, such as the left's revival of the German legal theorist and onetime Nazi Carl Schmitt, or the rediscovery of the Anglican theologian J. N. Figgis, by socialists seeking to revive the pluralism of the early twentieth century. (Both examples are discussed in more detail in the conclusion to this book.)

ENGAGING ON LIBERAL TERRAIN

Gamble's engagement with Hayek's work in the 1990s was developed most fully in an article, 'Hayek and the left' (which was abridged and published in the monthly magazine *Prospect* under the title 'Comrade

Hayek') and the final chapter of his book *Hayek: The iron cage of liberty*. Below I discuss three areas of Hayek's thought (concerning epistemology, markets and the state) which, Gamble argued, could offer insights for the left. For Gamble, at least in 1996, Hayek could be of use to *socialists*—hence his tongue-in-cheek description of 'Comrade Hayek'. However, I argue that the engagement with Hayek involves jettisoning much of what was understood as socialism during the twentieth century. Instead, I argue, the debate has now shifted on to more recognizably liberal grounds.

The limits of knowledge

Gamble argued that, 'One of Hayek's most important contributions was to revive the anti-rationalist, sceptical tradition' associated with Bernard Mandeville, David Hume, Adam Smith and Adam Ferguson.[29] Arguments that emphasize the limits of human reason are normally associated with the right and are historically rooted in ideas of human imperfection. Noel O'Sullivan argues that the British conservative tradition is based on an outlook which views human reason as limited.[30] There is also an important strand of anti-rational liberalism. In the twentieth century, this was most clearly found in Isaiah Berlin's value pluralism and Karl Popper's 'piecemeal social engineering'. It has more recently featured strongly in the work of John Gray.[31]

By contrast, the left have tended not to be so concerned with the limits of knowledge. Hayek argued that socialism, and an important strand within liberalism, relied upon 'constructivist rationalism', which knew of no theoretical limits to the scope of human reason. Constructive rationalism provided the basis for 'false individualism'.[32] It was the constructivist rationalists, Hayek believed, who instigated a tradition of thought that threatened the very existence of civilization: bulldozing established institutions if they did not fit in with rational plans. For Gamble to flirt with anti-rationalism marks a departure from a central, although often unstated, epistemological assumption in mainstream socialism as it existed for much of the previous century.

Hayek's anti-rationalism is predicated upon a theory of knowledge (which was discussed in more detail in Chapter 4) that Gamble finds compelling. Hayek argued that important knowledge could not be collected centrally in the way that the socialist planners and other 'con-

structive rationalists' believed. Instead, it existed in people's heads as
knowledge of time and place or, in his later work, as 'tacit' knowledge
('those things we know but cannot tell'). To Gamble, the idea of tacit
knowledge should be appropriated by the left, yet his engagement with
Hayek in this area challenges mainstream socialist views. One implication of the acceptance of the tacit nature of knowledge concerned the
devolution of power away from the state. He argued that:

> The logic of Hayek's approach, even if he himself does not always
> follow it through—is that there should be constant efforts to reform
> organisations to allow for specialised knowledge held by each indi-
> vidual to be utilised in the way in which decisions are taken. Central-
> ised models or decision-making are likely to be much more error-
> prone, and therefore less efficient in achieving objectives and maxi-
> mising welfare. [33]

Gamble supports Hayek's view that the 'agents' that possess tacit knowledge are individuals rather than groups. Gamble does not offer, as
Wainwright does, for example, an argument that tacit knowledge can be
shared imperfectly between group members, so that groups become
the key political actors. [34] Here Gamble's position is closer to those
liberals who have emphasized devolution of power to individuals than it
is to non-statist socialists, who have supported devolution of power to
groups or movements, such as guild socialists, Cole, Laski and, more
recently, Wainwright and Paul Hirst.

    Gamble argued that his acceptance of the tacit nature of knowledge
led to a scepticism about the state that 'reinforces those parts of the
socialist and liberal traditions which have always argued for autonomy
and independence of agents and strict curbs on centralised power'. [35]
Yet this acceptance of tacit knowledge in Gamble's argument was part
of a wider break with statist forms of socialism, such as the Fabian
tradition. Indeed, Gamble's argument is part of a wider move away
from what Hilary Wainwright in the previous chapter described as the
'powerful fantasy at the back of many a socialist mind' of the 'all-knowing state' that was often implicit in twentieth-century British socialism. [36]

    A related implication of Gamble's appropriation of tacit knowledge
concerns the retreat from public ownership. Writing in 1996 Gamble
noted that:

A great deal of socialist planning in the twentieth century assumed that an order could be rationally designed whose outcomes would be superior to those of an order which had arisen spontaneously. But that implied that those designing the order had enough knowledge to perform the task. Hayek's single most important contribution was his theoretical argument as to why they would not. [37]

This issue was, for much of the twentieth century, *the* shibboleth dividing left and right. By 1996 Gamble had conceded this ground to Hayek and the right. Collaborating with Gavin Kelly in 1998, Gamble argued that, 'For much of the twentieth century [ownership] has been the lode star by which left and right defined their attitudes towards economic and social organisation'. Hilary Wainwright made a similar claim in 1989, when, writing with Stephen Howe, she noted that, 'Divisions between the left and the right used to be based on how big a state there should be: and in particular, how much nationalisation?'[38] In conceding that the left must reject state ownership, through an engagement with Hayek's theory of knowledge, Gamble explicitly marks a shift in the history of twentieth-century political thought.

Markets and entrepreneurs

One implication of the argument for tacit knowledge that Gamble picked out was the idea that some agents must be proactive in finding out what other agents actually want if the economy and society are not to stagnate. To Gamble, Hayek's account of the market as a discovery process and the role of the entrepreneur within it should provide a further insight for the left:

> There is a crucial role for institutions which promote entrepreneurship, identifying new wants, new products, new forms of coordination and new types of association. The emphasis placed on centralised knowledge and administration in collectivist thought had tended to lead to the importance of entrepreneurs being downplayed. [39]

The claim made by Gamble and others on the left that entrepreneurship is a worthy activity marks another break with older left-wing argument. Entrepreneurship was admired by a strand in conservatism which stretched from the later works of W. H. Mallock to Enoch Powell and by most liberals, from Herbert Spencer to Hayek.[40] The language of entrepreneurship became particularly politicized during the 1980s, with the entrepreneur becoming a symbolic hero to the new right—someone who could lift Britain out of its relative decline. The left, on the other hand, had tended to be sceptical about entrepreneurial values. To Tawney, for example, writing after the First World War, the entrepreneur motivated by profit was morally questionable and contributed to an ethos of acquisitiveness in society.[41]

Breaking with the common views of entrepreneurship held by both left and right, Gamble argued that, 'The implication of this insight in Hayek is egalitarian'.[42] This is certainly not the conclusion that Hayek would have reached, but Gamble would argue that Hayek is committing 'ideological closure' here:

> Within his own thought there is a strong case for redistribution of both power and property rights in order to create a more flexible and dynamic society, and also to ensure that all individuals are full participants in the market order, taking responsibility for themselves and learning how to be self-reliant.[43]

Two aspects are worth highlighting in the way Gamble presents his account of entrepreneurship and the market. First, Gamble's discussion of *individual responsibility* above is part of the move away from a simple paternalist discourse, which had been powerful in socialist thought, to one of individual autonomy and its moral counterpart, personal responsibility. This move is found among several of Gamble's contemporaries on the left. Anthony Giddens, for example, places his arguments in these terms, arguing that a new individualism meant that government could no longer treat rights as unconditional claims but that they should be matched by new obligations: that there should be 'no rights without responsibility'.[44] This focus on the individual is more common in the liberal tradition than many older socialist arguments.

Second, to Gamble and others, private ownership was a necessary consequence of advocating the market and entrepreneurship. In the mid-1990s, around the same time as his engagement with Hayek's work, Gamble argued that the left needed to 'develop a distinctive approach to private ownership'.[45] Explicit discussions of *private* ownership marked another new direction for the left, as Gamble noted, again writing with Kelly:

> This is a very difficult agenda for many parts of the left because so much of its culture has been formed around hostility to markets and private property rights due to the concentration of ownership in capitalist societies. The dominant tradition of the left in this century has always thought in terms of using the powers of democracy and political action to constrain and control the forces of the market, and has neglected the powerful egalitarian weapons which markets could provide.[46]

Gamble goes further than most of his colleagues in his account of private ownership. Even those on the left who went furthest in arguing for the market, such as the 'market socialist' David Miller, whose work is discussed in Chapter 2, sought to combine an argument for the market with the predominantly 'socialised' (i.e., communal) ownership of the economy.[47] While Miller's attempts to present an argument for the market clings to its socialist roots, by incorporating a distinctly socialist form of ownership, Gamble's embrace of private ownership takes his argument onto recognizably liberal grounds. For Gamble, however, private ownership is defended not because it is derived from natural rights (as Spencer, among others, claimed) or because it allows the value of liberty to be realized and provides a bulwark against serfdom (as Hayek argued), but because private ownership allows individual empowerment in the market order and benefits society overall. In this, Gamble's argument evokes the new liberalism of the early twentieth century rather than liberalism in its Hayekian form.

For Gamble discussions of private ownership do not represent a 'capitulation to the New Right' because the implications are egalitarian.[48] However, he would not deny that he is taking the debate onto a new battleground for the left to fight on. Ownership matters to Gamble largely because it relates to questions of inequality. Gamble's engagement with Hayek is one way of approaching this issue: a more egalitarian distribution of private ownership could lead to a more flexible and dynamic society, in which individuals participate in the market and take responsibility for themselves. Yet this is a liberal account (albeit a left liberal one). It is based around a responsible, able individual operating in a fairly equal market society. It is more Mill than Marx.

The rejection of large-scale state ownership by the thinkers examined here was part of a much wider shift that gathered speed during the 'landslide' from the mid-1970s onwards. If socialism was essentially about state ownership, then Hayek's claim that the intellectual foundations of socialism have collapsed appears feasible. Although the rejection of planning did mark a break with socialism as it had been understood for much of the twentieth century, it did not necessarily mark victory for the right. Socialism always meant more than state planning, although this was an important element to it in the twentieth century. As Hobsbawm noted, 'there have been various phases in the Left–Right distinction' and it is possible that the debate about planning is only one.[49] The principled rejection of dirigisme, which is central to Gamble's thought, constitutes the end of one phase of that distinction.

The role of government and organizations

A final area in which Gamble believes the left can draw insights from Hayek's work concerns the nature of governments and organizations. Gamble argued that Hayek's concept of the spontaneous order or catallaxy, examined above, was a fruitful one for the left in considering the role of the government. Gamble did not accept Hayek's claim that the state's role should be as limited as possible. In fact, Gamble argued, there are times when 'made orders' are superior to spontaneous ones. The made order can provide a 'speed of response' to crisis such as famine, war or environmental catastrophe that the spontaneous one cannot, for example. What was important to Gamble was 'to ensure that government is making use of both catallaxies and made orders in order to tackle the problems it faces effectively'.[50]

Those at the centre could no longer claim any special expertise, derived from a rational account of knowledge, as Hayek showed, but, Gamble argued, what the centre could claim was 'knowledge about the general properties of the social system and the general conditions for institutional change and development'.[51] This knowledge could be used to steer public and private catallaxies in innovative and flexible directions, where power was dispersed as widely as possible in order to make the most efficient use of the knowledge that these catallaxies contain. Gamble concluded that:

> What Hayek offers us is a way of thinking about how the state can assist in the process of institutional change without imposing its own designs and trying to determine the outcomes of the process. In-

stead, the state sets the framework and helps point institutions in particular directions. It adopts an experimental approach, using trial and error in an attempt to establish new types of organisation.[52]

An implication of this view, to Gamble, was that those in government no longer believed that they could use the lever of state to bring about socialism for all, as, for example, the early Fabians did. Instead they acted, metaphorically, like gardeners, providing the right soil and carrying out the occasional bit of weeding to see what thrived. Gamble's account of the state is now closer to organic, new liberal understandings of the early twentieth century than it is to that found in most twentieth-century socialism.

Thus, in each of the areas in which Gamble argues that there are insights in Hayek's work, he shifts his argument away from socialism, as it was understood in Britain for much of the twentieth century, and on to grounds more obviously associated with liberalism: he accepts a far more limited view of human reason; a much greater role for the market, private ownership and entrepreneurship; and a much more organic approach to the growth of the state than most socialists had done. However, the liberal grounds onto which Gamble moves the argument remain a long way from Hayek's variant of 'classical' liberalism and owe more to the early new liberalism of Hobson, Hobhouse and others. This liberal shift in Gamble's argument is part of a wider move in the recent history of political thought, a move which I go on to discuss further in the final section of this chapter.

THE LIMITS OF ENGAGEMENT

The limit of Gamble's engagement with Hayek's work involved a dispute about the values that characterize modern society. For Hayek, it is liberty that makes the modern world possible; the pursuit of other values—notably equality—will lead to 'serfdom'. In this section, I reconstruct Gamble's Weberian interpretation of Hayek and examine his ambiguous description of Hayek's thought as an 'iron cage'. I then examine the limits of Gamble's engagement with Hayek's work, and his defence of equality.

The iron cage of liberty: Hayek, Weber and modernity

To Gamble, 'underpinning all Hayek's work is a particular conception of modernity'.[53] Hayek had, with many other thinkers of his scope, an account of the move from traditional to modern societies. In this respect, Hayek's argument is not unlike nineteenth-century accounts, such as Ferdinand Tönnies's description of the shift from *Gemeinschaft* to *Gesellschaft*; Herbert Spencer's portrayal of the move from militant to industrial societies or the description of the change from societies based on status to contract in the work of both Spencer and Henry Maine.[54] Comparisons between Hayek and Spencer seem particularly apt, given their shared narrative of a progressive rise in individualism subverted by collectivism. (Spencer's warnings of 'the coming slavery' also evoke a similar metaphor to Hayek's *The Road to Serfdom*.) In a later engagement with Hayek, Gamble compares his work with Spencer in more detail, noting that 'Spencer often seems to anticipate many of Hayek's arguments'.[55] However, Gamble points out that despite similarities, in practice, Hayek would have sanctioned quite ranging interventions from the state, providing they were carried out under the Rule of Law, far beyond what Spencer or strict libertarians, such as Nozick, would justify.[56] This is the difference between the carefully circumscribed minimal state of Spencer and the more flexible, 'limited' state of Hayek.

To Gamble, however, certainly in his 1996 book on Hayek, it is comparisons with Max Weber which are the most fruitful. The significance which Gamble gives to Weber in his interpretation of Hayek is demonstrated by the subtitle he chose for both his book on Hayek and the title of its concluding chapter: 'The Iron Cage of Liberty'[57]—a reworking of Talcott Parsons's translation of Weber's account of the 'iron cage' of capitalism and modernity.[58]

It has been argued that Parsons's translation of the 'stahlhartes Gehäuse' concept through the metaphor of an 'iron cage' to describe the human being under capitalism, would have better been translated as the 'shell as hard as steel'. In this new metaphor 'steel'—as a human-made, flexible product—becomes emblematic of modernity. The metaphor of a shell also suggests that capitalism has created a new kind of being, whereas a cage leaves the subject confined but with his powers intact.[59] Following this argument—and disregarding the iconic nature

of Parsons's translation—Gamble's book might have been better alter-
natively titled, *Hayek: The Steel Shell of Liberty*.

Yet, although both Hayek and Weber possessed an account of the
move from traditional society to modernity, the similarities between
them are not obviously clear. The choice of the rewording of Weber for
the subtitle of Gamble's book led to varying interpretations as to the
significance of the phrase among reviewers. This ambiguity is not made
clearer, as one reviewer notes, because, after the subtitle, Gamble uses
the phrase only once more in the book (as the title of his concluding
chapter) and does not explain it further.[60] This leaves the reader with
limited evidence as to Gamble's meaning, especially given that a Weberian interpretation of Hayek is unusual. As Gamble admitted, Weber
only features rarely in Hayek's overall output,[61] so the prominent allu-
sion to him seems an unusual choice by which to characterize his writings. (Weber is not mentioned at all, for example, in Hayek's *The Road
to Serfdom* and only in rare footnotes in *The Constitution of Liberty*.)

Given this room for ambiguity, several interpretations of Gamble's
subtitle have been made. One reviewer, Billy Jack, argued that the
phrase was chosen because Gamble believed that Hayek failed to ap-
preciate Weber's insight into the tragic implications of modernity.[62] A
second reviewer, Daniel Klein (without much further explanation) took
Gamble to mean that 'Hayekian liberalism scores poorly in achieving
socialism's "historic aims of liberty, equality, and solidarity"'.[63] The
most convincing interpretation, I argue, was made by Norman Barry,
and it is this interpretation that I follow, and expand upon, below.[64]

Gamble claimed that one of the main reasons 'for rethinking Hayek
is to assess his work as an account of the nature of modernity'.[65] Underlying all of Hayek's work, Gamble argued, is a meta-narrative about the
evolution of modern society, which was 'key to many aspects of his
thought'.[66] For Gamble, Hayek largely accepted Weber's account of the
processes that create modern society. Weber identified rationalization
of both means and ends ('Zweckrationalität') as the key process in the
progression from traditional to modern society. Traditional societies
were characterized as possessing communal values where relationships
were face-to-face. Rationalization of this kind undermined traditional
societies and created modern ones where values were individualist and
relationships were impersonal. For Gamble, there are considerable

similarities between Hayek and Weber's view of the creation of modernity.

However, while Hayek accepted Weber's account of modernization, he broke from Weber in his evaluation of modern society. Unlike Hayek, Weber's understanding of the modern world was, as Gamble noted, a tragic one. Weber argued that the process of rationalization, which brought about the modern world, was initially liberating, as traditional and 'enchanted' ways of life (notably, the commitment to religion) were questioned. However, for this sense of liberation from traditional constraints to continue, the institutions that provided the norms from which individuals were breaking free needed to remain. The process of rationalization undermined the traditional order and created new institutions that were efficient and bureaucratic—two characteristics of modernity. For Weber, with bureaucracy came the 'disenchantment of the world' as individuals became locked into vast impersonal organizations that sought to rationally maximize efficiency and where the meaning of individuals' actions were devalued, resulting in spiritual poverty.[67] To Weber, this processes of rationalization, and the disenchantment that eventually comes with it, are ultimately inescapable: that is why modern capitalism has created an 'iron cage'.[68] The only way in which individuals could apply meaning to their lives in this impersonal, disenchanted world, is to invent their own values—to ask, in Weber's phrase, 'Which of the warring gods should we serve?' Politically this could mean a choice between socialism and conservatism, but to Weber this choice would be essentially arbitrary, or at best based on consequentialist arguments.[69]

Hayek accepted Weber's characterization of the processes by which modern society emerges and the narrative of movement from an enchanted to a modern world. However, for Gamble, the two figures have a very different evaluation of modernity. As Gamble wrote, 'The structures of modern civilization, in Weber's view, constantly erode and marginalize individual freedom and autonomy. For Hayek, however, these structures, properly understood, are the expression of liberty'.[70] So, while for Weber these structures are rational, bureaucratic ones, for Hayek the 'iron cage of liberty' allows modern civilization to emerge within it. The spontaneous orders that emerge from the myriad interactions of individuals in the market place are the very expression of freedom. This difference between Weber and Hayek ties in with a criticism of Hayek raised, in passing, by Wainwright in the previous chapter. She pointed out that while Hayek claimed that the prime problem for economics was identifying the mechanisms for full use of knowledge, the examples of economic agency that he drew upon seemed limited to the self-employed entrepreneur and excluded those engaged in wage labour.[71] It is difficult to see Weberian bureaucracy as a Hayekian spontaneous order because Hayek assumed that the main actors are individual entrepreneurs, and not those labouring in Weber's 'iron cage'. For Weber, modernity creates an iron cage of bureaucracy; for Hayek, it creates freedom for the entrepreneur.

A further break between Hayek and Weber concerns their understanding of socialism. Whereas Weber viewed socialism as a part of modern society, Hayek saw it as an atavistic attempt to return to a lost pre-modern, more communal society.[72] Hayek detested the Marxist claim that socialism represented a stage beyond liberalism.[73] To Hayek the commitment to a particular kind of liberalism was the only commitment that one could make—the alternative, socialism, would lead to 'serfdom', as he famously put it.[74] To Hayek the liberty that developed with the processes of modernization provided the basis for modern civilization, and modern civilization would not survive without it. While Weber believed that the processes of rationalization and secularization that created liberty and the modern world led to the iron cage of bureaucracy; Hayek, in Gamble's phrase, believed that these processes of modernization created an 'iron cage of liberty'.

Hayek and Weber described the same iron cage: for Weber it initially offered freedom but soon locked us into disenchantment; for Hayek the initial promise of freedom remained, and the cage protected modern, civilized individuals from a return to the barbarism outside it. Seen in this way Hayek is one of the most passionate advocates of modernity. The spontaneous orders upon which modern society rests rely upon the unintended consequences of countless free interactions between individuals. To prevent individuals acting as they freely want to will prevent the structures that characterize modern society—such as language, law and the market—from arising. Liberty is the 'iron cage' that protects these institutions.

A 'new liberal' defence?

The limit of Gamble's engagement with Hayek's work involves a dispute about the values that characterize modern society. In this section, I examine the limits of Gamble's engagement with Hayek's work, and his defence of positive liberty. (The debate about positive and negative conceptions of liberty was set out in Chapter 3.) For Hayek, it was liberty that made the modern world possible; the pursuit of other values, or the 'confusion' of liberty with them, would, at worst, lead to 'serfdom'. Gamble challenged this: he argued that a positive conception of liberty was part of the modern world, too. In order to demonstrate the limits of his engagement with Hayek, Gamble contrasted Hayek's argument with Francis Fukuyama's well-known claim, made as the Berlin Wall fell in 1989, that liberal democracy was 'the end of history'.[75] The arguments of Hayek and Fukuyama are, on the face of it, similar: both were anti-socialist thinkers who saw forms of liberalism as the only viable option. However, Fukuyama differed from Hayek in arguing, not that socialism had been defeated but that it had been superseded—its insights had been absorbed; the rest had been rejected. Hayek, by contrast, saw liberalism and socialism as opposites. Fukuyama, according to Gamble's interpretation, recognized both socialism and liberalism as part of the same egalitarian-individualist modernist project, initiated by the French revolution.[76]

Fukuyama argued that liberal-capitalism was triumphant, but he did not argue that its form was fixed or invariable. He argued that societies with large public sectors and welfare programmes were as legitimate as those with minimal state intervention. To Fukuyama history has 'ended' because there was no longer any issue that could not be sorted out within the institutional framework that has been established. (This framework provides a Hegelian end-point, because it could provide for all human needs and reconcile all contradictions.) For Fukuyama, a plurality of types of liberal-capitalism existed incorporating different levels of state intervention.

Hayek's argument is more uncompromising than Fukuyama's, according to Gamble's reading. Whereas Fukuyama accepted state intervention, to Hayek, at his most polemical, almost all forms of state intervention were illegitimate. As Gamble noted, 'Hayek has no real answer to Fukuyama. He continued to believe to the end that no compromise is possible, and that the welfare state poses as great a long-term danger to the survival of individualistic Western civilisation as central planning and state socialism'.[77] Gamble used Fukuyama to show how narrow and one-sided Hayek's liberalism was. To Hayek, liberalism is based on the argument that the role of government is largely to facilitate a particular kind of liberty. To Fukuyama, many different varieties of liberalism are possible.

For Gamble, Hayek's narrow, negative account of liberty was justified by a false dichotomy between true and false individualism—a dichotomy of the kind common during the short twentieth century. Gamble argued that given Hayek's argument that moral views evolved, he never convincingly explained why the 'false' or 'constructive' side of individualism was not an authentic part of the Western tradition, while 'true individualism' should survive. This led Gamble to conclude that: 'Hayek's attempt to delegitimize one side of the Western tradition is one of the most significant ideological closures in his work. It prevents him from seeing the close ties which exist between liberalism and socialism'.[78]

To move beyond both Fukuyama and Hayek, Gamble discusses the arguments of Jeffrey Friedman. Friedman argued that Hayek's critique worked well against central planning, something Gamble acknowledged, but that his critique had been much less successful against the welfare state.[79] Following Friedman, Gamble argued that: '[T]he attempt to confine liberalism to negative liberty and proscribe other forms, as Hayek tries to do, is a hopeless task, which misconstrues the character of the cultural and ideological project of modernity. Negative liberty cannot be limited to property owners'.[80]

Still developing Friedman's argument, Gamble wrote that:

> Once individual freedom becomes an end in itself, the principles of self-determination and self-realization become central. Self-interest is condemned as being narrow and restrictive. *True freedom is conceived as liberation from the selfish appetites which lead to materialism and inequality.* The ideal of a community of citizens who are all responsible agents and equals is thus not rooted, as Hayek thinks, in some atavistic pre-modern impulses. It lies at the heart of the project of modernity which has developed within Western civilization.[81]

What is interesting in Gamble's account is that equality is now derived from a view of freedom—freedom from acquisitiveness and materialism. In this view, Gamble firmly rejects Hayekian conceptions of liberty in favour of something more akin to the new liberalism of T. H. Green a century before. Green's account of freedom as 'a positive power or capacity of doing or enjoying something *worth* doing or enjoying and that, too, something that we do or enjoy in common with others' (my italics) bears striking resemblance to Gamble's. [82]

Gamble also followed Friedman in his criticism of Fukuyama's 'end of history' thesis. Friedman argued that 1921 was a more significant date than 1989. He argued that the failure of 'war communism' in the Soviet Union and the introduction of the *New Economic Policy* (NEP) in that year marked the collapse of the Soviet project. (The NEP restored small-scale private ownership and reintroduced financial incentives by allowing the sale of some surpluses on the open market.) To Friedman these events did not just mark the failure of communism but also the failure of liberalism. He argued this because he believed that the goals of the communist revolutionaries were the ultimate expression of the goals of egalitarian-individualism, which guided both liberalism and socialism, and therefore the logical expression of the modernist project. To Friedman the failure of communism in 1921 meant the 'the attempt to launch a real experiment entailing an alternative to capitalism was abandoned'. [83] If Gamble were to accept this, then it would entail a further substantial break with the Marxism of his earlier writings, such as *Capitalism in Crisis*, published in 1976. Capitalism is now seen as part of the modern world, something that must be tamed, but which there is nothing beyond. The belief that socialism represented a stage beyond capitalism has been a central part of socialist thought. In following Friedman's account of liberty and his identification of the pre-Soviet era as a time when alternatives to capitalism were possible, Gamble's argument is again reminiscent of the arguments of the British new liberals and marks a break with the majority of earlier socialist thought.

CONCLUSIONS: THE DOMINANCE AND
DIVISION OF LIBERALISM

By 1996 Gamble was arguing that 'Hayek's approach has much to offer both liberals and conservatives, but ironically, perhaps most to socialists, as they seek to rethink their historic aims of liberty, equality, and solidarity'.[84] Yet the examination of Gamble's argument carried out in this chapter might instead lead us to ask how useful those terms are in describing the political landscape in the final decades of the twentieth century—a point I return to in the concluding chapter.

Gamble's engagement with the works of Hayek was part of a wider abandonment by the left of many of the concepts that had been most closely associated with the dominant forms of twentieth-century British socialism. Gamble, for example, rejected socialism's paternalism, its statism, its desire for a planned order and much of its collectivist basis. His belief in private ownership, markets, entrepreneurship, personal responsibility and the concentration on the individual owe more to the new liberalism of the early twentieth century than to any other tradition.

Running through the whole of Gamble's work is a commitment to positive liberty, which Hayek would have vehemently rejected. (Parallels can be drawn here with Raymond Plant's engagement with Hayek, discussed in Chapter 3, and his critique of the lack of any account of autonomy in Hayek's thought.[85]) For this reason it would be wrong to see Gamble's thought as a capitulation to the new right. In his reiteration of 'individual-egalitarianism' Gamble echoes the claim of new liberals that true freedom relies upon a high degree of equality to be 'effective'. To the new liberal, L. T. Hobhouse, writing in 1911, 'Liberal Socialism' (as he called it) must be democratic and 'make its account with the human individual. It must give the average man free play in the personal life for which he really cares. It must be founded on liberty, and must make not for the suppression but for the development of personality'.[86] Gamble's belief that the individual must participate and take responsibility echoes Hobhouse's claims.[87] By 2013, Gamble was even more explicit in the 'social liberal'[88] basis of his engagement with Hayek, arguing that: 'it is perfectly possible to derive a social-democratic or social-liberal Hayekian program that is true to the basic principles Hayek enunciated'.[89]

The account of Gamble's engagement with Hayek given in this chapter provides an example of the wider revival of liberalism in the years
after the end of the short twentieth century and its increasing separation into what could be described as its new and its classical strands.
Thus, the engagement of the British left with Hayek was carried out on
recognizably liberal terrain. Rather than demonstrating a capitulation to
classical liberalism (of the type that Hayek, loosely defined, was proposing) the left reasserted liberalism in its 'new' form. For many on the
left, this line of argument represented a shift of emphasis rather than a
categorical break.

The work of Gamble, and many of his colleagues at this time, constitutes a 'liberalization' of left-wing argument in the final decades of the
twentieth century as many socialists shifted away from more statist positions. In making this shift, they made a partial return to older debates.
The discussions between these left and right Hayekians bear some similarities to the debates between new (and before that Hegelian) liberals
with their Spencerian counterparts at the turn of the twentieth century.

This liberalization can be seen with the election of 'New Labour' in
1997 on a platform which owed much to earlier new liberal arguments.
David Marquand, among others, have noted this, writing that 'New
Labour has not advanced into astounding new territory, never before
glimpsed by a political thinker's eye; rather, it has picked up, after the
British left's 80-year detour, where Asquith and Lloyd George left
off'.[90] This element of Gamble's thought was noted in a letter published
in *The Guardian* in 1996, which noted that: 'It is deeply gratifying to us
Liberal Democrat trade unionists to see that Andrew Gamble and Gavin Kelly . . . have re-discovered principles set out by the Liberal Party
nearly 70 years ago in the Yellow Book—Britain's Industrial Future,
1928'.[91] Kelly went on to hold senior positions advising the Labour
government elected in 1997.

Gamble's engagement with the works of Hayek demonstrates the
transformation of socialism. If socialism survives in Gamble's thought, it
is as a liberal hybrid. Hayek, in this sense, is not so much 'Comrade
Hayek'—an inspiration for *socialists*—but a fellow liberal (although a
liberal of a very different kind to Gamble) and therefore someone
whose work could provide an inspiration, if only a partial one, for the
left as it reinvented itself at the end of the century. Gamble's comment

was tongue in cheek, but his engagement reflects 'Citizen Gamble', more than 'Comrade Hayek'.

By the 1990s, the political landscape in the UK was increasingly dominated by the liberal inheritance. Andrew Vincent, summing up political debate at this time concluded: 'Thus, in summary, we have seen not a debate between conservatism and socialism, but a debate between heterogeneous factions of liberalism, in fact, between variants of classical and new liberalism'. [92] The engagement of Gamble with the works of Hayek provides one case study of this liberalization, as Gamble's argument evokes an older new liberalism, which is pitted against Hayek's classical version, across the left–right political divide. Socialism, conservatism and liberalism are still in widespread currency but play a less clear role in mapping contemporary discourse than they did in the mid-twentieth century. As I argue in the concluding chapter, their transformations mark the end of a short twentieth century in political thought.

6

RESPONSES TO THE NEW RIGHT

The significance of the engagement

By the end of the twentieth century there was a commonly expressed belief that socialism had been demolished as an intellectual and political project, and that the left was unrecognizable from just a few years before. Friedrich Hayek claimed that the intellectual foundations of socialism had collapsed: that it was to be consigned to oblivion. Under this view socialism would perhaps be seen by future historians as nothing more than an 'exotic aberration . . . fated to vanish after briefly disturbing the main course of history'.[1] To Hayek, the battle was all but over.

Writing as the Soviet Union collapsed, the historian Perry Anderson included three further fates: transvaluation, transformation or redemption.[2] 'Transvaluation' would entail a complete historical break following demoralization, only for the ideas to re-emerge later in a new shape. After a period of demoralization and defeat (which might last decades or even centuries), some of socialism's ideas and objectives might be resurrected in a new form and new context and influence later movements for social change and social justice.

'Transformation' would mean a limited legacy is handed down that is found only as part of a new tradition. There would be no sharp break in continuity, as there would be under transvaluation. Instead the parties and movements of the left and centre-left might successfully adjust and evolve in the face of new circumstances, while retaining a recognizable identity and connection with the traditions of the past. It might mean the 'emergence of a new kind of movement for the radical transformation of society, in some respect acknowledging its debt to socialism, but in others criticizing and repudiating it quite sharply'.[3]

Finally, for 'redemption' to occur the old ideas must rise up free of any negative associations. That at the nadir of its fortunes socialism might be reborn. After all, as Anderson noted, '[b]y the end of the first third of the century, it looked to many observers as if liberalism might be destroying itself from within as a major historical force'.[4] It was during this middle third of the twentieth century that Hayek published his most famous warning against socialism, and by the 1960s his variety of classical liberalism could be dismissed as belonging to another age. Yet later in the twentieth century 'liberalism staged a remarkable recovery'.[5] Writing at the beginning of the 1990s, Anderson speculated that some new world crisis might make socialism once again relevant and necessary, although he conceded that as with the earlier rebirth of liberalism after 1945 this would have to be a socialism purged of its flaws and past mistakes, and reinvigorated by its inclusion of other traditions.[6] I return to these fates at the end of this book.

In this chapter I use the engagement of the British left with Hayek to reflect on several wider questions. First, in the decades since Anderson wrote, I examine the fate of socialism in, and after, the end of the twentieth century. I then look at the extent to which the engagement with Hayek can be understood as the part of a wider end to an ideological period—a 'short twentieth century'. This in turn allows me to reflect briefly on how ideologies, such as liberalism and socialism, change—and in particular on the role of enmity in that. Finally, I examine the impact these ideas had on the politics of the decades either side of the millennium, particularly the rise and fall of 'New Labour'.

THE FATE OF SOCIALISM

For those thinkers on the left who engaged with Hayek, what were the consequences for their political thought and how did their engagement reflect much wider shifts occurring on the left by the 1990s? In this section I argue the engagement with Hayek was part of a wider break

with the dominant socialism of twentieth century: an ideological transformation that I return to in the conclusion to this chapter.

Markets and the decline of state paternalism

For much of the twentieth century mainstream socialism had been
wedded to the state. Gamble, writing with Gavin Kelly, noted that 'the
political economy of the Left has always aimed at combining social
justice and economic efficiency':

> For much of the twentieth century, the favoured means has been a
> single measure, the common ownership of the means of produc-
> tion. . . . But increasingly common ownership came to be equated
> with state ownership . . . and this became the accepted definition of
> what socialism meant in practice for both its friends and enemies.[7]

The powerful and successful association of the state with 'slavery'
popularized by the new right, particularly in Hayek's *The Road to Serfdom*, led mainstream socialists to re-examine their attitudes. The engagement with Hayek's arguments among the thinkers I have examined
in this book, marks a radical challenge to the assumptions that underlay
the dominant view of the state on the British mainstream left.

Writing in the 1980s, the historian Rodney Barker asked what the
consequences were of the dominance of the state on British socialism.
He suggested:

> Not only a failure to develop a socialism which shares any of the
> libertarianism, anarchist, or even liberal attitudes towards the state
> which have certainly at times touched its attitudes to work, to art, or
> to civil liberties. But also, and especially from 1979 onwards, a total
> vulnerability to those on the new right who, with phrases directly
> derived from FA Hayek, assert that socialism means coercion by the
> state, and that the melange of cultural conservatism, military toryism,
> and economic liberalism, which they express means 'liberty'.[8]

In short, socialism was deeply paternalist. This paternalism is most associated with the Fabian tradition of socialism, and has various elements.
First, there was a belief in the authority of experts: there were those
with the knowledge to govern and those that needed governing. George

Bernard Shaw demonstrated this paternalism when he argued provocatively that: 'All Socialists are Tories. . . . The Tory is a man who believes
that those who are qualified by nature and training for public work, and
who are naturally a minority, have to govern the mass of the people.
That is Toryism. That is also Bolshevism'.[9] His Fabian colleague Beatrice Webb compared the role of the governing elite to Jesuits, while H.
G. Wells referred to them as a 'Samurai' class.[10] Fabian socialism, at any
rate, was about leadership on behalf of the people.

Second, Fabian paternalism was partly based on scepticism about
the ability of citizens to make their own choices. Wainwright's engagement with Hayek is inspired by what she sees as the failure of paternalist forms of socialism. She disparagingly cites Beatrice Webb, who re-
marked that 'the average sensual man can describe his problem but is
unable to prescribe a solution'.[11] This paternalism was infamously expressed by Douglas Jay, a Minister in several post-war Labour adminis-
trations, who stated that 'the gentleman in Whitehall knows best'. (The
sentence was picked up in the late 1940s and 1950s by the Conservative
Party and used in their election propaganda.[12]) There was a moral element to this form of its paternalism, too. Part of the reason that the
Webbs admired Soviet Russia was for its moral austerity and the Puri-
tanism of a country in which 'European dancing is taboo', 'promiscuity
is banned' and there was 'singularly little spooning in the Parks of Rest
and Culture'.[13] The later engagement with Hayek on the left, discussed
in this book, was partly inspired by a desire to reject this paternalism.

Despite the dominance of the Fabians, there has long been an anti-
paternalist strand on the left. Those authors who engaged with Hayek
echoed many of these earlier arguments. This anti-paternalism took
several forms. To the new liberal L. T. Hobhouse, the Fabian expert:

> sometimes looks strangely like the powers that be—in education, for
> instance, a clergyman under a new title, in business that very captain
> of industry who at the outset was the Socialist's chief enemy. Be that
> as it may, as the 'expert' comes to the front, and 'efficiency' becomes
> the watchword of administration, all that was human in Socialism
> vanishes out of it.[14]

To Hobhouse, the Fabians simply wanted to replace the capitalist with
the manager and the preacher with the schoolteacher—nothing
changed in the overall power relationships. The new liberal critique of

socialism at the start of the twentieth century finds a new form of expression in the Hayekian left at the century's end.

Within revisionist social democracy, anti-paternalism was a significant undercurrent. Anthony Crosland conceded that 'the Webbs have won their battle, and converted a generation to their standards', but he argued that:

> Now the time has come for a reaction: for a greater emphasis on private life, on freedom and dissent, on culture, beauty, leisure, and even frivolity. Total abstinence and a good filing-system are not now the right sign-posts to the socialist Utopia: or at least, if they are, some of us will fall by the wayside. [15]

This scepticism about the paternalist state is also found in older and more radical accounts of socialism. Joseph Lane issued an *Anti-Statist, Communist Manifesto*[16] in the 1880s, while William Morris felt that:

> it is necessary to point out that there are some Socialists who do not think that the problem of the organisation of life and necessary labour can be dealt with by a huge national centralisation, working by a kind of magic for which no one feels himself responsible; that on the contrary it will be necessary for the unit of administration to be small enough for every citizen to feel himself responsible for its details, and be interested in them; that individual men cannot shuffle off the business of life on to the shoulders of an abstraction called the State, but must deal with it in conscious association with each other. [17]

While the engagement with Hayek by some on the British left constituted a rejection of paternalist socialism, it also articulated themes that had long been part of a submerged tradition within socialism and the wider left.

The move away from the benevolent state took several forms after 1989: for example, the newfound importance placed in civil and civic rights. These rationalist approaches to constitutional planning are a far cry from Hayek's constitutional arguments, but they do shift the debate onto recognizably liberal grounds. The most obvious example of this development was the support among many on the British left for Charter 88—a pressure group created in 1988 to obtain a written constitution for Britain—of which Wainwright was a founding member.[18] Charter 88 gained popularity in response to the Conservative Government's use of the 'strong state'[19] to strip away existing tiers of democracy, the most obvious example being the abolition of the Greater London Council (GLC) in 1985, where Wainwright had worked in the early 1980s. It was the closure of the GLC, which was dominated by a broad coalition of left-wing groups clustered around the Labour Party, which led many on the left to question more explicitly their optimism in the constant benevolence of the state. By the 1980s the state could be viewed not as the solution, but as the problem, as Wainwright argued, 'tethering' the progress of socialism, rather than pulling it forward.[20]

In drawing on the constitution to protect the individual from the misuse of state power, as the supporters of Charter 88 did, the heritage of the argument is more obviously liberal than socialist. Comrades under the socialist state, depicted in class terms, are now citizens protected against the state by a written constitution, and viewed as individuals (albeit individuals shaped by a range of identities and solidarities). The argument owes more to the eighteenth-century radicalism of Thomas Paine, a writer whom Wainwright draws on at various points, than to the Fabians. Writing in 1998, just after New Labour's election, the journalist Jonathan Freedland reminded his readers that American radical liberalism started in the UK: Paine was both British and liberal, and it was, he argued, time to 'Bring Home the Revolution'.[21]

A second example of the move away from the benevolent state was the rediscovery of pluralism. For Wainwright and Miller this was an important consequence of the engagement with Hayek. This rediscovery also shows how the broader left at the end of the short twentieth century drew on traditions outside of mainstream twentieth-century socialism and social democracy. Paul Hirst argued, for example, for the revival of a pluralism that was explicitly derived, not just from socialists, such as Cole and Laski, but also from the Anglican and Whig theorist J. N. Figgis. Although the intellectual debt of other thinkers is less explicit, a discussion of pluralism can be found among many thinkers on the left after 1989 (an argument set out in Chapter 4). The pluralist revival is found in more or less radical forms. For Hirst and Wainwright, pluralism marked a radical departure towards associational forms of democracy. For more centrist thinkers, a more limited form of pluralism was a response to a view of globalization which saw that (in Daniel Bell's phrase) 'the nation state is becoming too small for the big problems of life, and too big for the small problems of life'.[22] This also led to calls for a 'new localism' on the left.[23] The revival of pluralism can be seen as a symptom of a wider rejection of twentieth-century conceptions of the role of the state after 1989.

The market, individual freedom and its consequences

If one aspect of the decline of the state was support for individual rights and pluralism, an even more significant change was a discovery by several thinkers on the left of the virtues of the market. Part of Hayek's argument for the market was made in terms of efficiency: socialism could not capture the knowledge necessary for successful economic planning. The acceptance of an epistemological argument for the market is often presented as a merely technical discussion about the efficient running of the economy. David Miller's discussion of central planning's ineffectiveness in responding to consumer demands (discussed in Chapter 2) is sometimes presented in this way. However, the argument that a tacit and individual account of knowledge drives the market contains implicit assumptions that challenge mainstream twentieth-century socialist and social democratic thought. These occur because to accept the market as a coordinating system is to accept many of the free and unpredictable decisions that individuals make within it.

Twentieth-century socialist and social democratic thought often contained a moral critique of the freely made choices of individuals in the market—from a critique of 'conspicuous consumption' to an attack on the sickness of an 'acquisitive society'.[24] W. G. Runciman pointed this out (perhaps with the ethical socialist R. H. Tawney in mind) noting that:

> For a very long time, British people have spent their money on accessories that moralising commentators regard as unnecessary and activities that those same commentators regard as harmful if not downright wicked.[25]

For David Miller an engagement with pro-market arguments led him to argue by 1989 that 'Freedom as a value has recently returned to prominence on the Left',[26] and he placed this value at the centre of his argument. The argument for freedom manifested itself in a newfound respect for individual choices made within the market—quirky or strange as those choices may be. As Miller wrote, 'Freedom is valuable precisely because of the possibility that people may make radically different choices about how they want to live their lives'.[27] The market can allow one the freedom to pursue a wide variety of lifestyles. However, the free choices that occur in the market also reflect and help to create an increasingly individualistic society and undermine the moral argument for solidarity that was a part of socialist and social democratic thought throughout the twentieth century—an issue that was discussed in Chapter 2.

In making individual liberty central to their arguments (most explicitly in the case of Plant and Miller), the thinkers I have examined in this book are drawing on a liberal strand, which was lacking in much twentieth-century socialism. But an acceptance of individual liberty also sets limits at what can be done by the state, the actions of which for most of the twentieth century many British socialists' assumed would be benevolent.

The search for a 'feasible' alternative

By the final decades of the twentieth century there was an increasing wariness of earlier socialists' ambitions for the future in the name of 'feasibility'. The engagement with Hayek reflected this broader shift. For example, the acceptance of some form of market, no matter how mediated, was often based on the acceptance of a much more limited view of human reason. Whether derived explicitly from Hayek or not, many socialists accepted his point that the kind of knowledge needed for successful economic planning simply did not exist. This was certainly the case for Gamble and Wainwright. The state was no longer given the role of primary economic coordinator, as it was perceived by the socialist and social democratic mainstream for much of the twentieth century.[28]

Miller set out explicitly to develop a 'feasible' form of socialism that eschews earlier utopian approaches. He argued that his writing was part of an attempt 'to recast the principle of socialism with the aim, broadly speaking, of bringing it more closely into line with the aspirations of the majority of the people (including the majority of workers) in advanced societies'.[29] Miller is not alone in stressing the 'feasibility' of his argument for socialism at the end of the twentieth century.[30] The move to less utopian and more feasible forms of socialism is part of a much longer historical shift.

The antecedents of this movement can be traced back to the recognition by Alexander Herzen and Karl Marx (in his later writings) that revolution was not imminent. However, it is in the decades after the end of the Second World War that the left has constantly narrowed its hopes in the name of 'feasibility'. In the twentieth century several factors created the conditions for a feasible socialism. The world wars are themselves partly responsible, creating a suspicion of grand theory.[31] There was increasing disenchantment with statist socialism, and in particular with the Soviet Union, which had provided a guiding star for many on the British left in the middle decades of the twentieth century. Stalin's show trials, the Nazi-Soviet Pact, Khrushchev's secret speech and, particularly, the crushing of the Hungarian and Czech uprisings meant that this star quickly faded. It was extinguished with the collapse of the Soviet Union after the revolutions of 1989. Finally, in the West, there were a series of disappointments for the left: the lack of long-term change following the demonstrations of 1968; the electoral popularity of governments inspired by the new right and, perhaps most importantly, a disenchantment with socialist and social democratic governments once in power. The abandonment of a radical programme by the French Socialists in 1983 symbolized this disenchantment more than any other event.[32]

By the early 1980s, the words 'feasible' or 'viable' were used constantly by socialist thinkers in putting forward their arguments, most famously by Alec Nove in *The Economics of Feasible Socialism*.[33] This shift is well summed up by the Labour advisor Michael Jacobs who wrote in 2002 that 'Over the last quarter of a century something very large, and not entirely understood, has happened to politics in western Europe. . . . It's a cultural, indeed a psychological, shift. A kind of spirit has been extinguished'.[34]

The engagement with Hayek can be seen as case study of much wider changes on the left in the late twentieth century: the decline of faith in the paternalist state, the discovery of constitutional freedoms, pluralism and the market and the development of 'feasible' socialism came from a variety of sources and engagements. These shifts allow me to reflect on various wider questions about political ideologies, including the question of the contemporary fate of socialism, which I raised at the start and to which I return at the conclusion of this chapter. Before then, however, I use the engagement with Hayek to explore some of the ways in which ideologies can change, and in particular the role of context and enmity in that process.

FIN DE SIÈCLE: ENEMIES AND IDEOLOGICAL CHANGE

The historian Eric Hobsbawm identified a 'short twentieth century' which ran from 1914 to 1991.[35] Hobsbawm's century replaces the historically arbitrary chronological periodization with a periodization by significant events, in this case the First World War and the collapse of the Soviet Union. For Hobsbawm, the short twentieth century, from a 'bird's eye view', was divided into three periods: an age of catastrophe dominated by two world wars; the post-war 'golden age' of economic growth and social transformation; and, from the early 1970s, the 'landslide'—a period of 'decomposition, uncertainly and crisis'.[36] (Hobsbawm's periodization was also discussed in Chapter 5.) This short twentieth century ended around the time of the collapse of the Soviet Union. '[T]here can be no serious doubt', Hobsbawm wrote, 'that in the late 1980s and early 1990s an era in world history ended and a new one began'.[37] Hobsbawm's assertion sparked a wider debate over the extent to which the collapse of the Soviet Union marked an end, not just to a distinct historical period, but of a unique ideological one as well.[38]

New and old ideological centuries

For some historians of political thought, such as Rodney Barker, the 1990s clearly marked the beginning of a new ideological period. Writing in 1995, he argued that:

> [T]he way in which political thinking is carried on now bears only superficial resemblances to the manner in which it was conducted in the 1940s. Arguments are different, but so are the key words and the things about which the arguments are conducted. Socialism, capitalism, class, cold war, equality, rationalism, modernization, society have been replaced or eclipsed by nationalism religion, pluralism, autonomy citizenship, post-modernism, and gender. Whether we ac-

cept Hobsbawm's date of 1991 or settle for 1979, 1989 or 1973, somewhere between 1945 and 1995 a transition has occurred.[39]

The most obvious way in which a new ideological century had begun was in the reported 'deaths' of two of the main players from the short twentieth century: socialism and conservatism. In a review of the Labour politician David Miliband's 1994 book, *Reinventing the Left*, Barker asked provocatively, 'Why are there no more socialists or conservatives?'[40] This scepticism about the use of the term 'socialism' was widespread. For about a year after his election as leader of the British Labour Party, Tony Blair would refer to himself, not as a socialist, but as a 'social-ist'.[41] The last sighting of this hyphenated construction in print may have been a year later, in his lecture on the fiftieth anniversary of the Labour landslide of 1945. Blair later settled on describing his project as part of 'a third way', drawing on Anthony Giddens' account of the concept. For Giddens, the third way lies between socialism and 'market fundamentalism'.[42] This period was replete with references to a third way, option or path. As early as 1988, Wainwright was arguing for 'a third option', by which she meant a politics which draws on 'socialist and republican traditions marginalized by social democracy and official communism'.[43] Giddens explicitly attempted to locate his work as social democratic, rather than socialist—and he tellingly entitled the first chapter of *The Third Way*, 'After Socialism'.[44]

If socialism, as it had been understood in the twentieth century disappeared, another departure marking the end of an era was that of conservatism.[45] The collapse of conservatism was hidden, to some extent, by the Constantinian relationship between party and ideology discussed in Chapter 5. As Shaw's comment, cited earlier in this chapter, shows, both 'Tory' conservatism and Fabian socialism shared a common paternalism in the twentieth century, built upon an understanding of society as hierarchical and class-based. Both themes were elitist and argued that leadership involved responsibilities to those less well off. The rise of the new right, significantly inspired by Hayek, led to the decline of paternalism for not only the left but for the right as well. The decline of the tory tradition in conservatism, illustrated by the purging of 'wets' in the early Thatcher governments, meant that conservatism, as it had been known in the twentieth century, joined socialism in having many of its components jettisoned. Just as in the period after the

First World War it was possible to talk about the 'death of liberalism',[46] by the last decades of the same century it was possible to talk about the 'deaths' of both socialism and conservatism, at least in their statist forms.

An examination of the engagement of the British left with Hayek provides one example of the end of an ideological era. The thinkers discussed in this book illustrate, if not the 'death of socialism', certainly a transformation. Plant's attempt to recast socialism in terms of autonomy and citizenship shifted the debate onto recognizably liberal terrain. Miller's embrace of the market included a defence of a particular understanding of freedom, pluralism and community which were all outside the mainstream of twentieth-century socialism. Andrew Gamble's rejection of paternalism, statism and the necessary superiority of the 'made' order, jettisoned many of the central themes of mainstream twentieth-century socialism, while his advocacy of private ownership, markets, entrepreneurship, personal responsibility and his focus on the individual owed more to the new liberalism of Hobson and Hobhouse than it did to earlier socialists. Wainwright moves away from traditional socialist conceptions of class in favour of social movements and is open about whether the changes she advocates can best be described as socialist.

From another perspective the 'short twentieth century' was merely a parenthesis within a longer period.[47] To several thinkers the intellectual landscape by the 1990s had more in common with the period before the short twentieth century began—perhaps the continuation of a long century dating back to the 1880s.[48] Under this view the short twentieth century becomes a long historical diversion, and political debate after 1989 carried on where it had left off before the creation of the Soviet Union. (For these thinkers the description of the 'Soviet century'—of 1917 to 1989 or 1991—is particularly apt, and loosely fits Hobsbawm's 'short twentieth century', which lasted from 1914 to 1991.) David Marquand provides an example of this when he describes 'the British left's 80-year detour'.[49] The thinkers discussed in this book provide some support for this reading, reflecting a rediscovery of neglected debates within liberalism and political pluralism from almost a century before.

The engagement of the British left with Hayek forced the debate onto liberal grounds. However, rather than demonstrating a capitulation to classical liberalism (of the type that Hayek was, loosely defined, proposing), the left tended to reassert a social form of liberalism. Thus, the debate between these new 'new liberals' and Hayekians bears many similarities to the debates between new (and before that Hegelian) liberals with Spencerian liberals before the short twentieth century began. Indeed, all of the four thinkers I looked at above placed freedom at the centre of their arguments, but they were also concerned with a more equal distribution of effective forms of that liberty. By contrast, socialists during the twentieth century, by and large, tended not to place freedom at the centre of their argument. This liberalization can be seen with the election of 'New Labour' in 1997 on a platform which owed much to earlier new liberal—and particularly new liberal—arguments. The historian Steven Fielding summed this shift up well, when he noted that the 'incorporation of elements from another party's past' was the 'most intriguing feature of New Labour's tradition'. Whatever its relation to New Labour, the engagement of the British left with Hayek was part of a wider liberalization of political debate in the final decades of the chronological twentieth century.

The liberal revival was accompanied by the rediscovery of political pluralism on the British left. In particular, the move away from class in favour of a free-floating radicalism based on social movements in the work of Hilary Wainwright more obviously evoked early twentieth-century pluralism than the work of any mainstream socialist thinkers. Miller also demonstrates a form of pluralism in his case for market socialism, which owes something to the socialist pluralism of Cole and early Laski in the first decades of the twentieth century. The rediscovery of pluralism was even more explicit in Paul Hirst (discussed in Chapter 4) and his attempt to place the pluralism 'back on the agenda'.

Sometime after 1989 one century in political thought ended. In the UK socialism, as it had been understood, died away—conservatism endured a similar fate although many of their components can still clearly be seen as contributing to a political landscape dominated by the two sides of the liberal tradition. In some respects political debate by the late 1990s echoed discussions almost a century before. There are new entrants. In particular, the centrality of gender and the immediate global reach of both environmental problems and economic markets in political discourse are perhaps the most significant differences between the terrain before and after the short twentieth century. Yet in terms of the revival of liberalism and political pluralism, important parallels do exist with earlier periods. The thinkers examined in this book provide one example of the end of one century and the resumption of another. The idea of the 'short twentieth century' is also helpful in explaining what led some thinkers on the British left to begin their engagement with Hayek.

Ideology and aversion: from enmity to enmities

The end of the short twentieth century marked the end of a particular period of enmity, one that was defined around a polar opposition between left and right. Hobsbawm makes this point when he argued that during the short twentieth century we were used to thinking 'in terms of binary opposites, 'capitalism' and 'socialism' as alternatives mutually excluding one another'.[50] For much of the twentieth century, on the left was communism, state planning and the Soviet Union and on the right was capitalism, the market and the United States. Attempts to combine elements of these distinct categories were rare. Political thought was understood largely in relation to binary opposites.

There are parallels in the work of the thinkers examined in this book on Hayek with the left's surprising engagement with the work the German legal theorist Carl Schmitt—an engagement primarily associated with Chantel Mouffe.[51] Schmitt, in large part because of his connections with the Nazi Party, was vilified by the left for much of the post-war period, and there was no detailed assessment of his work. A change in the way in which Schmitt's writings were received occurred during the 1990s when Mouffe, who is normally described as a 'post-Marxist', argued that there is much in Schmitt's thought that can usefully be reclaimed by the left.

Mouffe's writings on Schmitt contained a second parallel with the left's engagement with Hayek, which is relevant here. This parallel arises out of Schmitt's account of 'the political' as consisting of friend–enemy relations. Schmitt was opposed to liberal, democratic, legally rationalistic ideas of what constituted 'the political', which viewed the state conceptually prior to struggles within it. To Schmitt the state emerges out of struggle, which he argued was the essence of the political.[52] The political, therefore, only comes into being when different groups are in a relation of enmity to one another. Without endorsing Schmitt's account of the political, his recognition of the role of groups, group identity and the necessity of enmity in political thought is pertinent to any discussion of how former political enemies come to engage with one another's thought.

Ideologies are also formed through adversity. The importance of enmity is neglected in most major studies of political thought. Socialism may be in part about 'the constitutive nature of the human relationship, human welfare as a desirable objective, human nature as active, equality and history as an arena of (ultimately) beneficial change',[53] but it has also been about various aversions and enmities, too. In the twentieth century, socialism was commonly associated with a critique of the market and the 'selfish appetites' that drive it. To be a socialist was as much about developing a critical position against those ideologies that sought to promote capitalism as it was to develop an account of those concepts at socialism's core. These are aversions first and foremost: critical of the beliefs, values and concepts that make up alternative ideologies.

Rodney Barker has written of 'the importance of enemies' in political thought, noting that '[t]he identification of the values and practices which one opposes, and which may even be actively threatening, is one of the prior conditions and sustaining nourishments of political action'. He wrote that during the short twentieth century:

> Socialism was expounded as an opposition to capitalism, conservatism and liberalism as a defence against socialism. . . . Anthony Crosland . . . could organise his later work around an account of *The Conservative Enemy*. Hayek spent more time warning of the dangers of 'serfdom' than discussing the virtues of catallaxy.[54]

And, if one accepts that the destruction of a rival's case is as central to an ideology as the construction of your own argument, then changes in a rival's ideology can affect your own.

The engagement of the British left with Hayek cannot simply be viewed as part of the recent history of socialism. It can only be understood as part of the collapse of the exclusive and binary distinctions that dominated the politics of the (short) twentieth century. Hayek's reception from the left in the middle years of that century was overtly hostile, as Chapter 1 shows. He was viewed as a 'straw man' whose politics represented an enemy position. Herman Finer's book, *Road to Reaction*, published in 1945, was so vehement in its response to *The Road to Serfdom* that Hayek threatened legal action.[55] Hayek, especially later in

life, was equally dismissive of his detractors. As the short twentieth
century ended, new engagements were possible, freed from the binary
oppositions with which they had originally been associated. Miller's
'market socialism', for example, brought together terms that to some
older critics were simply oxymoronic, as Chapter 2 shows. What happened with the collapse of the Soviet Union was not so much the 'disappearance of enemies'[56]—political thought is still defined against the
views of others—but the collapse of the binary distinctions that had
dominated and defined the short twentieth century. Gamble's concept
of 'ideological closure' can be understood in these terms. The politics of
the short twentieth century confined debates to relationships of enmity.
Gamble reflects on how this might have affected Hayek's own arguments:

> In changed circumstances, Hayek might have presented his argu-
> ment rather differently. If he had not been so shaped intellectually
> by his long ideological struggle against socialism, he might have given
> greater weight to other options for preserving economic liberty, such
> as finding ways to empower all citizens and to create a more cohesive
> and far society.[57]

The collapse of binary distinctions provided a new political landscape
after the short twentieth century. It was cluttered with terms that do
not fit easily onto those older relationships of enmity. Many of these
terms reflect debates about various forms of identity: feminism, nationalism, multiculturalism, religion, fundamentalism and gender add to
existing debates about class and capital.

In the next section I look briefly at the the party political left's
engagement with the market in Britain, before returning to the question of the fate of socialism in the conclusion.

LABOUR AND THE MARKET

By the 1990s, the battles that the left was fighting were not the same as
they had been a generation before. The engagement with Hayek can be
seen as symptomatic of this change. The 'modernization' of the Labour
Party—for much of the twentieth century the vehicle for a wide variety
of different aspirations for the left—was partly informed by the debates

discussed in this book. All of the thinkers examined had some relationship to the Labour Party. For Miller and Plant, one reason to engage with Hayek was the electoral failure of the Party in 1983. Hilary Wainwright was part of an alternative path, working for Ken Livingstone on the radical Greater London Council of the early 1980s. In the mid-1990s Gamble's ideas of stake-holding fed into Tony Blair's modernization of the Labour Party. His co-author at the time, Gavin Kelly, went on to be a senior adviser to both Blair and Gordon Brown.

The making of New Labour

The broad arguments for the market set out by Hayek were pithily summarized in phrases that entered the political philosophy of Thatcherism: the state was inefficient and the market ensured freedom.[58] This analysis remains powerful in the Conservative Party, which maintained a strong attack on Labour's 'statism' while the party was in office after 1997, and which continues to this day.[59]

Whatever social democrats thought of these arguments, by the 1980s they were manifested in the electoral success of the right in Britain to which the left had to respond. In the wake of the 1983 general election defeat—in which, among other things, Labour had set out manifesto commitments to renationalize recently privatized industries—the Fabian Society called together a group of sympathetic academics to discuss what had 'gone wrong'. This Socialist Philosophy Group (SPG), discussed in Chapters 2 and 3, met on a regular basis to begin 'rethinking and reconstructing socialist ideas'. The aim of the group was to find a 'political philosophy' or narrative for the Labour Party.[60] Many of the papers presented engaged, for the first time since the socialist calculation debates of the 1920s and 1930s, with the idea of the market; most were brought together in a 1989 collection, edited by Julian Le Grand and Saul Estrin, called *Market Socialism*, which remains influential today and shaped New Labour's views on the market.

The chapters in *Market Socialism* ranged broadly across the left, from the proto-Blairism of Julian Le Grand to David Miller's more radical claim—discussed in Chapter 2 —that it was 'quite possible to be for markets and against capitalism'.[61] Yet across the spectrum of opinion of the Socialist Philosophy Group four important points were made. First, there was a widespread acceptance of the epistemological difficulties of coordinating a planned system. Second, there was recognition that the right's efforts to argue against the state on the grounds of freedom had gained public purchase, and by contrast, contemporary socialism did not provide a sufficient account of liberty. Third, there was agreement that the pro-market arguments put forward by the right had to be taken seriously. Indeed to Plant and Miller—and to Andrew Gamble, who was not a member of the Group—there was a guarded acceptance of the virtues of a market economy. Finally, there was an agreement that none of this necessitated the kind of policies that the Thatcher government was pursuing.

The arguments of the Socialist Philosophy Group were influential in the modernization of the Labour Party. Raymond Plant, for example, worked closely with the party's Deputy Leader, Roy Hattersley, in the run up to the publication of his book *Choose Freedom* in 1987, while Julian Le Grand later became a Senior Policy Advisor to Tony Blair. The overall message of the SPG was broadly in keeping with the tenor of the Kinnock Policy Reviews of 1980s, which adopted a much more positive approach to the market. Yet some of the subtlety of the group's views on markets was lost during the New Labour years.

Despite the engagement with Hayek by several thinkers influential in the Labour Party, elected politicians of the left tended to be more suspicious. While Raymond Plant could both write about Hayek and represent the Labour Party from the electorally sheltered position of the House of Lords, the politician that Plant most influenced, Roy Hattersley—an elected Member of Parliament and Labour's Deputy Leader from 1983–1992—was much more wary of Hayek. Writing in 2010, Hattersley reiterated his intellectual indebtedness to Plant (discussed in Chapter 3) but argued that, 'it always seemed to me that he is overgenerous in his attitude towards Friedrich Hayek'.[62] It may be that while those thinkers largely based in academia were freed from what Gamble described as 'ideological closure', by the end of the relationship of enmity that characterized the short twentieth century, some politicians still faced a 'partisan closure' as well. They continued to reject an engagement with someone whom they were aware would not score them electoral benefit and whom was still largely associated with the opposition—in this case the Conservative Party.

New Labour in retrospect: markets and the left

By the time the Conservatives left office in 1997, after four tumultuous terms, the growth model that they bequeathed to Labour—based on the largely Hayekian tenets of deregulation, market expansion and an entrepreneurial culture—appeared a successful one. As in the post-war period, a settlement with the market seemed to have been reached—although in a rather different position. From 1992–2007, the British economy grew at a gradual and steady rate, and unemployment remained relatively low. This new settlement allowed Labour to push through the minimum wage, tax the proceeds of growth and spend the money on public services and various forms of welfare support and subsidy. New Labour could combine, as Tony Blair claimed, 'fairness with economic efficiency'. An accommodation with the market enabled the achievement of important social democratic goals. Hayek could provide some of the foundations, if not for socialism, then for a political platform that owed something to the left.

New Labour introduced a series of pro-market policies while ensuring that services were well funded and that there were limits to the inequalities that market-based policies would cause. For example, while private 'Independent Sector Treatment Centres' provided health care to NHS patients, treatment remained free at the point of use. To give just a few examples, New Labour's pro-market policies included support for individual budgets in health and social care allowing users to shape the service provided (a policy that Hayek would have approved); the introduction of quasi-markets within public services (especially in health care and welfare); support for further privatization (for example, of National Air Traffic Systems); the private provision of public infrastructure (via forms of Public Private Partnerships); and, most controversially, the acceptance of a deregulated financial sector. The latter followed the 'prawn cocktail offensive', which promised light-touch financial regulation and convinced the City that Labour was not a threat, symbolizing Labour modernization in the early 1990s. In the wake of the financial crisis, light-touch regulation seems particularly foolhardy, although during the New Labour years tax receipts from the City flooded into public services after a long arid spell. In 2007, for example, the total tax contribution of the financial services sector in the UK amounted to around 14 percent of government receipts—a significant sum.[63] Overall, New Labour was heavily reliant on a successful market economy to achieve its goals. For some critics, New Labour had simply introduced a form of left neo-liberalism, the heritage of which owed more to Hayek and the Thatcher reforms than to 'Old' Labour's socialist roots. [64] Many in the Labour Party would describe their policies as a form of social democratic revisionism, they were relaxed about 'whatever works'—market or state—in achieving their aims.[65]

After the financial and then economic crisis of 2007/2008, New Labour's embrace of the market revealed many of the vulnerabilities of market-led approaches. First, Blairites in particular tended to say little about the market's distributive failings. They were, as Peter Mandelson famously commented, 'intensely relaxed about people getting filthy rich'. Several commentators noted the failure to bring down income inequality during the New Labour years—though serious attempts were made to help those at the bottom through tax credits, the introduction of the minimum wage and investment in public services. The thinkers examined in this book all had substantial contributions to make about the extent of equality in society—from Plant's claim for the importance of making freedom of equal value to all, to Gamble's argument that a 'revised Hayekian' would remember that economic liberty was the result of measures to equalize power.[66] New Labour was far more radical in its embrace of the market than it was in considering the forms of equality needed to ensure the market's success.

Second, while New Labour was relaxed about the means it pursued, it was sometimes less clear in setting out its ends. Increased public spending improved public services, but for what purpose? With seeming sympathy for the Hayekian argument (set out in Chapter 3) that the pursuit of traditional socialist goals, such as greater equality, suppressed freedom and were electorally unpopular, New Labour failed to articulate the values behind its decision to increase public spending. This left Labour's successes—investment in the health service and education, tax credits for those who were worse off, for example—deeply vulnerable to attack once a government of the right was elected and committed to austerity cuts. New Labour failed to articulate a vision for the social democratic policies that it did introduce.

Finally, New Labour was complacent that the market could provide constant economic growth: that 'boom and bust' was over. Just as the first generation of post-war revisionists found with collapse of the Keynesian consensus in the 1970s, New Labour discovered that they could not rely on sharing the proceeds growth to achieve their goals. As Michael Jacobs wrote in 2013, 'Over the past five years . . . the primary problem facing Western societies has not been a consequence of the failure of the state, but of the failure of markets'.[67] The recession that began in 2008 revealed the extent to which the UK economy had become unbalanced, and the vulnerability of an economic strategy that is reliant on the vagaries of global markets to secure its ends. New Labour's failure to articulate clear values, which social democratic policies helped to attain, meant that once the economic storm broke, their reforms were left deeply vulnerable to erosion. Like the post-war social democrats, New Labour was reliant on constant economic growth to share the proceeds of growth fairly and had no clear normative justification for continued redistribution once that growth faltered.

CONCLUSIONS: NEW CENTURIES, HYBRID IDEOLOGIES

Which of the possibilities for socialism set out by Anderson at the start of this chapter—destruction, redemption, transformation or transvaluation—best explains the contemporary fate of socialism?

Socialism has not been consigned to oblivion. Many of the concepts that form the ideology—notably the ideal of greater equality—remain at the heart of contemporary debate. What is now missing, compared with mid-twentieth-century socialism, is faith in the means available to reach those goals, in particular faith in the ability of the state to achieve social ends without unintended consequence, inefficiency or the suppression of liberty.

It is this gap which makes Anderson's second possibility—redemption—unlikely. On the centre left, few thinkers believe that a return to the overarching state of the post-war consensus can bring about the kind of outcomes that they desire. The poisonousness of Soviet socialism tainted even moderate democratic forms of social democracy that existed in Western Europe. As Miller wrote in 1989, 'Socialism is no longer an unsullied idea; *faute de mieux*, people will identify it with the unattractive form of statism that has emerged over the last half-century in Eastern Europe'.[68] Despite the ongoing economic crisis caused by the widespread overreach of financial markets, radical socialism has not been forgiven its failings, nor has more moderate forms of social democracy convinced voters of its feasibility. Most of Europe turned to governments of the right to sort out capitalism's failings. In the decades since the fall of the Berlin Wall redemption has not looked likely.

The question remaining, therefore, is whether the fate of socialism lies in 'transvaluation' or 'transformation'; whether the ideology has been so comprehensively displaced that we are likely to see a complete historical break, or whether a limited legacy can continue. By the beginning of the twenty-first century, many writers on the left adopted a resigned, eulogistic tone. Tony Judt's *Ill Fares the Land* epitomized this attitude, lamenting what had been lost in the old social democracy but unclear on what was to come.[69] Socialism in its radical and traditional forms was in deep trouble, and there was no obvious cavalry waiting to ride in and save the day. The left at the start of the new century were waiting for radical change but were unsure what it would look like or how to bring it about. This book has stressed the importance of context in reshaping ideology, and it may only be through some form of crisis—environmental, nuclear or economic—that a transvaluation of socialism could occur.[70]

The arguments explored in this book are part of a rather more limited change: an ongoing 'transformation' of socialism. The transformation of socialism after the short twentieth century is often a form of 'hybridization'. Socialist ideas are found mixed with aspects other ideologies. In different ways, Gamble and Plant make a case that mixes elements of socialism with liberalism. Plant, like Hobhouse almost a century before, at times refers to himself as a 'liberal socialist'.[71] Similarly, Miller and Wainwright draw on arguments that owe as much to pluralism as they do to socialism. In Wainwright's case in particular, feminism is added to the blend. The boundaries between socialism and other ideologies have blurred, so that many contemporary arguments are made on what would have been the dividing line between fairly discrete sets of argument. This makes classification of argument difficult, as Michael Freeden noted when he described the 'perimeter problem of market socialism'[72] or said of Raymond's Plant's work, 'Whether this is left-liberalism masquerading as democratic socialism depends entirely on where one wishes to draw the boundary line between the two; indeed, on whether they can be separated by so crude a device as a line'.[73] Hybridization means ideological debate occurs in what would have been the grey areas between the main ideologies of the twentieth century. Socialism is not dead, but in many cases its decedents have merged with other ideologies and created something new—or if not new, configured differently to those ideologies that dominated the short twentieth century. As Barker has commented in 2009, we have torn up the ideological maps, but we are still squabbling over the compass to find our way around.[74]

The engagement with Hayek by some members of the British left in the late twentieth century was significant. It is a way of reflecting on the changing conditions that made engagement with an enemy possible: the end of one century in political thought, and the collapse of the relationships of enmity that defined it. It was also part of a much wider transformation of socialism, which saw its survival largely as a hybrid with other ideologies. Finally, the writers who engaged with Hayek were part of a 'modernization' of the party political left: a modernization that began by emphasising change, openness, conciliation and the absorption of other doctrines, but which left the party dependent upon market-led growth to secure its ends, and—like earlier revisionist socialists—vulnerable when that growth stopped.

NOTES

1. HAYEK AND THE LEFT

1. A. Gamble, *Hayek: The Iron Cage of Liberty* (Cambridge: Polity, 1996), 192.

2. F. A. Hayek, *New Studies in Philosophy, Politics, Economics and the History of Ideas* (London: Routledge, 1978), 305.

3. M. Thatcher, *The Path to Power* (London: HarperCollins, 1995), 50.

4. J. Cassidy, "The Price Prophet", *New Yorker*, February 7, 2000, accessed 1 June 2014, http://www.hooverdigest.org/003/cassidy.html.

5. H. Wainwright, *Arguments for a New Left: Answering the Free-Market Right* (Oxford: Blackwell, 1994), 5.

6. C. Mouffe, ed., *The Challenge of Carl Schmitt* (London: Verso, 1999).

7. The essay is reprinted in J. Anderson, *Studies in Empirical Philosophy* (Sydney, NSW: Sydney University Press, 2005).

8. M. Thatcher, "Speech accepting an honorary degree from Hofstra University", March 27, 2000, accessed 1 June 2014, http://www.margaretthatcher.org/document/108387.

9. J. Gray, *Hayek on Liberty* (London and New York: Routledge, 1989), 4.

10. E. Butler, *Hayek: His Contribution to the Economic Thought of Our Times* (Worcester: Billing and Sons Ltd, 1983), 5.

11. Butler, *Hayek*, 5.

12. F. Hayek, *Hayek on Hayek: An Autobiographical Dialogue* (London: Routledge, 1994), 4–5.

13. Butler, *Hayek*, 5.

14. Hayek, *Hayek on Hayek*, 6.

15. Butler, *Hayek*, 5.

16. L. van Mises, *Socialism: An Economic and Sociological Analysis* (London: J. Cape, 1936, original 1922).

17. The series was later published as F. Hayek, *Prices and Production* (London: Routledge, 1934).

18. A. Seldon, "Obituary: Professor F. A. Hayek", *The Independent*, March 25, 1992, accessed 1 June 2014, www.lexisnexis.com/uk/business.

19. Cassidy, "The Price Prophet".

20. Cassidy, "The Price Prophet".

21. N. McInnes, "The Road Not Taken: Hayek's Slippery Slope to Serfdom", *The National Interest*, Spring 1998, accessed 21 April 2014, www.lexisnexis.com/uk/business.

22. Atticus, *Sunday Times*, March 29, 1992, accessed 21 April 2014, www.lexisnexis.com/uk/business.

23. Cassidy, "The Price Prophet". *The Road to Serfdom* was published in 1944.

24. McInnes, "The Road Not Taken".

25. H. Macmillan, *The Middle Way. A Study of the Problem of Economic and Social Progress in a Free and Democratic Society* (London: Macmillan & Co., 1938).

26. F. Hayek, *The Road to Serfdom* (London: Routledge, 1944), iv.

27. McInnes, "The Road Not Taken".

28. Quoted in Cassidy, "The Price Prophet".

29. S. Brittan, "Champion of Liberty and Law: The Work of the Late Friedrich Von Hayek", *Financial Times*, March 25, 1992, 19.

30. Although the phrase is popularly attributed to Winston Churchill, as an insult directed at Clement Attlee, it has also been argued that Churchill actually made the comment about an earlier British Prime Minister, Ramsay MacDonald. Others claim that Churchill was not the source at all but that the phrase derives from the humorist J. B. Morton or 'Beachcomber' (N. Rees, 'The Vagueness Is All', 1993, accessed 14 August 2006, http://archive.today/DGGUG#selection-45.5-47.33).

31. The effect of *The Road to Serfdom* on the 1945 General Election is discussed in R. Cockett, *Thinking the Unthinkable: Think-Tanks and the Economic Counter-Revolution, 1931–1983* (London: Harper Collins, 1994), 90–99.

32. Brittan, "Champion of Liberty and Law".

33. H. Finer, *Road to Reaction* (Boston: Little, Brown and Company, 1945), 15.

34. Finer, *Road to Reaction*, ix.

35. B. Wootton, *Freedom under Planning* (Chapel Hill: University of North Carolina Press, 1945), also quoted in B. Seligman, "The Study of Man: Dice, Dr. Hayek and the Consumer", *Commentary* 1, 5 (1946): 84.

36. E. Durbin, "Professor Hayek on Economic Planning and Political Liberty", *The Economic Journal* 55, 220 (1945).

37. McInnes, "The Road Not Taken".

38. Cockett, *Thinking the Unthinkable*, 101.

39. C. Merriam, "Book Reviews: Friedrich A. Hayek, the Road to Serfdom", *The American Journal of Sociology* 50, 3 (1944): 234.

40. Merriam, "Book Reviews", 235.

41. G. Orwell, "Review: *The Road to Serfdom* by F. A. Hayek, the *Mirror of the Past* by K. Zilliacus" in *The Collected Essays, Journalism and Letters of George Orwell. Volume 3: As I Please. 1943–1945*, ed. S. Orwell and I. Angus (Harmondsworth: Penguin, 1982, originally 1968), 143. It demonstrates the enduring statures of these two thinkers at the end of the twentieth century to note that Orwell and Hayek both had two books in *National Review*'s list of the top ten best non-fiction books of the previous hundred years. *The Road to Serfdom* was at number four, sandwiched between Orwell's *Homage to Catalonia* (at three) and *Collected Essays* (at five). Hayek's *The Constitution of Liberty* was at number nine (*National Review*, "The 100 Best Non-Fiction Books Of The Century", May 3, 1999, accessed 1 June 2014, http://www.nationalreview.com/100best/100_books.html).

42. Orwell, "Review", 144.

43. B. Crick, *George Orwell: A Life* (Harmondsworth: Penguin, 1992, originally 1980), 538.

44. Crick, *George Orwell*, 28. From the right, the American 'neo-conservative' Norman Podhoretz has argued that Orwell's review of *The Road to Serfdom* reflects his disillusion with socialism and that 'Orwell did indeed defect from the left' after a youthful flirtation (N. Podhoretz, "Revenge of the Smelly Little Orthodoxies", *National Review*, January 27, 1997, accessed 1 June 2014, http://www.netcharles.com/orwell/ctc/docs/smelly.htm). Certainly, the disillusioned tone of Orwell's review is also found in his final books, *Animal Farm* (1945) and *Nineteen Eighty-Four* (1949). However, Podhoretz's account is not convincing because it does not explain why 'Orwell for some reason never gave up calling himself a socialist', nor—despite his assertion that Orwell 'spilled far more ink attacking and even ridiculing socialists than he ever did in criticizing the Right'—does Podhoretz acknowledge in any detail that Orwell's position, even as it was laid out relatively late in his career, was recognizably if at times quirkily socialist. See, for example, *The Lion and the Unicorn: Socialism and the English Genius* (1941).

45. Keynes quoted in R. Harrod, *The Life of John Maynard Keynes* (London: Macmillan, 1951), 436–37.

46. This libertarian strand gives some support to 'the Anarchists' Orwell' discussed in J. Rodden, *The Politics of Literary Reputation: The Making and*

Claiming of 'St. George' Orwell (New York and Oxford: Oxford University Press, 1989), 153, and presented, above all, in the biography of him by his friend George Woodcock, *The Crystal Spirit: A Study of George Orwell* (Harmondsworth: Penguin, 1970, originally 1967).

47. Other reviews of *The Road to Serfdom* are found in the second volume of J. Wood and R. Woods (eds.), *Friedrich A. Hayek: Critical Assessments, Volume II* (London: Routledge, 1991). Both Schumpeter and Roll noted that the book was written against the spirit of the age. Schumpeter's review argued that *The Road to Serfdom* 'takes surprisingly little account of the political structure of our time' while Eric Roll's comment that Hayek had written 'a wholly unhistorical book' was motivated by the same thought (30–68).

48. Cockett, *Thinking the Unthinkable*, 322. The term 'consensus' should be used with some caution. The traditional reading of consensus was laid out by Paul Addison in *The Road to 1945: British Politics and the Second World War* (London: Cape, 1975) and explained contemporary politics at the time of writing as derived from a war-generated elite consensus. However, the idea of a period of post-war consensus is increasingly contested. Harriet Jones has noted that the concept is more popular with political scientists than with historians in H. Jones and M. Kandiah (eds.), *The Myth of Consensus: New Views on British History, 1945–64* (Basingstoke: Macmillan, 1996), xiii–xvii. In the same book Peter Catterall goes even further, arguing that the concept is 'an example of contemporary political perspectives skewing the understanding of contemporary history' (x). As a sketch of intellectual history, the idea of 'a post-war consensus' remains helpful, although revisionist interpretations provide a useful warning against exaggerating both the duration to which the term applies and its extent.

49. Butler, *Hayek*, 4.

50. E. Hobsbawm, *Age of Extremes: The Short Twentieth Century 1914–1991* (London: Michael Joseph, 1994), 5–12 and Part Two.

51. Cassidy, "The Price Prophet".

52. F. Hayek, *The Constitution of Liberty* (London: Routledge, 1960), 398.

53. Hayek, *The Constitution of Liberty*, 409.

54. Hayek, *The Constitution of Liberty*, 398.

55. M. Pirie, "Why F. A. Hayek Is a Conservative" in *Hayek on the Fabric of Human Society*, ed. E. Butler and M. Pirie (London: Adam Smith Institute, 1987).

56. Cockett, *Thinking the Unthinkable*, 336–43.

57. Seldon, "Obituary", 33.

58. Cockett, *Thinking the Unthinkable*, 123.

59. Cockett, *Thinking the Unthinkable*, 123.

60. Cockett, *Thinking the Unthinkable*, 123–24.

61. Cockett, *Thinking the Unthinkable*, 125.

62. D. Collard, *The New Right: A Critique* (London: Fabian Society, 1968).

63. Gamble, *Hayek*, 10.

64. F. Hayek, *Law, Legislation and Liberty, Volume 1: Rules and Order* (London: Routledge and Kegan Paul, 1973); F. Hayek, *Law, Legislation and Liberty, Volume 2: The Mirage of Social Justice* (London: Routledge and Kegan Paul, 1976); F. Hayek, *Law, Legislation and Liberty, Volume 3: The Political Order of a Free People* (London: Routledge and Kegan Paul, 1979).

65. Cassidy, "The Price Prophet".

66. M. Thatcher, "House of Commons PQs", March 10, 1981, accessed 1 June 2014, http://www.margaretthatcher.org/document/104593.

67. R. Lewis, "The Prophet of Socialist Doom", *Daily Mail*, March 25, 1992, accessed 21 April 2014, www.lexisnexis.com/uk/business.

68. Cassidy, "The Price Prophet".

69. Merriam-Webster, "Engage", accessed 21 April 2014, http://www.m-w.com/dictionary/engage.

70. Merriam-Webster, "Engage".

71. J. Ayto, *20th Century Words* (Oxford: Oxford University Press, 1999), 273.

72. Finer, *Road to Reaction*.

73. J. Tomlinson, *Hayek and the Market* (London and Winchester, MA: Pluto Press, 1990) xii.

74. P. Anderson, *A Zone of Engagement* (London: Verso, 1992), ix.

75. D. Miller, *Market, State and Community: Theoretical Foundations of Market Socialism* (Oxford: Clarendon, 1989); J. Roemer, *A Future for Socialism* (Cambridge, MA: Harvard University Press, 1994).

76. Roemer, *A Future for Socialism*, 2.

77. T. Burczak, "Socialism after Hayek", *Rethinking Marxism* 9, 3 (1997); T. Burczak, *Socialism after Hayek* (Ann Arbor: University of Michigan Press, 2006).

78. Another example of the economists' use of Hayek is found in J. Birner and R. Van Zipj (eds.), *Hayek, Coordination and Evolution: His Legacy in Philosophy, Politics, Economics and the History of Ideas* (London: Routledge, 1994), which featured chapters on Hayek's legacy from the economist and Labour Peer Meghnad Desai. The collection also featured a contribution from Raymond Plant, whose work is discussed in Chapter 3.

79. A. Sen, "Comment: An Enduring Insight into the Purpose of Prosperity", *Financial Times* , September 21, 2004, 21.

80. Sen, "Comment".

81. Sen, "Comment".

82. Tomlinson, *Hayek and the Market*, xi; Wootton, *Freedom under Planning*. Tomlinson dismisses Finer's 1945 book on Hayek for the reasons given earlier in this chapter regarding Finer's limited detailed engagement with Hayek's wider work.

83. Tomlinson, *Hayek and the Market*, xi.

84. Tomlinson, *Hayek and the Market*, xi.

85. Tomlinson, *Hayek and the Market*, xi.

86. Seldon, "Obituary", 33.

87. Tomlinson, *Hayek and the Market*, viii.

88. R. Blackburn, *"Fin-De-Siècle:* Socialism after the Crash", *New Left Review* 185 (1991): 36.

89. For example, in H. Wainwright, *Reclaim the State: Experiments in Popular Democracy* (London: Seagull, 2009) and A. Gamble, "Hayek on Liberty", *Critical Review* 25, 3–4 (2013).

2. THE RISE AND FALL OF
MARKET SOCIALISM

1. Hayek, *The Road to Serfdom*, 24.

2. In this chapter I am not primarily concerned with whether the normative arguments for market socialism can be successfully applied. There is substantial literature on the difficulties which market socialism might face in practice. John Gray gives a brief but useful early summary of some of these problems (J. Gray, "Marxian Freedom, Individual Liberty and the End of Alienation", *Social Philosophy and Policy* 3, 2 (1986): 174–80.

3. D. Miller, "Why Markets?", in Estrin and Le Grand, *Market Socialism*, 25.

4. A. De Jasay provides an example of this kind of approach in *Market Socialism: a scrutiny—'this square circle'* (London: IEA, 1990).

5. D. Miller, "Socialism and the Market", *Political Theory* 5, 4 (1977): 473.

6. Quoted in W. Greenleaf, *The British Political Tradition. Volume 2: The Ideological Heritage* (London and New York: Routledge, 2003, originally 1983), 7.

7. L. T. Hobhouse, *Liberalism* (New York: Oxford University Press, 1964, originally 1911), 29; the example is from Greenleaf, *The British Political Tradition*, 11.

8. Greenleaf, *The British Political Tradition*, 11.

9. Greenleaf, *The British Political Tradition*, 11.

10. Greenleaf, *The British Political Tradition*.

11. Greenleaf, *The British Political Tradition*, 14–15.

12. W. Greenleaf, "Laski And British Socialism", *History of Political Thought* II, 3 (1981): 577.

13. M. Bevir, "New Labour: A Study in Ideology", *British Journal of Politics and International Relations* 2, 3 (2000): 278.

14. Bevir, "New Labour: A Study in Ideology", 283.

15. Bevir, "New Labour: A Study in Ideology", 282.

16. Bevir, "New Labour: A Study in Ideology", 283.

17. Bevir, "New Labour: A Study in Ideology", 288.

18. Bevir, "New Labour: A Study in Ideology", 285.

19. Bevir, "New Labour: A Study in Ideology", 283.

20. Bevir, "New Labour: A Study in Ideology", 283.

21. Bevir, "New Labour: A Study in Ideology", 283.

22. Freeden, *Ideologies and Political* Theory, 75–91.

23. Barker, *Political Ideas in Modern Britain*, 7.

24. N. Harte, *The University of London 1836–1986: An Illustrated History* (London: Athlone, 1986), 159.

25. Miller, *Market, State and Community*, vii.

26. Miller, *Market, State and Community*, 6.

27. S. Estrin and D. Winter, "Planning in a Market Socialist Economy", in Estrin and Le Grand, *Market Socialism*.

28. Miller, *Market, State and Community*, 6–7.

29. G. Orwell, *Nineteen Eighty-Four* (Harmondsworth: Penguin, 1949), and S. and B. Webb, *Soviet Communism: a new civilization*, 2nd ed. (London, New York: Longmans, Green, 1937).

30. A. Crosland, "The Transition to Capitalism", in *New Fabian Essays*, ed. R. Crossman (London: Turnstile, 1952); and A. Crosland, *The Future of Socialism* (London: Robinson Publishing, 2006, originally 1956), xii.

31. T. Stark, *A New A–Z of Income and Wealth* (London: Fabian Society, 1988).

32. Crosland, "The Transition to Capitalism", 43.

33. Crosland, "The Transition to Capitalism", 67–68.

34. Miller, *Market, State and Community*, 9.

35. See, for example, D. Lipsey, "Too Much Choice", *Prospect* 117, December 2005 and J. Le Grand, "Too Little Choice", *Prospect* 118, January 2006.

36. J. Le Grand, *The Other Invisible Hand: Delivering Public Services through Choice and Competition* (Princeton, NJ: Princeton University Press, 2007).

37. An example is found in D. Reay and H. Lucey, "The Limits of 'Choice': Children and Inner City Schooling", *Sociology* 37, 1 (2003).

38. Estrin and Le Grand, *Market Socialism*.

39. Estrin and Le Grand, *Market Socialism*, v.

40. D. Miller, "The Resurgence of Political Theory", *Political Studies* 38, 3 (1990).

41. J. Rawls, *A Theory of Justice* (Cambridge, MA: Harvard University Press, 1971). Although harbingers of this resurgence are found in Peter Laslett's announcement of the revival of political theory as early as 1956 (see P. Laslett, ed., *Philosophy, Politics and Society: A Collection* [Oxford: Blackwell, 1956]), and it was in 1962 that Rawls' essay "Justice as Fairness" appeared in the second series of this collection (see J. Rawls, "Justice as Fairness" in P. Laslett and W. G. Runciman, eds., *Philosophy, Politics & Society: 2nd Series: A Collection* [Oxford: Blackwell, 1962]).

42. In particular in Rawls, *A Theory of Justice*, and R. Nozick, *Anarchy, State and Utopia* (Oxford: Blackwell, 1974).

43. Miller, "Socialism and the Market", 474.

44. Miller, "Socialism and the Market", 474.

45. M. Cowling, "The Sources of the New Right: Irony, Geniality and Malice", *Encounter* LXXIII, 4 (1989).

46. Miller, *Market, State and Community*, 2.

47. Estrin and Le Grand, *Market Socialism*, v.

48. In a detailed exploration of the concept, John Roemer has identified five waves of market socialism in the twentieth century. Roemer does not include Mill in his account, and breaks the calculation debate into three stages. See Roemer, *A Future for Socialism*, ch. 4.

49. J. Gray, "John Stuart Mill: The Crisis of Liberalism", in *Plato to NATO: Studies in Political Thought*, ed. B. Redhead (Penguin: Harmondsworth, 1984), 154.

50. See, for example, Mill's account in his *Principles of Political Economy* (Oxford: Oxford University Press, 2008), Bk IV, ch.7.

51. Although Lange is typically described as a market socialist, this has been contested. See D. Ramsey Steele, *From Marx to Mises: post-capitalist society and the challenge of economic calculation* (La Salle, IL: Open Court, 1992), 154–57. A useful summary of the calculation debate is found in Gamble, *Hayek*, ch. 3.

52. Further discussion can be found in S. Estrin, "Yugoslavia—the Case of Self-Managing Market Socialism", *Journal of Economic Perspectives* 5, 4 (1991).

53. Discussions of 'market socialism' in China can be found in J. Petras, "Contradictions of Market Socialism in China 1", *Journal of Contemporary Asia* 18, 1 (1988); J. Petras, "Contradictions of Market Socialism in China 2", *Journal of Contemporary Asia* 18, 2 (1988); P. Bowles and G. White, "The Dilemmas of Market Socialism—Capital-Market Reform in China 1 Bonds", *Journal of Development Studies* 28, 3 (1992); and P. Bowles and G. White,

"The Dilemmas of Market Socialism—Capital-Market Reform in China 2 Shares", *Journal of Development Studies* 28, 4 (1992).

54. See J. Carens, *Equality, Moral Incentives, and the Market: An Essay in Utopian Politico-Economic Theory* (Chicago: University of Chicago Press, 1980); A. Nove, "Market Socialism", *Acta Oeconomica* 40, 3–4 (1989); Nove, *The Economics of Feasible Socialism*; C. Pierson, *Socialism after Communism: The New Market Socialism* (Cambridge: Polity, 1995); Roemer, *A Future for Socialism*; J. Roemer, "Market Socialism —a Blueprint", *Dissent* 38, 4 (1991).

55. D. Miller and S. Estrin, "A Case for Market Socialism—What Does It Mean—Why Should We Favor It", *Dissent* 34, 3 (1987).

56. Important statements of the argument are to be found in D. Miller, "Socialism and the Market"; Miller and Estrin, "A Case for Market Socialism"; Miller, *Market, State and Community*; and D. Miller, "A Vision of Market Socialism—How It Might Work—and Its Problems", *Dissent* 38, 3 (1991).

57. Miller, "Why Markets?", in Estrin and Le Grand, 30.

58. Miller, "Why Markets?", in Estrin and Le Grand, 32.

59. Miller, "Why Markets?", in Estrin and Le Grand, 32.

60. Miller, "Why Markets?", in Estrin and Le Grand, 33.

61. An example of this kind of argument is found in R. McChesney, *Rich Media, Poor Democracy: communication politics in dubious times* (Urbana and Chicago: University of Illinois Press, 1999).

62. Leon Trotsky, quoted in the epigraph to Chapter IX of Hayek, *The Road to Serfdom*.

63. Miller, *Market, State and Community*, 10.

64. Miller, *Market, State and Community*, 10.

65. Miller, *Market, State and Community*, 327.

66. Miller, *Market, State and Community*, 330.

67. D. Miller, "In What Sense Must Socialism Be Communitarian?", *Social Philosophy & Policy* 6, 2 (1989): 54.

68. Patrick Diamond has argued that British socialist revisionism pre-dates Crosland. See P. Diamond, *New Labour's Old Roots: Revisionist Thinkers in Labour's History 1931–1997*, (Exeter: Imprint Academic, 2004).

69. Miller, *Market, State and Community*, 5.

70. Miller, *Market, State and Community*, 321.

71. Miller, "In What Sense Must Socialism Be Communitarian?", 52–60.

72. Miller, "In What Sense Must Socialism Be Communitarian?", 55.

73. Miller, "In What Sense Must Socialism Be Communitarian?", 55–56.

74. Miller, *Market, State and Community*, 321.

75. P. Hirst, *The Pluralist Theory of the State* (London and New York: Routledge, 1989), ch. 1.

76. R. Barker, "Pluralism, Revenant or Recessive?", in *The British Study of Politics in the Twentieth Century*, ed. J. Hayward (Oxford: Oxford University Press, 1999).

77. D. Miller, *Anarchism* (London: Dent, 1984).

78. Crosland, *The Future of Socialism*, 165.

79. Wainwright, *Arguments for a New Left*, 274; Miller, "Why Markets?", 29.

80. F. Hayek, *The Fatal Conceit: The Errors of Socialism* (London: Routledge, 1988), 18–19.

81. L. Colley, *Britons: Forging the Nation 1707–1837* (New Haven and London: Yale University Press, 1992); A. Pilkington, "Cultural Representations and Changing Ethnic Identities in a Global Age", in *Developments in Sociology*, ed. M. Holborn (Ormskirk: Causeway Press, 2002).

82. Miller, *Market, State and Community*, 232; D. Goodhart, "Too Diverse? Is Britain Becoming Too Diverse to Sustain the Mutual Obligations Behind a Good Society and the Welfare State?", in *Prospect*, February, 2004.

83. Raymond Plant cited in Miller, *Market, State and Community*, 231–32.

84. Miller, *Market, State and Community*, 233.

85. An argument made in greatest detail in D. Miller, *On Nationality* (Oxford: Clarendon Press, 1995).

86. Miller, *Market, State and Community*, 238.

87. In particular G. Orwell, "Notes on Nationalism", in *George Orwell Essays* (Harmondsworth: Penguin, 1984, originally 1945) and *The Lion and the Unicorn: Socialism and the English Genius* (Harmondsworth, Penguin, 1982, originally 1941) and R. Blatchford, *Britain for the British* (London: Clarion Press, 1902).

88. Pierson, *Socialism after Communism*, ch. 1.

89. At its most radical this thesis claims 'The Death of Class'. See J. Pakulski and M. Waters, *The Death of Class* (London: Sage, 1996). I discuss this argument further in Chapter 4.

90. R. Plant, "To a Communal Market; Commentary", *The Times*, April 10, 1989, accessed 14 April 2014, www.lexisnexis.vom/uk/business.

91. Miller, "Why Markets?", 29.

92. D. Miller, "What Kind of Equality Should the Left Pursue?", in *Equality*, ed. J. Franklin (London: IPPR, 1997), 98.

93. The many contested meanings of 'market socialism' make this kind of conceptual search methodologically problematic. A prime example concerns many of the more recent articles which use the term 'market socialism' to describe the market reforms carried out in China in recent years. These reforms owe little to the British market socialism discussed in this chapter. Nor does the graph take into account the selection of journals surveyed or the rise

in the number of journals which occurred during the period examined. Furthermore, this kind of search obviously does not include works that include arguments with ideational similarities to market socialism but that do not use the term. Despite these problems, the exercise provides a useful indication, if no more, of the rise and fall of academic debate on market socialism in recent decades.

94. G. Cohen, "The Future of a Disillusion", *New Left Review*, 190 (1991), 15.

95. Miller, "In What Sense Must Socialism Be Communitarian?", 55.

96. Estrin and Le Grand, *Market Socialism*.

97. Even those on the left who were sceptical about globalization, such as Hirst, had to engage in a debate with those who thought globalization a real limit to what the left could achieve. See P. Hirst and G. Thompson, *Globalization in Question: The International Economy and the Possibilities of Governance* (Cambridge: Polity, 1996).

98. See, for example, A. Giddens, *The Third Way: the renewal of social democracy*, (Cambridge: Polity, 1998).

99. Freeden, *Ideologies and Political Theory*, 477.

3. REVISIONISM REVISED

1. J. Willman, "Man in the News: The Seeds of a Political Storm—Raymond Plant", *Financial Times*, 3 April 1993, accessed 21 April 2014, www.lexisnexis.com/uk/business.

2. Estrin and Le Grand, *Market Socialism*, v.

3. R. Plant, *Hegel* (London: Allen & Unwin, 1973); R. Plant, *Community and Ideology: An Essay in Applied Social Philosophy* (London: Routledge and Kegan Paul, 1974).

4. A. Vincent and R. Plant, *Philosophy, Politics and Citizenship: The Life and Thought of the British Idealists* (Oxford: Wiley-Blackwell, 1984).

5. R. Plant, *Social and Moral Theory in Casework* (London: Routledge and Kegan Paul, 1970).

6. R. Plant, "Should Blood Be Bought and Sold? (Part I)", *Journal of Medical Ethics: The Journal of the Institute of Medical Ethics* 3 (1977) and "How Should Health Care Be Distributed? (Part II)", *Journal of Medical Ethics: The Journal of the Institute of Medical Ethics* 4 (1978).

7. R. Titmuss, *The Gift Relationship: From Human Blood to Social Policy* (London: Allen & Unwin, 1970).

8. R. Plant, *Equality, Markets and the State* (London: Fabian Society, 1984).

9. J. Lloyd, "New Markets for Socialist Ideas", *Financial Times*, November 17, 1986, accessed 21 April 2014, www.lexisnexis.com/uk/business.

10. B. Gould, *Socialism and Freedom* (Basingstoke: Macmillan, 1985).

11. R. Hattersley, *Choose Freedom: The Future for Democratic Socialism* (London: Michael Joseph, 1987).

12. R. Plant, "Master of the Market: Commentary", *The Times*, 8 May 1989, accessed 21 April 2014, www.lexisnexis.com/uk/business

13. R. Plant, "Socialism, Markets and End States", in *Market Socialism*, ed. S. Estrin and J. Le Grand (Oxford: Clarendon, 1989).

14. R. Plant, "Hayek On Social Justice: A Critique" in J. Birner and R. Van Zipj (eds), *Hayek, Coordination and Evolution: His Legacy in Philosophy Politics Economics and the History of Ideas* (London: Routledge, 1994).

15. R. Plant, *Modern Political Thought* (Oxford, UK, and Cambridge, MA: Blackwell, 1991), especially 78–97.

16. R. Plant, *The Neo-liberal State* (Oxford: Oxford University Press, 2010), Preface.

17. Estrin and Le Grand, *Market Socialism.*

18. Plant, "Socialism, Markets and End States", 51.

19. Hegel has been the dominant influence upon Plant, who has published widely on the philosopher. Plant commented in 1997 that 'Major thinkers in this century . . . are scarcely comprehensible without understanding their relation to Hegel' and specifically cited the new liberal T. H. Green, as a thinker who worked in Hegel's 'shadow'. R. Plant, *Hegel* (St. Ives: Phoenix, 2003, originally 1997), 3.

20. Plant, "Master of the Market".

21. R. Plant, interview with the author, Houses of Parliament, 5 June 2007.

22. J. Espada, *Social Citizenship Rights: A Critique of F.A. Hayek and Raymond Plant* (London: Macmillan, 1996), 1.

23. Espada, *Social Citizenship Rights*, x.

24. Espada, *Social Citizenship Rights*, 100.

25. Hayek, *Law, Legislation and Liberty, Volume 2.*

26. Plant, "Socialism, Markets and End States", 57.

27. K. Marx, *Critique of the Gotha Program* (originally 1875), Part I, accessed 21 April 2014, http://www.marxists.org/archive/marx/works/1875/gotha/index.htm.

28. J. Gray, *Isaiah Berlin* (London: HarperCollins, 1995).

29. J. Gray, "Positional Goods, Classical Liberalism and the Politicisation of Poverty", in *Dilemmas of Liberal Democracy: Readings in Fred Hirsch's Social Limits to Growth*, ed. A. Ellis and K. Kumar (London: Tavistock, 1983), 181; cited in Plant, "Socialism, Markets and End States", 59.

30. Plant, "Socialism, Markets and End States", 63.

31. Cited in Plant, "Socialism, Markets and End States", 59.

32. Plant, "Socialism, Markets and End States", 63.

33. R. Plant, *The Plant Report: Democracy, Representation and Elections, Report of the Working Party on Elections* (London: Labour Party, 1993).

34. Willman, "Man in the News".

35. Hattersley, *Choose Freedom*.

36. M. Evans, *Charter 88: A Successful Challenge to the British Political Tradition?* (Aldershot: Dartmouth, 1995).

37. Willman, "Man in the News".

38. Willman, "Man in the News".

39. Willman, "Man in the News".

40. Plant, *The Plant Report*.

41. Plant, "Socialism, Markets and End States".

42. Cited in Plant, "Socialism, Markets and End States", 52; R. Plant, "Market Place for Everyone: Labour's Constitutional Changes Reflect a Move Away from Dogma Towards Greater Social Justice", *The Guardian*, 20 March 1995, accessed 21 April 2014, www.lexisnexis.com/uk/business and elsewhere.

43. Plant, "Socialism, Markets and End States", 65.

44. Forms of this argument are found in R. Plant, H. Lesser and P. Taylor-Gooby, *Political Philosophy and Social Welfare: Essays on the Normative Basis of Welfare Provision* (London: Routledge and Kegan Paul, 1980); Plant, "Socialism, Markets and End States"; Plant, *Modern Political Thought*, 90–94 and elsewhere.

45. Plant, *Modern Political Thought*, 92.

46. Plant, *Modern Political Thought*, 92.

47. Plant, *Modern Political Thought*, 93.

48. R. Plant, "Hayek on Social Justice: A Critique", in *Hayek, Coordination and Evolution: His Legacy in Philosophy, Politics, Economics and the History of Ideas*, ed. J. Birner, R. Van Zijp (London: Routledge, 1994), 170–71.

49. R. Plant, "No Man Is an Island—except in Ignorance", *The Times*, 1 January 1990, accessed 21 April 2014, www.lexisnexis.com/uk/business.

50. Plant, "No Man Is an Island".

51. This argument for liberty is found in Hayek, *The Constitution of Liberty*, ch. 1. Negative concepts of liberty are often presumed to support right-wing argument, but negative liberty can be compatible with holding a left of centre position. The most explicit attempt to do this has come from G. A. Cohen, who first made a left-wing argument for negative freedom in G. Cohen, "Capitalism, Freedom and the Proletariat", in *The Idea of Freedom*, ed. A. Ryan (Oxford: Oxford University Press, 1979), which provided an early response to the claims of the new right on this form of liberty . The paper was

revised as "Capitalism, Freedom and the Proletariat", in *Liberty*, ed. D. Miller (Oxford, Oxford University Press, 1991).

52. In a well-known response to this claim Gerald MacCallum has pointed out that freedom is always both 'freedom from' and 'freedom to', and so it is both negative and positive. He argued that discussions of freedom, although they do not always make explicit each component, take the form of a 'triadic relation' encompassing both negative and positive liberty: 'x is (is not) free from y to do (not do, become, not become) z', where x ranges over agents, y ranges over 'preventing conditions' and z ranges over actions or conditions of character or circumstance. See G. MacCallum, "Negative and Positive Freedom", in *Liberty*, ed. D. Miller (Oxford: Oxford University Press, 1991), 102.

53. This is related to the distinction made famous by Isaiah Berlin in his seminal essay, "Two Concepts of Liberty", in *The Proper Study of Mankind: An Anthology of Essays*, ed. H. Hardy and R. Hausheer (London: Pimlico, 1998).

54. Plant, "Socialism, Markets and End States", 65; R. Plant, "Hayek on Social Justice: A Critique", 171–72.

55. These are arguments taken up in R. Plant 'Political Theory without Foundations', *History of the Human Sciences* 5, 3 (1992).

56. R. Plant, *Equality, Markets and the State* (London: Fabian Society, 1984), 7.

57. Plant, Lesser and Taylor-Gooby, *Political Philosophy and Social Welfare*, 33.

58. J. Mill, "On Liberty", in *Utilitarianism, on Liberty, Considerations on Representative Government*, ed. G. Williams (London: Everyman, 1993); J. Raz, *The Morality of Freedom*, (Oxford: Clarendon, 1988).

59. Plant, Lesser and Taylor-Gooby, *Political Philosophy and Social Welfare*, 38.

60. A. Gewirth, *Reason and Morality* (Chicago and London: University of Chicago Press, 1978) and *Human Rights: Essays in Justification and Applications* (Chicago and London: University of Chicago Press, 1982).

61. Plant, *Equality, Markets and the State*, 6 and 27.

62. N. Bobbio, *Left and Right: The Significance of a Political Distinction* (Cambridge: Polity, 1996), 62.

63. A. Sen, "Equality of What? The Tanner Lecture on Human Values", lecture at Stanford University, 22 May, 1979, accessed 21 April 2014, http://tannerlectures.utah.edu/_documents/a-to-z/s/sen80.pdf.

64. Plant, "Socialism, Markets and End States", 64; R. Plant, "Hardly Poor by Choice", *The Times*, 2 April 1990, accessed 21 April 2014, www.lexisnexis.com/uk/business.

65. Plant, *Equality, Markets and the State*, 26.

66. K. Hoover and R. Plant, *Conservative Capitalism in Britain and the United States: A Critical Appraisal* (London: Routledge, 1989), 220.

67. Plant, "Socialism, Markets and End States", 68. The argument is also made in Plant's earlier work, where the authors write that equality before the law, plus the Hayekian argument for value pluralism result in there being 'no moral grounds for saying that some people deserve to have more effective basic liberty'. Hoover and Plant, *Conservative Capitalism in Britain and the United States*, 211; also cited in Espada, *Social Citizenship Rights*, 112.

68. Hoover and Plant, *Conservative Capitalism in Britain and the United States*, 224; also cited in Espada, *Social Citizenship Rights*, 117.

69. There are similarities between Rawls and Hayek, in particular their shared Kantian conception of the Rule of Law. Indeed as Andrew Lister has noted, Hayek commented that the differences between himself and Rawls are 'more verbal than substantial' and that—despite Rawls's use of the term 'social justice'—they both agree on 'the essential point' that that principles of justice apply to the rules of institutions and social practices, not to distributions of particular things across specific persons. A. Lister, "The 'Mirage' of Social Justice: Hayek Against (and For) Rawls", Oliver Smithies Lecture, 10 May 2011, at Balliol College, Oxford, accessed 1 June 2014, http://social-justice.politics.ox.ac.uk/materials/SJ017_Lister_MirageofSocialJustice.pdf.

70. J. Rawls, *A Theory of Justice* (Cambridge, MA: Harvard University Press, 1971), 303.

71. Espada, *Social Citizenship Rights*, 118.

72. K. Popper, *Unended Quest: An Intellectual Autobiography* (London: Routledge, 2002), 36.

73. Notably, in D. Lipsey and D. Leonard, eds., *The Socialist Agenda: Crosland's Legacy* (London: Cape, 1981); D. Leonard, ed., *Crosland and New Labour* (London: Palgrave, 1998); and R. Plant, M. Beech and K. Hickson, eds., *The Struggle for Labour's Soul* (London and New York: Routledge, 2004).

74. Plant, interview.

75. Many of whom contributed to the earlier revisionist text *New Fabian Essays*. See R. Crossman, ed., *New Fabian Essays* (London: Turnstile Press, 1952). Outside of the limits of time and geography imposed in this book, the German revisionist thinker Eduard Bernstein is of particular note. Although Bernstein's work had limited influence on the British labour movement when it was first published, it was of influence on the first wave of post-war British revisionists. Crosland, in particular, was influenced by Bernstein's thought. The twenty-one-year-old Crosland wrote to a friend in 1940, 'I am engaged on a great revision of Marxism, & will certainly emerge as the modern Bernstein'—quoted in D. Leonard, "Introduction" in Crosland, *The Future of Socialism*, xii.

76. The train metaphor is from Rodney Barker. This is not to say there was not significant dissent in the wider parliamentary party before 1951, particularly from the Keep Left Group. See, for example, J. Schneer, "Hopes Deferred or Shattered: The British Labour Left and the Third Force Movement, 1945–49", *The Journal of Modern History* 56, 2, June 1984.

77. Aneurin Bevan, *In Place of Fear* (New York: Simon and Schuster, 1952). Nationalization was not the only area of debate between right and left of the party; there were also significant differences over foreign policy, among other areas.

78. Crosland, "The Transition to Capitalism"; A. Crosland, *Socialism Now, and Other Essays*, (London: Cape, 1974), 44.

79. Crosland, *The Future of Socialism*, XXIV, I.

80. Estrin and Le Grand, *Market Socialism*, v.

81. Plant, interview.

82. D. Spender, *There's Always Been a Woman's Movement in this Century* (Kitchener, Ont., Canada: Pandora Press, 1983).

83. See, for example, Patrick Diamond's discussion in *New Labour's Old Roots: Revisionist Thinkers in Labour's History 1931–1997* (Exeter: Imprint Academic, 2004).

84. Plant, interview.

85. Plant, interview.

86. Plant, "Hardly Poor by Choice".

87. Crosland, *The Future of Socialism*, XXV, IV.

88. E. Durbin, "Professor Hayek and economic planning and political liberty", *The Economic Journal* 55 (1945), 357.

89. M. Freeden, *Ideologies and Political Theory: A Conceptual Approach* (Oxford: Clarendon Press, 1996), 479.

90. D. Marquand, "Can Labour kick the winning habit?", *New Statesman*, 23 October 1998, 26.

91. The fight over Crosland's legacy continues. See, for example, S. Meredith, "Mr Crosland's Nightmare? New Labour and Equality in Historical Perspective", *British Journal of Politics and International Relations* 8, 2 (2006); K. Hickson, "Reply to Stephen Meredith: Mr. Crosland's Nightmare? New Labour and Equality in Historical Perspective", *British Journal of Politics and International Relations* 9, 1 (2007); S. Meredith, "New Labour and Equality: A Response to Hickson", *British Journal of Politics and International Relations* 9, 1 (2007).

92. Le Grand quoted in Backbencher, "My First Vote", *Guardian*, 18 June 2003, accessed 15 April 2014, http://politics.guardian.co.uk/backbencher/story/0,10599,980148,00.html.

93. Plant, *Equality, Markets and the State*, 9.

94. Plant, *Equality, Markets and the State*, 9–10.

4. SOCIAL MOVEMENTS AND PLURALISM

1. R. Blackburn, *"Fin-De-Siècle"*, 36.
2. R. Blackburn, "Themes", *New Left Review* I, 185 (1991), 4.
3. Hayek, "The Use of Knowledge in Society".
4. While Hayek Anglicizes Lange's name, I have elsewhere kept with the Polish spelling, 'Oskar', to remain consistent with other non-English names used in this book.
5. Hayek, "The Use of Knowledge in Society", 89.
6. Blackburn, *"Fin-De-Siècle"*, 35.
7. Blackburn, *"Fin-De-Siècle"*, 36.
8. Blackburn, *"Fin-De-Siècle"*, 32.
9. Blackburn, *"Fin-De-Siècle"*, 35.
10. Blackburn, *"Fin-De-Siècle"*, 35, footnote 51.
11. The argument is laid out several times in Wainwright's work, including H. Wainwright, "The New Left After Communism", *Studies in Political Economy* 38, Summer (1992): 155–66; H. Wainwright, 'A New Kind of Knowledge for a New Kind of State', in *A Different Kind of State*, ed. G. Albo, D. Langille and L. Panitch (Toronto: OUP, 1993); Wainwright, *Arguments for a New Left*; and Wainwright, *Reclaim the State*.
12. Wainwright, *Arguments for a New Left*, 5.
13. T. Wright, "Arguments for a New-Left—Wainwright, H.", *Political Quarterly* 66, 1 (1995): 101.
14. J. Bockman, *Markets in the Name of Socialism: The Left-Wing Origins of Neoliberalism* (Stanford: Stanford University Press, 2011).
15. Wainwright, *Arguments for a New Left*, 2.
16. Wainwright, *Arguments for a New Left*, ix.
17. Wainwright, *Arguments for a New Left*, 13.
18. Wainwright, *Arguments for a New Left* , 4.
19. R. Barker, "Hooks and Hands, Interests and Enemies: Political Thinking as Political Action", *Political Studies* 48, 2 (2000).
20. Gray, *Hayek on Liberty*, 148.
21. Cited in Blackburn, *"Fin-De-Siècle"*, 40.
22. R. Kurzweil, *The Age of Spiritual Machines: When Computers Exceed Human Intelligence* (Harmondsworth: Viking, 1999).
23. F. Hayek, "Economics and Knowledge", in *Individualism and Economic Order* (Chicago and London: University of Chicago Press, 1948, originally

1936), 79. The reconstruction of Hayek's argument in this area is largely based on arguments that he set out in this relatively early paper.

24. Hayek, "Economics and Knowledge", 79.
25. Hayek, "Economics and Knowledge", 79.
26. Hayek, "Economics and Knowledge", 81.
27. Hayek, "Economics and Knowledge", 80.
28. Hayek, "Economics and Knowledge", 80.
29. Hayek, "Economics and Knowledge", 84.
30. Hayek, "Economics and Knowledge", 84.
31. Hayek, "Economics and Knowledge", 86.
32. Hayek, "Economics and Knowledge", 87.
33. Hayek, "Economics and Knowledge", 86–89.
34. Hayek, *Law, Legislation and Liberty*, 113.
35. Gamble, *Hayek*, x.
36. Wainwright, *Arguments for a New Left*, 57.
37. Wainwright, *Arguments for a New Left*, 57.
38. Wainwright, *Arguments for a New Left*, 58.
39. Wainwright, *Arguments for a New Left*, 58.
40. Wainwright, *Arguments for a New Left*, 61.
41. Wainwright, *Arguments for a New Left*, 59.
42. A point made by Rodney Barker. R. Barker, personal communication, 18 February 2003.
43. Wainwright, *Arguments for a New Left*, 60.
44. Wainwright, *Arguments for a New Left*, 61.
45. Wainwright, *Arguments for a New Left*, 60.
46. Wainwright, *Arguments for a New Left*, 60.
47. Wainwright, *Arguments for a New Left*, 60.
48. The phrase 'God's finger' is generally attributed to the nineteenth-century French economist Frédéric Bastiat. See L. von Mises, *Theory and History* (Auburn, AL: Ludwig von Mises Institute, 2007, originally 1957), 168, accessed 24 June 2011, http://mises.org/Books/theoryhistory.pdf. The quote is from Wainwright, *Arguments for a New Left*, 60–61.
49. Wainwright, *Arguments for a New Left*, 13.
50. Wainwright, *Arguments for a New Left*, 279–80.
51. H. Wainwright with M. Little, *Public Service Reform . . . But not as we know it! A story of how democracy can make public services genuinely efficient* (Great Britain: Picnic Publishing, 2009).
52. Paul Anderson, "Togetherness", *New Statesman & Society*, 4 February 1994, 45.
53. Wright, "Arguments for a New-Left—Wainwright, H.", 102. Wright does, however, give her 'full marks for intellectual cheek' for her 'ambitious'

and 'quirky adoption of Hayek' in Wright, "Arguments for a New-Left—Wainwright, H.", 101–3.

54. Paul Anderson, "Togetherness", 45.

55. Paul Anderson, "Togetherness", 45.

56. Wainwright, *Arguments for a New Left*, 280.

57. Wainwright, "The New Left After Communism", 23.

58. Wainwright, "The New Left After Communism", 23.

59. Wainwright, *Arguments for a New Left*, 190.

60. Wainwright, *Arguments for a New Left*, 190.

61. Wainwright, *Reclaim the State*, esp. 42–69.

62. Wainwright, *Reclaim the State*, 198.

63. S. Griffiths, "Review of H. Wainwright, 'Reclaim the State' ", *Renewal* 11, 4 (2003): 89–91.

64. A view put forward by W. H. Greenleaf, *The British Political Tradition*, but also found more widely. See, for example, D. MacShane, "Labour's Good Book", *Prospect*, September 2006.

65. R. Barker, *Politics, People and Government* (Basingstoke: Macmillan, 1994), 81–83.

66. H. Wainwright, "Untethering the Left", *New Statesman & Society*, 24 February 1989, 16–17.

67. Wainwright, *Arguments for a New Left*, 285.

68. Notably Wootton, *Freedom Under Planning*, who argued that there could be freedom under central planning provided that there was parliamentary democracy and a substantial private sector.

69. Wainwright, *Arguments for a New Left*, 3.

70. Wainwright, *Arguments for a New Left*, 4. Wainwright is dismissive of Wootton. However, Wootton is arguably not as paternalist as Wainwright depicts her to be, allowing an important role in her thought for the responsible citizen as a break on the misuse of state power.

71. Wainwright, *Arguments for a New Left*, 109.

72. As George Bernard Shaw provocatively claimed. See G. B. Shaw, *Ruskin's Politics* (London: Ruskin, Centenary Council, 1921), 15.

73. D. Jay, *The Socialist Case* (London: Faber and Faber, 1937), ch. 30.

74. Wainwright, *Arguments for a New Left*, ch. 1.

75. H. Wainwright, *Red Pepper Newsletter*, May 1993, 2.

76. E. Wood, *The Retreat from Class: a new 'true' socialism* (London: Verso Editions, 1986).

77. S. Rowbotham, L. Segal and H. Wainwright, *Beyond the Fragments* (London: Merlin Press, 1979), 3.

78. Rowbotham, Segal and Wainwright, *Beyond the Fragments*, 4.

79. R. Barker, *Political Ideas in Modern Britain: In and after the twentieth century* (London and New York: Routledge, 1997), 262.

80. S. Cohen, "Book Review", *Capital and Class* 55 (1995): 163.

81. J. Gray, personal communication, April 2003.

82. Wainwright, *Arguments for a New Left*, 285.

83. Wainwright, *Arguments for a New Left*, 284.

84. Wainwright, *Arguments for a New Left*, 284.

85. J. Gray and D. Willetts, *Is Conservatism Dead?* (London: Profile Books, 1997).

86. R. Barker, 'Pluralism, revenant or recessive?', in *The British Study of Politics in the Twentieth Century*, ed. J. Hayward (Oxford: Oxford University Press, 1999).

87. Hirst, *The Pluralist Theory of the State*, 1.

88. Hirst, *The Pluralist Theory of the State*, 3.

89. Hirst, *The Pluralist Theory of the State*, 2.

90. P. Hirst, "Associational Democracy", in *Prospects for Democracy: North, South, East, West*, ed. D. Held (Cambridge: Polity, 1993); P. Hirst, *Associative Democracy* (Cambridge: Polity, 1994).

91. Hirst, *The Pluralist Theory of the State*, 114.

92. R. Eisfeld, "The Emergence and Meaning of Socialist Pluralism", *International Political Science Review* 17, 3 (1996), 276.

93. J. Grahl, "Agenda for a new Left: Answering the free-market right—Wainwright, H.", *New Left Review* 214 (1995): 156.

94. R. Barker, "The pluralism of British pluralism", *Journal of Political Ideologies 14*, 1 (2009).

95. C. Laborde, *Pluralist Thought and the State in Britain and France, 1900–1925* (Basingstoke: Macmillan, 2000), ch. 1.

96. D. Elson, "Market Socialism or Socialization of the Market?", *New Left Review* 172 (1988); Wainwright, *Arguments for a New Left*, 153, 170–72; Blackburn, "*Fin-De-Siècle*", 47–48.

97. MacShane, "Labour's Good Book", 15.

98. The globalization of political issues is discussed in U. Beck, *Risk Society: Towards a New Modernity* (London: Sage Publications, 1992).

99. By contrast, other thinkers have been more sceptical over the claims of globalization, arguing that the term is used by many on the left to justify the narrowing of earlier hopes (for example, P. Hirst and G. Thompson, *Globalization in Question: The International Economy and the Possibilities of Governance* (Cambridge: Polity, 1996).

100. A. Gamble and A. Payne, eds., *Regionalism and World Order* (Basingstoke: Macmillan, 1996).

101. Wainwright, *Reclaim the State*, 180–203.

102. A. Gamble, *Politics and Fate* (Cambridge: Polity, 2000) and A. Gamble, *Between Europe and America: The Future of British Politics* (Basingstoke: Palgrave, 2002).

103. D. Miller, *Justice for Earthlings: Essays in Political Philosophy* (Cambridge: Cambridge University Press, 2013).

5. THE REVIVAL OF LIBERALISM

1. A. Gamble, "Comrade Hayek", *Prospect*, March (1996), accessed 21 April 2014, www.lexisnexis.com/uk/business.

2. P. Walton, A. Gamble and J. Coulter, "Image of man in Marx", *Social Theory and Practice* I (1970); P. Walton, A. Gamble and J. Coulter, "Philosophical anthropology in Marxism", *Social Research* 37 (1970) and P. Walton, J. Coulter and A. Gamble, "Marx and Marcuse", *The Human Context* III (1971).

3. P. Walton and A. Gamble, *From Alienation to Surplus Value* (London: Sheed and Ward, 1972), 227.

4. Walton and Gamble, *From Alienation to Surplus Value*, 227.

5. Deutscher Prize, accessed 1 June 2014, http://www.deutscherprize.org.uk/; A. Gamble and P. Walton, *Capitalism in Crisis* (London and Basingstoke: Macmillan Press Ltd., 1976), Preface.

6. Hobsbawm, *Age of Extremes*, 6.

7. Gamble and Walton, *Capitalism in Crisis*, 5.

8. Crosland, *Socialism Now*, 44.

9. Crosland, *The Future of Socialism*, 30–32.

10. A. Gamble, "The free economy and the strong state: The rise of the social market economy", in *The Socialist Register*, ed. R. Miliband and J. Saville (London: Merlin Press, 1979).

11. Gamble and Walton, *Capitalism in Crisis*, 198. Alternatives to the impasse are also discussed in A. Gamble, *Britain in Decline* (London: Macmillan, 1981), chs. 5–6.

12. Gamble and Walton, *Capitalism in Crisis*, 197.

13. A. Crosland, *The Conservative Enemy; a Programme of Radical Reform for the 1960s*, (London: J. Cape, 1962).

14. Gamble, 'The free economy and the strong state", in Miliband and Saville, *The Socialist Register*.

15. A. Gamble, *The Free Economy and the Strong State: The Politics of Thatcherism* (Durham, NC: Duke University Press, 1988).

16. Gamble, "The free economy and the strong state", in Miliband and Saville, *The Socialist* Register, 6.

17. A. Gamble, "Review of *The Collected Works of FA Hayek: Vol. III, the trend of economic thinking—essays on political economists and economic history*", *Political Studies* 40 (1992): 760.

18. A. Gamble, "Review of J. Birner and R. Van Zijp (Eds.), *Hayek Co-Ordination and Evolution: His Legacy in Philosophy, Politics, Economics and the History of Ideas*", *History of Political Thought* 16, 2 (1995): 278.

19. Gamble, "Review of J. Birner and R. Van Zijp", 278.

20. A search using the *International Bibliography of the Social Sciences* revealed no uses of the term as a major part of any work in the social sciences before Gamble's own.

21. Gamble, *Hayek*, x.

22. Gamble, "Review of 'The Collected Works of FA Hayek' ", 278.

23. Gamble, *Hayek*, 4.

24. Perry Anderson, *Spectrum: From Right to Left in the World of Ideas* (London: Verso, 2005), xi.

25. N. Lamont, "Lamont tells MPs of his 'uncomfortable experience", *The Independent*, June 10, 1993, accessed 1 June 2014, www.lexisnexis.com/uk/business. Gamble used the phrase as the title of an article on Conservative decline. See A. Gamble, "In government, but not in power", *New Statesman & Society* 6 (1993): 272.

26. A. Gamble, "The crisis of conservatism", *New Left Review* 214 (1995): 8.

27. R. Barker, "A future for liberalism or a liberal future?" in *The Liberal Political Tradition: Contemporary Reappraisals*, ed. J. Meadowcroft (Cheltenham: Edward Elgar Publishing Ltd, 1996).

28. The metaphor that some information is 'sticky' is also used in a different way in management studies by Eric von Hippel in his description of information which is difficult to acquire, transfer and use for problem solving. See E. von Hippel, " 'Sticky Information' and the Locus of Problem Solving: implications for innovation", *Management Science* 40, April (1994).

29. A. Gamble, "Hayek and the Left", *Political Quarterly* 67 (1996): 49. In this article, Gamble draws an important distinction between 'anti-rationalism' and 'irrationalism'. The former, he argues, does nothing more than place *limits* on the extent of effective planning, it does not rule it out in toto.

30. N. O'Sullivan, *Conservatism* (London: Dent and Sons, 1976), ch. 4.

31. K. Popper, *The Open Society and Its Enemies* (London: Routledge, 1945); J. Gray, *Isaiah Berlin* (London: HarperCollins, 1995) and J. Gray, "The case for decency", *New York Review of Books* 53 (2006).

32. Hayek, *Individualism and the Economic Order*, ch.1.

33. Gamble, "Hayek and the Left", 50.

34. Wainwright, *Arguments for a New Left*.

35. Gamble, "Hayek and the Left", 50.

36. Wainwright, *Arguments for a New Left*, 61.

37. Gamble, "Hayek and the Left", 49–50.

38. G. Kelly and A. Gamble, "Owners and citizens", *Political Quarterly* 69 (1998): 344; S. Howe and H. Wainwright, "Change from below", *New Statesman & Society* 2 (1989): 16.

39. Gamble, "Hayek and the Left", 50.

40. This line of argument is found in W. Mallock, *The Limits of Pure Democracy* (London: Chapman & Hall, 1918); W. Mallock, *A Critical Examination of Socialism* (London: J. Murray, 1908); E. Powell, *Reflections of a Statesman: The Writings and Speeches of Enoch Powell* (London: Bellew Publishing, 1991) and H. Spencer, *The Man Versus the State* (New York: Appleton, 1884).

41. R. H. Tawney, *The Acquisitive Society* (London: G. Bell, 1921) and R. Tawney, *Equality* (London: Allen & Unwin, 1931).

42. Gamble, "Hayek and the Left", 51.

43. Gamble, "Hayek and the Left", 51.

44. Giddens, *The Third Way*, 34–37 and 65–66.

45. Kelly and Gamble, "Owners and citizens", 63.

46. A. Gamble and G. Kelly, "How to raise the stakes", *The Guardian*, January 15, 1996, accessed 1 June 2014, www.lexisnexis.com/uk/business.

47. Miller, *Market, State and Community*, in particular 49–53.

48. Kelly and Gamble, "Owners and citizens", 64.

49. E. Hobsbawm, *The New Century* (St. Ives: Abacus, 2000), 96.

50. Gamble, "Hayek and the Left", 51.

51. Gamble, "Hayek and the Left", 51.

52. Gamble, "Hayek and the Left", 51–52.

53. Gamble, *Hayek*, 177.

54. Notably H. Spencer, *The Man Versus the State* (New York: Appleton, 1884); H. Maine, *Ancient Law: Its Connection with the Early History of Society and Its Relation to Modern Ideas* (London: Oxford University Press, 1959, originally 1863). The comparison was also noted by Gamble, *Hayek*, 181.

55. A. Gamble, "Hayek on Liberty", *Critical Review* 25, 3–4 (2013): 351.

56. Gamble, "Hayek on Liberty", 352.

57. Gamble, *Hayek*.

58. M. Weber, *The Protestant Ethic and the Spirit of Capitalism*, trans. Talcott Parsons (London: Allen & Unwin, 1930).

59. P. Baehr, "The 'Iron Cage' and the 'Shell as Hard as Steel': Parsons, Weber, and the *Stahlhartes Gehäuse* Metaphor in the Protestant Ethic and the Spirit of Capitalism", *History and Theory* 40, 2 (2001).

60. D. Klein, "Review of Gamble, *A.—Hayek: The Iron Cage of Liberty*", *Constitutional Political Economy* 8, 3 (1997): 258.

61. Gamble, *Hayek*, 177.

62. B. Jack, "Review of Andrew Gamble, *Hayek: The Iron Cage of Liberty*", accessed 1 August 2014, http://web.archive.org/web/20070701212250/http://people.sunyit.edu/~harrell/billyjack/.

63. D. Klein, "Review of Gamble, A.—*Hayek: The Iron Cage of Liberty*", *Constitutional Political Economy* 8, 3 (1997): 258.

64. N. Barry, "Review of Gamble, A., *Hayek: The Iron Cage of Liberty*", *Economic Affairs* 17, 2 (1997): 44.

65. Gamble, *Hayek*, 4.

66. Gamble, *Hayek*, 31.

67. M. Weber, *Science as a Vocation* (London: Routledge and Kegan Paul, 1948), 155.

68. Weber, *The Protestant Ethic and the Spirit of Capitalism*.

69. M. Weber, *Science as a Vocation*,152–53.

70. Gamble, *Hayek*, 181.

71. Wainwright, *Arguments for a New Left*, 55.

72. Hayek, *The Fatal Conceit*, 18–19.

73. Gamble, *Hayek*, 58–59.

74. Hayek, *The Road to Serfdom*.

75. F. Fukuyama, "The End of History", *The National Interest*, Summer 1989.

76. Gamble, *Hayek*, 185.

77. Gamble, *Hayek*, 184. In a later work Gamble discusses how flexible Hayek's view of state intervention is. See Gamble, "Hayek on Liberty". There is certainly a disjuncture between *The Road to Serfdom*, in which Hayek argued that almost any state intervention outside specific constraints would lead to serfdom, and Hayek's later, more policy-orientated work. One example of this flexibility is found in *The Constitution of Liberty* (ch.15, s.12), where Hayek lists those service activities in which government can legitimately intervene.

78. Gamble, *Hayek*, 182.

79. J. Friedman, "The new consensus: II, the democratic welfare state", *Critical Review* 4 (1990); J. Friedman, "The new consensus: I, the Fukuyama thesis" *Critical Review* 3 (1989).

80. Gamble, *Hayek*, 185.

81. Gamble, *Hayek*, 185–86 (my italics).

82. T. H. Green, "Liberal legislation and freedom of contract", in *Liberty*, ed. D. Miller (Oxford: Oxford University Press, 1993), 21. There is a striking resemblance to some of the language used by ethical socialists, such as R. H. Tawney against acquisitiveness here, too. A point I develop in the concluding chapter.

83. Gamble, *Hayek*, 185.

84. Gamble, *Hayek*, 194.

85. A point made in Gamble, "Hayek on Liberty", 346.

86. L. T. Hobhouse, *Liberalism* (New York: Oxford University Press, 1964, originally 1911), ch. 8.

87. Gamble also discusses 'political ignorance in a market society' and the role of instruction, deliberation and debate in protecting the market order in "Hayek on Liberty", 354–59.

88. Gamble, "Hayek on Liberty", 359.

89. Gamble, "Hayek on Liberty", 360–61.

90. P. Sylvester, "Letters: 'Tony Blair's stake in the future'", *The Guardian*, 16 January 1996, accessed 1 June 2014, www.lexisnexis.com/uk/business.

91. D. Marquand, "Can Labour kick the winning habit?", *New Statesman*, October 23, 1998, 26

92. A. Vincent, "New ideologies for old?", *The Political Quarterly* 69 (1998): 57.

6. RESPONSES TO THE NEW RIGHT

1. Hayek quoted in Gamble, *The Free Economy and the Strong State*, 27; Anderson, *A Zone of Engagement*, 368.

2. Anderson, *A Zone of Engagement*, 367–75. Anderson used the term 'mutation' rather than 'transformation'. The term 'transformation' is rather broader and does not draw on a biological metaphor, so allows me to discuss the nature of that change later in this chapter.

3. Anderson, *A Zone of Engagement*, 371–72.

4. Anderson, *A Zone of Engagement*, 373.

5. Anderson, *A Zone of Engagement*, 373.

6. Andrew Gamble also reflects on these possible fates in his chapter "Coming to Terms with Capitalism: Austerity Politics and the Public Household", *Progressive Politics after the Crash: Governing from the Left*, ed. O. Cramme, P. Diamond and M. McTernan, (Padstow, Cornwall: I. B. Tauris, 2013).

7. A. Gamble and G. Kelly, "The New Politics of Ownership", *New Left Review* I, 220 (1996): 62.

8. R. Barker, " 'The Fabian State' in Fabian Essays", in *Socialist Thought*, ed. B. Pimlott, (London: Heinemann, 1984), 36.

9. G. B. Shaw, *Ruskin's Politics* (London: Ruskin Centenary Council, 1921), 15.

10. Barker, *Political Ideas in Modern Britain*, 50.

11. Wainwright, *Arguments for a New Left*, 109.

12. D. Jay, *The Socialist Case* (London: Faber and Faber, 1937), ch. 30. Jay's *Times* obituarist wrote that this statement was 'a classic statement of Fabian arrogance and elitism' (cited in R. Toye, "'The Gentleman in Whitehall' Reconsidered: The Evolution of Douglas Jay's Views on Economic Planning and Consumer Choice 1937–1947", *Labour History Review* 67, 2 [2002], 188). Margaret Thatcher also attacked the phrase in her autobiography. Jay's comment even made it into Matthew Parris's edited collection, *Read My Lips: A Treasury of Things Politicians Wish They Hadn't Said* (London: Penguin, 1997). However, Richard Toye has noted that Jay's comment has been taken out of context. Toye argued that the polemical use of the phrase by his political enemies meant that 'Jay's views on economic planning and consumer choice have frequently been misrepresented' (Toye, " 'The Gentleman in Whitehall' Reconsidered", 187).

13. Webb and Webb, *Soviet Communism*; also quoted in V. Bogdanor, "Why Fabianism Could Not Survive", *New Statesman: Special Compilation Edition: The Third Way?*, December, 2001.

14. L. Hobhouse, *Democracy and Reaction* (Brighton: Harvester, 1972, originally 1905), 230; also cited in Barker, *Political Ideas in Modern Britain*, 28.

15. Crosland, *The Future of Socialism*, Conclusion IV.

16. J. Lane, *Anti-Statist, Communist Manifesto* (Sanday: Cienfuegos Press, New Anarchist Library, 1978, originally 1887).

17. W. Morris, "Looking Backward", in *News from Nowhere and Other Writings*, ed. C. Wilmer (Harmondsworth: Penguin, 1993, originally 1889), 358.

18. M. Evans, *Charter 88: A Successful Challenge to the British Political Tradition?* (Aldershot: Dartmouth, 1995).

19. Gamble, *The Free Economy and the Strong State*.

20. Wainwright, "Untethering the Left".

21. J. Freedland, *Bring Home the Revolution: How Britain Can Live the American Dream* (London: Fourth Estate, 1998), esp. ch. 9.

22. A. Giddens, *Where Now For New Labour?* (Cambridge: Polity, 2002), 43–47. The quote is from D. Bell, "The World and the United States in 2013", *Daedalus* (Summer 1997): 14.

23. For example, D. Corry and G. Stoker, *New Localism: Refashioning the Centre Local Relationship* (London: New Local Government Network, 2002).

24. T. Veblen, *Theory of the Leisure Class: An Economic Study in the Evolution of Institutions* (New York: Macmillan, 1899); Tawney, *The Acquisitive Society*.

25. W. Runciman, "What Happened to the Labour Party?", *London Review of Books*, 22 June 2006, 20.

26. D. Miller, "Why Markets?", 32.

27. D. Miller, "Why Markets?", 32.

28. See, for example, G. B. Shaw and H. Wilshire, eds., *Fabian Essays in Socialism* (New York: Humboldt Publishing Co., 1891, originally 1889) for this account of the state.

29. Miller, "In What Sense Must Socialism Be Communitarian?", 51–52.

30. Nove, *The Economics of Feasible Socialism.*

31. As found, for example, in K. Popper, *The Open Society and its Enemies* (London: Routledge, 1945).

32. Grahl, "Agenda for a New Left".

33. Nove, *The Economics of Feasible Socialism.*

34. M. Jacobs, "Reason to Believe", *Prospect*, October, 2002.

35. Hobsbawm, *Age of Extremes.* For Hobsbawm the 'short century' ended in 1991. However, he admits that 'I chose that date for reasons of expediency' (E. Hobsbawm, *The New Century* [St Ives: Abacus, 2000], 2) and that 'singling out a particular date is a convention and not something that historians are ready to fight for' (Hobsbawm, *The New Century*, 3). While Hobsbawm chose the final dissolution of the Soviet Union to mark the end of the century, the collapse on the Berlin Wall in 1989 marked a more obvious end. As such, the choice of 1989 seems at least as appropriate a date as 1991 for the 'short twentieth century' to end, a point also made by R. Barker, "Political Ideas since 1945, or How Long Was the Twentieth Century?", in *Ideas and Think Tanks in Contemporary Britain*, ed. M. Kandiah and A. Seldon (London: Frank Cass, 1996) 3.

36. R. Barker, "Political Ideas since 1945", 6.

37. E. Hobsbawm, *Age of Extremes*, 5. Hobsbawm's work has been criticized for failing to take sufficient notice of 'The World Outside Europe'. See G. Therborn, "The Autobiography of the Twentieth Century", *New Left Review* I, 214 (1995). The claims made here are rather more parochial and focused on the experience in Britain.

38. E. Hobsbawm, "The Crisis of Today's Ideologies", *New Left Review* I, 192 (1992); M. Mann, "As the Twentieth Century Ages", *New Left Review* I, 214 (1995); Therborn, "The Autobiography of the Twentieth Century" and Barker, "Political Ideas since 1945".

39. Barker, "Political Ideas since 1945", 6.

40. R. Barker, "Why Are There No More Socialists or Conservatives?", *Contemporary Politics* 1, 2 (1995).

41. David Selbourne coined this term in his communitarian tract *The Principle of Duty: An Essay on the Foundations of the Civic Order* (London: Sinclair-Stevenson, 1994), and it was first used by Blair in a 1994 speech to a *Guardian/Whatever Next?* conference (later issued as T. Blair, *Socialism: Fa-*

bian Tract 565 [London: Fabian Society, 1994]—this time spelled with no hyphen).

42. Giddens, *The Third Way*, 3.

43. H. Wainwright, "A Third Option", *New Statesman & Society* 1, 29–30, (1988): 34.

44. Giddens, *The Third Way*, 3.

45. Gray and Willetts, *Is Conservatism Dead?*

46. G. Dangerfield, *The Strange Death of Liberal England* (New York: G. P. Putnam and Sons, 1980, originally 1935).

47. The phrase is from François Furet and is discussed in Perry Anderson, *New World Old World* (London: Verso, 2011), 164.

48. The idea of the 'long twentieth century' is discussed in R. Barker, "How long was the twentieth century? Lecture at Gresham College", 14 October 2008, accessed 1 June 2014, http://www.gresham.ac.uk/lectures-and-events/how-long-was-the-twentieth-century.

49. Marquand, "Can Labour Kick the Winning Habit?", 26.

50. Hobsbawm, *Age of Extremes*, 4.

51. Mouffe, *The Challenge of Carl Schmitt*.

52. C. Schmitt, *The Concept of the Political* (Chicago: University of Chicago Press, 1996). Although in Schmitt's account, as Mouffe eventually recognized, this enmity existed between polities not within them, and so defined the polity but cannot, pace Schmitt's own arguments, define politics.

53. Freeden, *Ideologies and Political Theory*, 425–26.

54. Barker, "Political Ideas since 1945", 16; Barker, *Political Ideas in Modern Britain*, 279.

55. McInnes, "The Road Not Taken".

56. A term used by Rodney Barker in "Political Ideas since 1945", 16.

57. Gamble, "Hayek on Liberty", 360.

58. The claim, also made by some on the Thatcherite wing of the Conservative Party that the market rewards according to effort would not be supported by Hayekians, who acknowledge that there is no necessary link between effort or desert and reward in the market—unlike adherents of rather less sophisticated arguments of Samuel Smiles, for example.

59. R. Hayton, *Reconstructing Conservatism* (Manchester: Manchester University Press, 2013); S. Griffiths, "What was progressive in progressive conservatism?", *Political Studies Review* 12, 1 (2014).

60. Plant, interview.

61. Miller, "Why Markets?", 25.

62. R. Hattersley, "Response to Simon Griffiths", in *British Party Politics and Ideology after New Labour*, ed. S. Griffiths and K. Hickson (Basingstoke: Palgrave Macmillan, 2010), 85.

63. pwc, "The Total Tax Contribution of UK Financial Services (5th edition)", December 2012, accessed 1 June 2014, http://www.cityoflondon.gov.uk/business/economic-research-and-information/research-publications/Documents/research-2012/Total_tax_Contribution_OnlineVersion_PDF.pdf, 5.

64. P. Kerr, "Cameron Chameleon and the Current State of Britain's 'Consensus'", *Parliamentary Affairs*, 60, 1 (2007).

65. Diamond, *New Labour's Old Roots*.

66. Gamble, "Hayek and Liberty", 362.

67. M. Jacobs, "Beyond the Social Market: Rethinking Capitalism and Public Policy", *The Political Quarterly* 84, 1 (2013): 16.

68. M. Jacobs, "Beyond the Social Market", 6.

69. T. Judt, *Ill Fares the Land: A Treatise on Our Present Discontents* (St. Ives: Penguin Press, 2010).

70. These 'spectres' are discussed in A. Gamble, *The Spectre at the Feast: Capitalist Crisis and the Politics of Recession* (Basingstoke: Palgrave Macmillan, 2009).

71. R. Plant, "Response to Roy Hattersley and Kevin Hickson", *Political Quarterly* 83, 1 (2012): 14–15.

72. Freeden, *Ideologies and Political Theory*, 477.

73. Freeden, *Ideologies and Political Theory*, 479.

74. R. Barker, "Tearing up the ideological maps, and squabbling over the compass", Lecture at Gresham College, 3 March 2009, accessed 1 June 2014, http://www.gresham.ac.uk/lectures-and-events/tearing-up-the-ideological-maps-and-squabbling-over-the-compass.

BIBLIOGRAPHY

Addison, P. *The Road to 1945: British Politics and the Second World War*. London: Cape, 1975.

Anderson, J. *Studies in Empirical Philosophy*. Sydney University Press, 2005.

Anderson, Paul. "Togetherness". *New Statesman & Society*. 4 February 1994.

Anderson, Perry. *A Zone of Engagement*. London: Verso, 1992.

Anderson, Perry. *Spectrum: From Right to Left in the World of Ideas*. London: Verso, 2005.

Anderson, Perry. *New World Old World*. London: Verso, 2011.

Atticus, *Sunday Times*, March 29, 1992. Accessed 21 April 2014. www.lexisnexis.com/uk/business.

Ayto, J. *20th Century Words*. Oxford: Oxford University Press, 1999.

Backbencher. "My First Vote". *Guardian*. 18 June 2003. Accessed 15 April 2014. http://politics.guardian.co.uk/backbencher/story/0,10599,980148,00.html.

Baehr, P. "The 'Iron Cage' and the 'Shell as Hard as Steel': Parsons, Weber, and the *Stahlhartes Gehäuse* Metaphor in the Protestant Ethic and the Spirit of Capitalism". *History and Theory* 40, 2 (2001).

Barker, R. " 'The Fabian State' in Fabian Essays". In *Socialist Thought*, edited by B. Pimlott. London: Heinemann, 1984.

Barker, R. *Politics, People and Government*. Basingstoke: Macmillan, 1994.

Barker, R. "Why Are There No More Socialists or Conservatives?" *Contemporary Politics* 1, 2 (1995).

Barker, R. "A future for liberalism or a liberal future?" In *The Liberal Political Tradition: Contemporary Reappraisals*, edited by J. Meadowcroft. Cheltenham: Edward Elgar Publishing Ltd, 1996.

Barker, R. "Political Ideas since 1945, or How Long Was the Twentieth Century?" In *Ideas and Think Tanks in Contemporary Britain*, edited by M. Kandiah and A. Seldon. London: Frank Cass, 1996.

Barker, R. *Political Ideas in Modern Britain: In and after the twentieth century*. London and New York: Routledge, 1997.

Barker, R. "Pluralism, revenant or recessive?" In *The British Study of Politics in the Twentieth Century*, edited by J. Hayward. Oxford: Oxford University Press, 1999.

Barker, R. "Hooks and Hands, Interests and Enemies: Political Thinking as Political Action". *Political Studies* 48, 2 (2000).

Barker, R. "How long was the twentieth century?" Lecture at Gresham College. 14 October 2008. Accessed 1 June 2014. http://www.gresham.ac.uk/lectures-and-events/how-long-was-the-twentieth-century.

Barker, R. "The pluralism of British pluralism". *Journal of Political Ideologies* 14, 1 (2009).

Barker, R. "Tearing up the ideological maps, and squabbling over the compass". Lecture at Gresham College, 3 March 2009. Accessed 1 June 2014. http://www.gresham.ac.uk/lectures-and-events/tearing-up-the-ideological-maps-and-squabbling-over-the-compass.

Barry, N. "Review of Gamble, A., *Hayek: The Iron Cage of Liberty*". *Economic Affairs* 17, 2 (1997).

Beck, U. *Risk Society: Towards A New Modernity*. London: Sage Publications, 1992.

Bell, D. "The World and the United States in 2013". *Daedalus*, Summer 1997.

Berlin, I. "Two Concepts of Liberty". In *The Proper Study of Mankind: An Anthology of Essays*, edited by H. Hardy and R. Hausheer. London: Pimlico, 1998.

Bevan, A. *In Place of Fear*. New York: Simon and Schuster, 1952.

Bevir, M. "New Labour: A Study in Ideology". *British Journal of Politics and International Relations* 2, 3 (2000).

Birner, J., and R. Van Zipj, eds. *Hayek, Coordination and Evolution: His Legacy in Philosophy, Politics, Economics and the History of Ideas*. London: Routledge, 1994.

Blackburn, R. "*Fin-De-Siècle*—Socialism after the Crash". *New Left Review* 185 (1991).

Blackburn, R. "Themes". *New Left Review* I, 185 (1991).

Blair, T. *Socialism: Fabian Tract 565*. London: Fabian Society, 1994.

Blatchford, R. *Britain for the British*. London: Clarion Press, 1902.

Bobbio, N. *Left and Right: The Significance of a Political Distinction*. Cambridge: Polity, 1996.

Bockman, J. *Markets in the Name of Socialism: The Left-Wing Origins of Neoliberalism*. Stanford: Stanford University Press, 2011.

Bogdanor, V. "Why Fabianism Could Not Survive". *New Statesman: Special Compilation Edition: The Third Way?*, December 2001.

Bowles, P., and G. White. "The Dilemmas of Market Socialism—Capital-Market Reform in China 1 Bonds". *Journal of Development Studies* 28, 3 (1992).

Bowles, P., and G. White. "The Dilemmas of Market Socialism—Capital-Market Reform in China 2 Shares". *Journal of Development Studies* 28, 4 (1992).

Brittan, S. "Champion of Liberty and Law: The Work of the Late Friedrich Von Hayek". *Financial Times*. March 25, 1992.

Burczak, T. "Socialism after Hayek". *Rethinking Marxism* 9, 3 (1997).

Burczak, T. *Socialism after Hayek*. Ann Arbor: University of Michigan Press, 2006.

Butler, E. *Hayek: His Contribution to the Economic Thought of Our Times*. Worcester: Billing and Sons Ltd, 1983.

Carens, J. *Equality, Moral Incentives, and the Market: An Essay in Utopian Politico-Economic Theory*. Chicago: University of Chicago Press, 1980.

Cassidy, J. "The Price Prophet". *New Yorker*, February 7, 2000. Accessed 1 June 2014. http://www.hooverdigest.org/003/cassidy.html.

Cockett, R. *Thinking the Unthinkable: Think-Tanks and the Economic Counter-Revolution, 1931–1983*. London: Harper Collins, 1994.

Cohen, G. "Capitalism, Freedom and the Proletariat". In *The Idea of Freedom*, edited by A. Ryan. Oxford: Oxford University Press, 1979.

Cohen, G. "Capitalism, Freedom and the Proletariat". In *Liberty*, edited by D. Miller. Oxford: Oxford University Press, 1991.

Cohen, G. "The Future of a Disillusion". *New Left Review* 190 (1991).

Cohen, S. "Book Review". *Capital and Class* 55 (1995).

Collard, D. *The New Right: A Critique*. London: Fabian Society, 1968.

Colley, L. *Britons: Forging the Nation 1707–1837*. New Haven and London: Yale University Press, 1992.

Corry, D., and G. Stoker, *New Localism: Refashioning the Centre Local Relationship*. London: New Local Government Network, 2002.

Cowling, M. "The Sources of the New Right: Irony, Geniality and Malice". *Encounter* LXXIII, 4 (1989).

Crick, B. *George Orwell: A Life*. Harmondsworth: Penguin, 1992, originally 1980.

Crosland, A. "The Transition to Capitalism". In *New Fabian Essays*, edited by R. Crossman. London: Turnstile, 1952.

Crosland, A. *The Future of Socialism*. London: Robinson Publishing, 2006, originally 1956.
Crosland, A. *The Conservative Enemy; a Programme of Radical Reform for the 1960s*. London: J. Cape, 1962.
Crosland, A. *Socialism Now, and Other Essays*. London: Cape, 1974.
Crossman, R., ed. *New Fabian Essays*. London: Turnstile, 1952.
Dangerfield, G. *The Strange Death of Liberal England*. New York: G. P. Putnam and Sons, 1980, originally 1935.
De Jasay, A. *Market Socialism: a scrutiny—'this square circle'*. London: IEA, 1990.
Diamond, P. *New Labour's Old Roots: Revisionist Thinkers in Labour's History 1931–1997*. Exeter: Imprint Academic, 2004.
Durbin, E. "Professor Hayek and economic planning and political liberty". *The Economic Journal* 55 (1945).
Eisfeld, R. "The Emergence and Meaning of Socialist Pluralism". *International Political Science Review* 17, 3 (1996).
Elson, D. "Market Socialism or Socialization of the Market?" *New Left Review* 172 (1988).
Espada, J. *Social Citizenship Rights: A Critique of F. A. Hayek and Raymond Plant*. London: Macmillan, 1996.
Estrin, S. "Yugoslavia—the Case of Self-Managing Market Socialism". *Journal of Economic Perspectives* 5, 4 (1991).
Estrin, S., and J. Le Grand (eds). *Market Socialism*. Oxford: Clarendon, 1989.
Estrin, S., and D. Winter. "Planning in a Market Socialist Economy". In *Market Socialism*, edited by S. Estrin and J. Le Grand. Oxford: Clarendon, 1989.
Evans, M. *Charter 88: A Successful Challenge to the British Political Tradition?* Aldershot: Dartmouth, 1995.
Evans, M. *Charter 88: A Successful Challenge to the British Political Tradition?* Aldershot: Dartmouth, 1995.
Finer, H. *Road to Reaction*. Boston: Little, Brown and Company, 1945.
Freeden, M. *Ideologies and Political Theory: A Conceptual Approach*. Oxford: Clarendon Press, 1996.
Freedland, J. *Bring Home the Revolution: How Britain Can Live the American Dream*. London: Fourth Estate, 1998.
Friedman, J. "The new consensus: I, the Fukuyama thesis". *Critical Review* 3 (1989).
Friedman, J. "The new consensus: II, the democratic welfare state". *Critical Review* 4 (1990).
Fukuyama, F. "The End of History". *The National Interest*, Summer 1989.
Gamble, A. "The free economy and the strong state: The rise of the social market economy". In *The Socialist Register*, edited by R. Miliband and J. Saville. London: Merlin Press, 1979.
Gamble, A. *The Free Economy and the Strong State: The Politics of Thatcherism*. Durham, NC: Duke University Press, 1988.
Gamble, A. "Review of *The Collected Works of FA Hayek: Vol. III, the trend of economic thinking—essays on political economists and economic history*". *Political Studies* 40 (1992).
Gamble, A. "In government, but not in power". *New Statesman & Society* 6 (1993).
Gamble, A. "Review of J. Birner and R. Van Zijp (Eds.), *Hayek Co-Ordination and Evolution: His Legacy in Philosophy, Politics, Economics and the History of Ideas*". *History of Political Thought* 16, 2 (1995).
Gamble, A. "The crisis of conservatism". *New Left Review* 214 (1995).
Gamble, A. *Hayek: The Iron Cage of Liberty*. Cambridge: Polity, 1996.
Gamble, A. "Comrade Hayek". *Prospect*, March 1996. Accessed 21 April 2014. www.lexisnexis.com/uk/business.
Gamble, A. "Hayek and the Left". *Political Quarterly* 67 (1996).
Gamble, A. *Politics and Fate*. Cambridge: Polity, 2000.
Gamble, A. *Between Europe and America: The Future of British Politics*. Basingstoke: Palgrave, 2002.

Gamble, A. *The Spectre at the Feast: Capitalist Crisis and the Politics of Recession*. Basingstoke: Palgrave Macmillan, 2009.

Gamble, A. "Coming to Terms with Capitalism: Austerity Politics and the Public Household". In *Progressive Politics after the Crash: Governing from the Left*, edited by O. Cramme, P. Diamond and M. McTernan. Padstow, Cornwall: I. B. Tauris, 2013.

Gamble, A. "Hayek on Liberty". *Critical Review* 25, 3–4 (2013).

Gamble, A., and G. Kelly. "The New Politics of Ownership". *New Left Review* I, 220 (1996).

Gamble, A., and G. Kelly. "How to raise the stakes". *The Guardian*, January 15, 1996. Accessed 1 June 2014. www.lexisnexis.com/uk/business.

Gamble, A., and A. Payne, eds. *Regionalism and World Order*. Basingstoke: Macmillan, 1996.

Gamble, A., and P. Walton. *Capitalism in Crisis*. London and Basingstoke: Macmillan Press Ltd., 1976.

Gewirth, A. *Reason and Morality*. Chicago and London: University of Chicago Press, 1978.

Gewirth, A. *Human Rights: Essays in Justification and Applications*. Chicago and London: University of Chicago Press, 1982.

Giddens, A. *The Third Way: the renewal of social democracy*. Cambridge: Polity, 1998.

Giddens, A. *Where Now For New Labour?* Cambridge: Polity, 2002.

Goodhart, D. "Too Diverse? Is Britain Becoming Too Diverse to Sustain the Mutual Obligations Behind a Good Society and the Welfare State?" *Prospect*, February 2004.

Gould, B. *Socialism and Freedom*. Basingstoke: Macmillan, 1985.

Grahl, J. "Agenda for a new left: Answering the free-market right—Wainwright, H". *New Left Review* 214 (1995).

Gray, J. "Positional Goods, Classical Liberalism and the Politicisation of Poverty". In *Dilemmas of Liberal Democracy: Readings in Fred Hirsch's Social Limits to Growth*, edited by A. Ellis and K. Kumar. London: Tavistock, 1983.

Gray, J. "John Stuart Mill: The Crisis of Liberalism". In *Plato to NATO: Studies in Political Thought*, edited by B. Redhead. Penguin: Harmondsworth, 1984.

Gray, J. "Marxian Freedom, Individual Liberty and the End of Alienation". *Social Philosophy and Policy* 3, 2 (1986).

Gray, J. *Hayek on Liberty*. London and New York: Routledge, 1989.

Gray, J. *Isaiah Berlin*. London: HarperCollins, 1995.

Gray, J. "The case for decency". *New York Review of Books* 53 (2006).

Gray, J., and D. Willetts. *Is Conservatism Dead?* London: Profile Books, 1997.

Green, T. "Liberal legislation and freedom of contract". In *Liberty*, edited by D. Miller. Oxford: Oxford University Press, 1993.

Greenleaf, W. "Laski And British Socialism". *History of Political Thought* II, 3 (1981).

Greenleaf, W. *The British Political Tradition. Volume 2: The Ideological Heritage*. London and New York: Routledge, 2003, originally 1983.

Griffiths, S. "Review of H. Wainwright, 'Reclaim the State'". *Renewal* 11, 4 (2003).

Griffiths, S. "What was progressive in progressive conservatism?" *Political Studies Review* 12, 1 (2014).

Harrod, R. *The Life of John Maynard Keynes*. London: Macmillan, 1951.

Harte, N. *The University of London 1836–1986: An Illustrated History*. London: Athlone, 1986.

Hattersley, R. *Choose Freedom: The Future for Democratic Socialism*. London: Michael Joseph, 1987.

Hattersley, R. "Response to Simon Griffiths". In *British Party Politics and Ideology after New Labour*, edited by S. Griffiths and K. Hickson. Basingstoke: Palgrave Macmillan, 2010.

Hayek, F. *Prices and Production*. London: Routledge, 1934.

Hayek, F. "Economics and Knowledge". In *Individualism and Economic Order*. Chicago and London: University of Chicago Press, 1948, originally 1936.

Hayek, F. *The Road to Serfdom*. London: Routledge, 1944.

Hayek, F. *The Constitution of Liberty*. London: Routledge, 1960.

Hayek, F. *Law, Legislation and Liberty, Volume 1: Rules and Order*. London: Routledge and Kegan Paul, 1973.

Hayek, F. *Law, Legislation and Liberty, Volume 2: The Mirage of Social Justice*. London: Routledge and Kegan Paul, 1976.

Hayek, F. *Law, Legislation and Liberty, Volume 3: The Political Order of a Free People*. London: Routledge and Kegan Paul, 1979.

Hayek, F. *The Fatal Conceit: The Errors of Socialism*. London: Routledge, 1988.

Hayek, F. *Hayek on Hayek: An Autobiographical Dialogue*. London: Routledge, 1994.

Hayek, F. A. *New Studies in Philosophy, Politics, Economics and the History of Ideas*. London: Routledge, 1978.

Hayton, R. *Reconstructing Conservatism*. Manchester: Manchester University Press, 2013.

Hickson, K. "Reply to Stephen Meredith: Mr. Crosland's Nightmare? New Labour and Equality in Historical Perspective". *British Journal of Politics and International Relations* 9, 1 (2007).

Hirst, P. *The Pluralist Theory of the State*. London and New York: Routledge, 1989.

Hirst, P. "Associational Democracy". In *Prospects for Democracy: North, South, East, West*, edited by D. Held. Cambridge: Polity, 1993.

Hirst, P. *Associative Democracy*. Cambridge: Polity, 1994.

Hirst P., and G. Thompson. *Globalization in Question: The International Economy and the Possibilities of Governance*. Cambridge: Polity, 1996.

Hobhouse, L. *Democracy and Reaction*. Brighton: Harvester, 1972, originally 1905.

Hobhouse, L. *Liberalism*. New York: Oxford University Press, 1964, originally 1911.

Hobsbawm, E. "The Crisis of Today's Ideologies". *New Left Review* I, 192 (1992).

Hobsbawm, E. *Age of Extremes: The Short Twentieth Century 1914–1991*. London: Michael Joseph, 1994.

Hobsbawm, E. *The New Century*. St. Ives: Abacus, 2000.

Hoover, K., and R. Plant. *Conservative Capitalism in Britain and the United States: A Critical Appraisal*. London: Routledge, 1989.

Howe S., and H. Wainwright. "Change from below". *New Statesman & Society* 2 (1989).

Jack, B. "Review of Andrew Gamble, *Hayek: The Iron Cage of Liberty*". Accessed 20 July 2006. http://web.archive.org/web/20070701212250/http://people.sunyit.edu/~harrell/billy jack/.

Jacobs, M. "Reason To Believe". *Prospect*, October 2002.

Jacobs, M. "Beyond the Social Market: Rethinking Capitalism and Public Policy". *The Political Quarterly* 84, 1 (2013).

Jay, D. *The Socialist Case*. London: Faber and Faber, 1937.

Jones, H., and M. Kandiah, eds. *The Myth of Consensus: New Views on British History, 1945–64*. Basingstoke: Macmillan, 1996.

Judt, T. *Ill Fares the Land: A Treatise on Our Present Discontents*. St. Ives: Penguin Press, 2010.

Kelly, G., and A. Gamble. "Owners and citizens". *Political Quarterly* 69 (1998).

Kerr, P. "Cameron Chameleon and the Current State of Britain's 'Consensus' ". *Parliamentary Affairs* 60, 1 (2007).

Klein, D. "Review of Gamble, A.—*Hayek: The Iron Cage of Liberty*". *Constitutional Political Economy* 8, 3 (1997).

Kurzweil, R. *The Age of Spiritual Machines: When Computers Exceed Human Intelligence*. Harmondsworth: Viking, 1999.

Laborde, C. *Pluralist Thought and the State in Britain and France, 1900–1925*. Basingstoke: Macmillan, 2000.

Lamont, N. "Lamont tells MPS of his 'uncomfortable experience'". *The Independent*, 10 June 1993, accessed 1 June 2014, www.lexisnexis.com/uk/business.

Lane, J. *Anti-Statist, Communist Manifesto*. Sanday: Cienfuegos Press, New Anarchist Library, 1978, originally 1887.

Laslett, P., ed. *Philosophy, Politics and Society: A Collection*. Oxford: Blackwell, 1956.

Le Grand, J. *Motivation, Agency, and Public Policy: Of Knights and Knaves, Pawns and Queens*. Oxford: Oxford University Press, 2003.

Le Grand, J. "Too Little Choice". *Prospect* 118, January 2006.

Le Grand, J. *The Other Invisible Hand: Delivering Public Services through Choice and Competition*. Princeton, NJ: Princeton University Press, 2007.

Leonard, D., ed. *Crosland and New Labour*. London: Palgrave, 1998.

Lewis, R. "The Prophet of Socialist Doom". *Daily Mail*, March 25, 1992. Accessed 21 April 2014. www.lexisnexis.com/uk/business.

Lipsey, D. "Too Much Choice". *Prospect* 117, December 2005.

Lipsey, D., and D. Leonard, eds. *The Socialist Agenda: Crosland's Legacy*. London: Cape, 1981.

Lister, A. "The 'Mirage' of Social Justice: Hayek Against (and For) Rawls". Oliver Smithies Lecture, Balliol College, Oxford, 10 May 2011. Accessed 1 June 2014. http://social-justice.politics.ox.ac.uk/materials/SJ017_Lister_MirageofSocialJustice.pdf.

Lloyd, J. "New Markets for Socialist Ideas". *Financial Times*, November 17, 1986. Accessed 21 April 2014. www.lexisnexis.com/uk/business.

MacCallum, G. "Negative and Positive Freedom". In *Liberty*, edited by D. Miller. Oxford: Oxford University Press, 1991.

Macmillan, H. *The Middle Way. A Study of the Problem of Economic and Social Progress in a Free and Democratic Society*. London: Macmillan & Co., 1938.

MacShane, D. "Labour's Good Book". *Prospect*, September 2006.

Maine, H. *Ancient Law: Its Connection with the Early History of Society and Its Relation to Modern Ideas*. London: Oxford University Press, 1959, originally 1863.

Mallock, W. *A Critical Examination of Socialism*. London: J. Murray, 1908.

Mallock, W. *The Limits of Pure Democracy*. London: Chapman & Hall, 1918.

Mann, M. "As the Twentieth Century Ages". *New Left Review* I, 214 (1995).

Marquand, D. "Can Labour kick the winning habit?" *New Statesman*. 23 October 1998.

Marx, K. *Critique of the Gotha Programme*. Accessed 21 April 2014. http://www.marxists.org/archive/marx/works/1875/gotha/index.htm.

McChesney, R. *Rich Media, Poor Democracy: communication politics in dubious times*. Urbana and Chicago: University of Illinois Press, 1999.

McInnes, N. "The Road Not Taken: Hayek's Slippery Slope to Serfdom". *The National Interest*, Spring 1998. Accessed 21 April 2014. www.lexisnexis.com/uk/business.

Meredith, S. "Mr Crosland's Nightmare? New Labour and Equality in Historical Perspective". *British Journal of Politics and International Relations* 8, 2 (2006).

Meredith, S. "New Labour and Equality: A Response to Hickson". *British Journal of Politics & International Relations* 9, 1, February (2007).

Merriam, C. "Book Reviews: Friedrich A. Hayek, *The Road to Serfdom*". *The American Journal of Sociology* 50, 3 (1944).

Mill, J. "On Liberty". In *Utilitarianism, on Liberty, Considerations on Representative Government*, edited by G. Williams. London: Everyman, 1993.

Mill, J. *Principles of Political Economy*. Oxford: Oxford University Press, 2008.

Miller, D. "Socialism and the Market". *Political Theory* 5, 4 (1977).

Miller, D. *Anarchism*. London: Dent, 1984.

Miller, D. "In What Sense Must Socialism Be Communitarian?" *Social Philosophy & Policy* 6, 2 (1989).

Miller, D. "Why Markets?" In *Market Socialism*, edited by S. Estrin and J. Le Grand. Oxford: Clarendon: 1989.

Miller, D. *Market, State and Community: Theoretical Foundations of Market Socialism*. Oxford: Clarendon, 1989.

Miller, D. "The Resurgence of Political Theory". *Political Studies* 38, 3 (1990).

Miller, D. "A Vision of Market Socialism—How It Might Work—and Its Problems". *Dissent* 38, 3 (1991).

Miller, D. *On Nationality*. Oxford: Clarendon Press, 1995.

Miller, D. "What Kind of Equality Should the Left Pursue?" In *Equality*, edited J. Franklin. London: IPPR, 1997.

Miller, D. *Justice for Earthlings: Essays in Political Philosophy*. Cambridge: Cambridge University Press, 2013.

Miller D., and S. Estrin. "A Case for Market Socialism—What Does It Mean—Why Should We Favor It?" *Dissent* 34, 3 (1987).

Morris, W. "Looking Backward". In *News from Nowhere and Other Writings*, edited by C. Wilmer. Harmondsworth: Penguin, 1993, originally 1889.

Mouffe, C., ed. *The Challenge of Carl Schmitt*. London: Verso, 1999.

National Review. "The 100 Best Non-Fiction Books of the Century". May 3, 1999. Accessed 1 June 2014. http://www.nationalreview.com/100best/100_books.html.

Nove, A. "Market Socialism". *Acta Oeconomica* 40, 3–4 (1989).

Nozick, R. *Anarchy, State and Utopia*. Oxford: Blackwell, 1974.

Orwell, G. *The Lion and the Unicorn: Socialism and the English Genius*. Harmondsworth: Penguin, 1982, originally 1941.

Orwell, G. *Nineteen Eighty-Four*. Harmondsworth: Penguin, 1949.

Orwell, G. "Notes on Nationalism". In *George Orwell Essays*. Harmondsworth: Penguin, 1984, originally 1945.

Orwell, G. "Review: *The Road to Serfdom* by F. A Hayek, the *Mirror of the Past* by K. Zilliacus". In *The Collected Essays, Journalism and Letters of George Orwell. Volume 3: As I Please. 1943–1945*, edited by S. Orwell and I. Angus. Harmondsworth: Penguin, 1982, originally 1968.

O'Sullivan, N. *Conservatism*. London: Dent and Sons, 1976.

Pakulski, J., and M. Waters. *The Death of Class*. London: Sage, 1996.

Parris, M., ed. *Read My Lips: A Treasury of Things Politicians Wish They Hadn't Said*. London: Penguin, 1997.

Petras, J. "Contradictions of Market Socialism in China 1". *Journal of Contemporary Asia* 18, 1 (1988).

Petras, J. "Contradictions of Market Socialism in China 2". *Journal of Contemporary Asia* 18, 2 (1988).

Pierson, C. *Socialism after Communism: The New Market Socialism*. Padstow, Cornwall: I. B. Turns, 1995.

Pilkington, A. "Cultural Representations and Changing Ethnic Identities in a Global Age". In *Developments in Sociology*, edited by M. Holborn. Ormskirk: Causeway Press, 2002.

Pirie, M. "Why F. A. Hayek Is a Conservative". In *Hayek on the Fabric of Human Society*, edited by E. Butler and M. Pirie. London: Adam Smith Institute, 1987.

Plant, R. *Social and Moral Theory in Casework*. London: Routledge and Kegan Paul, 1970.

Plant, R. *Hegel*. London: Allen & Unwin, 1973.

Plant, R. *Community And Ideology: An Essay In Applied Social Philosophy*. London: Routledge and Kegan Paul, 1974.

Plant, R. "Should Blood Be Bought and Sold (Part I)?" *Journal of Medical Ethics: The Journal of the Institute of Medical Ethics* 3 (1977).

Plant R. "How Should Health Care Be Distributed? (Part II)". *Journal of Medical Ethics: The Journal of the Institute of Medical Ethics* 4 (1978).

Plant, R. *Equality, Markets and the State*. London: Fabian Society, 1984.

Plant, R. "To a Communal Market; Commentary". *The Times*, April 10, 1989. Accessed 14 April 2014. www.lexisnexis.vom/uk/business.

Plant, R. "Master of the Market: Commentary". *The Times*, 8 May 1989. Accessed 21 April 2014. www.lexisnexis.com/uk/business.

Plant, R. "Socialism, Markets and End States". In *Market Socialism*, edited S. Estrin and J. Le Grand. Oxford: Clarendon, 1989.

Plant, R. "No Man Is an Island—except in ignorance". *The Times*, 1 January 1990. Accessed 21 April 2014. www.lexisnexis.com/uk/business.

Plant, R. "Hardly Poor by Choice". *The Times*, 2 April 1990. Accessed 21 April 2014. www.lexisnexis.com/uk/business.

Plant, R. *Modern Political Thought*. Oxford, UK, and Cambridge, MA: Blackwell, 1991.

Plant, R. "Political Theory without Foundations". *History of the Human Sciences* 5, 3 (1992).

Plant, R. "Hayek on Social Justice: A Critique". In *Hayek, Coordination and Evolution: His Legacy in Philosophy Politics Economics and the History of Ideas*, edited J. Birner and R. Van Zipj. London: Routledge, 1994.

Plant, R. "Market Place for Everyone: Labour's Constitutional Changes Reflect a Move Away from Dogma Towards Greater Social Justice". *The Guardian*. 20 March 1995. Accessed 21 April 2014. www.lexisnexis.com/uk/business.

Plant, R. *Hegel: The Great Philosophers*. St. Ives: Phoenix, 2003, originally 1997.

Plant, R. *The Neo-liberal State*. Oxford: Oxford University Press, 2010.

Plant, R. "Response to Roy Hattersley and Kevin Hickson". *Political Quarterly* 83, 1 (2012).

Plant, R. *The Plant Report: Democracy, Representation and Elections, Report of the Working Party on Elections*. London: Labour Party, 1993.

Plant, R., M. Beech and K. Hickson, eds. *The Struggle for Labour's Soul*. London and New York: Routledge, 2004.

Plant, R., H. Lesser and P. Taylor-Gooby. *Political Philosophy and Social Welfare: Essays on the Normative Basis of Welfare Provision*. London: Routledge and Kegan Paul, 1980.

Podhoretz, N. "Revenge of the Smelly Little Orthodoxies". *National Review*, January 27, 1997. Accessed 1 June 2014. http://www.netcharles.com/orwell/ctc/docs/smelly.htm.

Popper, K. *The Open Society and its Enemies*. London: Routledge, 1945.

Popper, K. *Unended Quest: An Intellectual Autobiography*. London: Routledge, 2002.

Powell, E. *Reflections of a Statesman: The Writings and Speeches of Enoch Powell*. London: Bellew Publishing, 1991.

pwc. "The Total Tax Contribution of UK Financial Services (5th edition)". December 2012. Accessed 1 June 2014. http://www.cityoflondon.gov.uk/business/economic-research-and-information/research-publications/Documents/research-2012/Total_tax_Contribution_OnlineVersion_PDF.pdf, 5.

Ramsey Steele, D. *From Marx to Mises: post-capitalist society and the challenge of economic calculation*. La Salle, IL: Open Court, 1992.

Rawls, J. "Justice as Fairness". In *Philosophy, Politics & Society: 2nd Series: A Collection*, edited by P. Laslett and W. G. Runciman. Oxford: Blackwell, 1962.

Rawls, J. *A Theory of Justice*. Cambridge, MA: Harvard University Press, 1971.

Raz, J. *The Morality of Freedom*. Oxford: Clarendon, 1988.

Reay, D., and H. Lucey. "The Limits of 'Choice': Children and Inner City Schooling". *Sociology* 37, 1 (2003).

Rees, N. "The Vagueness Is All". *The "Quote . . . Unquote" Newsletter* 2, 2, April 1993. Accessed 1 June 2014. http://archive.today/DGGUG#selection-45.5-47.33.

Rodden, J. *The Politics of Literary Reputation: The Making and Claiming of 'St. George' Orwell*. New York and Oxford: Oxford University Press, 1989.

Roemer, J. "Market Socialism—A Blueprint". *Dissent* 38, 4 (1991).

Roemer, J. *A Future for Socialism*. Cambridge, MA: Harvard University Press, 1994.

Rowbotham, S., L. Segal and H. Wainwright, *Beyond the Fragments*. London: Merlin Press, 1979.

Runciman, W. "What Happened to the Labour Party?" *London Review of Books*, 22 June 2006.

Schmitt, C., *The Concept of the Political*. Chicago: University of Chicago Press, 1996.

Schneer, J. "Hopes Deferred or Shattered: The British Labour Left and the Third Force Movement, 1945–49". *The Journal of Modern History* 56, 2 (1984).

Selbourne, D. *The Principle of Duty: An Essay on the Foundations of the Civic Order*. London: Sinclair-Stevenson, 1994.

Seldon, A. "Obituary: Professor F. A. Hayek". *The Independent*. March 25, 1992. Accessed 1 June 2014. www.lexisnexis.com/uk/business.

Seligman, B. "The Study of Man: Dice, Dr. Hayek and the Consumer". *Commentary* 1, 5 (1946).

Sen, A. "Equality of What? The Tanner Lecture on Human Values". Lecture at Stanford University, 22 May 1979. Accessed 21 April 2014. http://tannerlectures.utah.edu/_documents/a-to-z/s/sen80.pdf.

Sen, A. "Comment: An Enduring Insight into the Purpose of Prosperity". *Financial Times*, September 21, 2004.

Shaw G., and H. Wilshire, eds. *Fabian Essays in Socialism*. New York: Humboldt Publishing Co., 1891, originally 1889.

Shaw, G. *Ruskin's Politics*. London: Ruskin Centenary Council, 1921.

Spencer, H. *The Man Versus the State*. New York: Appleton, 1884.

Spender, D. *There's Always Been a Woman's Movement in this Century*. Kitchener, Ont., Canada: Pandora Press, 1983.

Stark, T. *A New A–Z of Income and Wealth*. London: Fabian Society, 1988.

Sylvester, P. "Letters: 'Tony Blair's stake in the future' ". *The Guardian*, 16 January 1996. Accessed 1 June 2014. www.lexisnexis.com/uk/business.

Tawney, R. *The Acquisitive Society*. London: G. Bell, 1921.

Tawney, R. *Equality*. London: Allen & Unwin, 1931.

Thatcher, M. "House of Commons PQs". March 10, 1981. Accessed 1 June 2014. http://www.margaretthatcher.org/document/104593.

Thatcher, M. *The Path to Power*. London: HarperCollins, 1995.

Thatcher, M. "Speech accepting an honorary degree from Hofstra University". March 27, 2000. Accessed 1 June 2014. http://www.margaretthatcher.org/document/108387.

Therborn, G. "The Autobiography of the Twentieth Century". *New Left Review* I, 214 (1995).

Titmuss, R. *The Gift Relationship: From Human Blood to Social Policy*. London: Allen & Unwin, 1970.

Tomlinson, J. *Hayek and the Market*. London and Winchester, MA: Pluto Press, 1990.

Toye, R. "The Gentleman in Whitehall' Reconsidered: The Evolution of Douglas Jay's Views on Economic Planning and Consumer Choice 1937–1947". *Labour History Review* 67, 2 (2002).

Veblen, T. *Theory of the Leisure Class: An Economic Study in the Evolution of Institutions*. New York: Macmillan, 1899.

Vincent, A. "New ideologies for old?" *Political Quarterly* 69 (1998).

Vincent, A. and R. Plant. *Philosophy, Politics and Citizenship: The Life and Thought of the British Idealists*. Oxford: Wiley-Blackwell, 1984.

von Hippel, E. " 'Sticky Information' and the Locus of Problem Solving: implications for innovation". *Management Science* 40, April (1994).

von Mises, L. *Socialism: An Economic and Sociological Analysis*. London: J. Cape, 1936, originally 1922.

von Mises, L. *Theory and History*. Auburn, AL: Ludwig von Mises Institute, 2007, originally 1957. Accessed 24 June 2011. http://mises.org/Books/theoryhistory.pdf.

Wainwright, H. "A Third Option". *New Statesman & Society* 1, 29–30 (1988).

Wainwright, H. "Untethering the Left". *New Statesman & Society*, 24 February 1989.

Wainwright, H. "The New Left after Communism". *Studies in Political Economy* 38, Summer (1992).

Wainwright, H. "A New Kind of Knowledge for a New Kind of State". In *A Different Kind of State*, edited by G. Albo, D. Langille and L. Panitch. Toronto: OUP, 1993.

Wainwright, H. *Red Pepper Newsletter*, May 1993.

Wainwright, H. *Arguments for a New Left: Answering the Free-Market Right*. Oxford: Blackwell, 1994.

Wainwright, H. *Reclaim the State: Experiments in Popular Democracy*. London: Verso, 2003.

Wainwright, H., with M. Little. *Public Service Reform . . . But not as we know it! A story of how democracy can make public services genuinely efficient*. Great Britain: Picnic Publishing, 2009.

Walton, P., A. Gamble and J. Coulter. "Philosophical anthropology in Marxism". *Social Research* 37 (1970).

Walton, P., A. Gamble and J. Coulter. "Image of man in Marx". *Social Theory and Practice* I (1970).

Walton, P., and A. Gamble. *From Alienation to Surplus Value*. London: Sheed and Ward, 1972.

Walton, P., J. Coulter and A. Gamble. "Marx and Marcuse". *The Human Context* III (1971).

Webb, S., and B. Webb. *Soviet Communism: A new civilization*. London and New York: Longmans, Green, 1937.

Weber, M. *The Protestant Ethic and the Spirit of Capitalism*. Tranlated by Talcott Parsons. London: Allen & Unwin, 1930.

Weber, M. *Science as a Vocation*. London: Routledge and Kegan Paul, Ltd, 1948.

Willman, J. "Man in the News: The Seeds of a Political Storm—Raymond Plant". *Financial Times*, 3 April 1993. Accessed 21 April 2014. www.lexisnexis.com/uk/business.

Wood, E. *The Retreat from Class: a new 'true' socialism*. London: Verso Editions, 1986.

Wood J., and R. Woods, eds. *Friedrich A. Hayek: Critical Assessments, Volume II*. London: Routledge, 1991.

Woodcock, G. *The Crystal Spirit: A Study of George Orwell*. Harmondsworth: Penguin, 1970, originally 1967.

Wootton, B. *Freedom under Planning*. Chapel Hill: University of North Carolina Press, 1945.

Wright, T. "Arguments for a New-Left—Wainwright, H.". *Political Quarterly* 66, 1 (1995).

INDEX

arguments, 52; and Wainwright's
arguments, 21, 69–74, 81–83, 87, 93
Kun, Béla, 4
Kurzweil, Ray, 75

Laborde, Cécile, 90
The Labour Party (UK): 1983 General
Election, 3, 13, 18, 49; and class, 43;
and crisis of the 1970s, 97; and
electoral failure, 32; and Miller, 23;
New, 1, 3, 32, 45, 58, 64–66, 95, 118,
126, 132, 137–140; and Plant, 49–50,
52, 55; during post-war period, 7, 9,
63, 83, 91–92, 124; and socialism, 11,
131; and Wainwright, 82, 125
Lamont, Norman, 101
the 'landslide', 9, 96–97, 107, 130
Lane, Joseph, 41, 125
Lange, Oskar, 35, 70
Laski, Harold, 25, 40, 87–90, 104, 126,
133
Law, Legislation and Liberty, 13, 33
left-liberalism, 65–66, 142. *See also*
liberalism, new
left-right distinction, 60, 70–71, 105, 106,
108, 119, 134, 160n77
Le Grand, Julian, 18, 29, 32, 34, 45, 52,
66, 137–138
Lenin, Vladimir, 79
Lerner, Abba, 70, 72
Liberal Socialism, 117, 142
liberal-capitalism and Fukuyama, 114
liberalism, 2, 25, 26, 46, 99, 119, 122, 133,
135; anti-rationalist, 103; classical, 22,
109, 118, 140; 'death of', 132;
economic, 22, 47, 123; and Hayek,
11–12; Hegelian, 50, 111; left, 65–66,
142; and market socialism, 19; and
Marxism, 113; new, 20, 25, 51, 64–66,
95, 107, 109, 114–118, 132; political,
33; radical, 126; revival of, 118, 122;
social, 47, 132; and socialism, 142. *See
also* libertarianism; neo-liberalism
libertarianism, 3, 8–9, 26, 29, 33–34, 40,
65, 69, 72, 84, 90, 93, 110, 123
liberty, 10, 21, 26, 30, 39–40, 65, 86, 128,
137, 158n52; and the left, 50, 79, 87,
125; and markets, 13, 36, 39–40, 44,
46, 66, 127–128, 137–138; and

modernity, 110–116; negative, 10, 56,
59, 107, 112, 136, 157n51; positive,
20–21, 59–60, 62, 114, 116–117, 123,
132, 140; value of, 60–61, 140
light-touch financial regulation, 139
Livingstone, Ken, 136
Lloyd, John, 50
Luard, Evan, 64

Mach, Ernest, 76
Mackintosh, John, 64
Macmillan, Harold, 6
Maine, Henry, 110
Mallock, William Hurrell, 105
Mandelson, Peter, 140
Mandeville, Bernard, 103
'market fundamentalism', 131
markets: arguments against, 39–40, 140;
arguments for,. *See also* knowledge
36–37, 52, 55–56, 59; and community,
41–44; financial, 139–141; and
freedom,; liberty 39–40, 127–128; and
Gamble, 95, 97, 105–107, 109, 112,
116; and growth, 3, 139–140; and
Hayek, 4, 6, 11; and ideology, 2; and
the left, 17, 23–24; and Miller, 36–37,
39–44; and New Labour, 3, 136–140;
and paternalism, 123; and Plant,
55–56, 59; 'socialised', 90; and think
tanks, 12; and Wainwright, 74–77; See
also *market socialism*
Marquand, David, 118, 132
Marx, Karl, 39, 42, 44, 54, 129
Marxism, 15, 37, 65, 95–98, 107, 113, 116;
post-, 134
Marxism Today, 43
Merriam, Charles, 8
Miliband, David, 131
Mill, John Stuart, 25, 34, 59–60, 107
Miller, David, 1, 126, 127–128, 133, 135,
141; engagement with Hayek, 15,
18–21, 23–47; and Gamble, 107; and
Labour, 137; and Plant, 49–50, 52,
132, 136; and Wainwright, 71, 92, 126,
142
minimum wage, 139–140
Modena, 78, 80
modernity, 110–115
Mont Pelerin Society, 12–13

Morris, William, 30, 41–42, 87, 125
Mouffe, Chante, 134
Myrdal, Gunnar, 13

nationalism, 19, 38, 42, 136
nationalization, 13, 52, 63, 71, 105, 137
Nazism, 3, 6, 102, 134
Nazi-Soviet pact, 129
neo-liberalism, 11, 20, 52–54, 56–57, 59, 60–62, 63–64, 69, 72–73, 81, 83, 88, 139
New Economic Policy (NEP), USSR, 116
New Labour. *See* The Labour Party (UK)
New Left Review, 18, 70, 72
The New Republic, 7
new right, 1, 9, 11, 13–14, 16, 18, 20, 29–30, 33–34, 46, 49–50, 55, 63, 92, 99, 101–102, 105, 107, 117, 123, 129, 131
'New Times', 43, 100
Nove, Alexander, 18, 35, 73, 129
Nozick, Robert, 33, 110

orders: made, 108, 132; spontaneous, 11, 21, 77, 105, 108, 112–113
Orwell, George, 8–9, 30, 42, 84, 147n41, 147n44
O'Sullivan, Noel, 103
ownership: private, 23, 106–107, 109, 116–117; social or communal, 23, 34, 37, 107; state or public, 104–105, 107, 123, 132

Paine, Thomas, 82, 126
Parsons, Talcott, 110
paternalism, 2, 9, 15, 21, 40–41, 46, 66, 83, 87, 93, 106, 117, 123–129, 131–132
Pierson, Christopher, 35
Pilkington, Andrew, 42
Pinochet, Augusto, 74
Pirie, Madsen, 11
Plant, Raymond, 1, 11, 15, 18, 128, 132, 136, 142; engagement with Hayek's arguments, 18–21, 49–67; and Gamble, 117; and Labour, 137–138, 140; and Miller, 32, 38, 42–43
pluralism, 2, 19, 21, 40–41, 44, 46, 69, 83, 87–90, 93, 102, 126–127, 129–130, 132–133, 142. *See also* value pluralism

Polanyi, Michael, 12, 76
political theory, rise of, 33–34, 152n41
'poll' tax, 101
Popper, Karl, 12, 62, 103
Porto Alegre, 82
poverty, 32, 80, 87
Powell, Enoch, 97, 105
'Prawn cocktail offensive', 139
price system, 36–37, 70–71, 76–77
privatization, 13, 137, 139
progress, 32, 82, 110–111. *See also* modernity
Prospect, 42, 95, 102
Proudhon, Pierre-Joseph, 41
Public Private Partnerships, 139

quasi-markets, 32, 139

rationalism and critiques, 11, 54, 103, 125, 130
rationalization, 111–113
The Reader's Digest, 6, 9
Red Pepper, 1, 69, 84
religion, 112, 130, 136
rights, 107, 125–127; property, 56, 106–107; and responsibilities, 57, 107; and social movements, 83; social or welfare, 38, 53; workers', 39
The Road to Serfdom, 1, 3, 6–9, 12–13, 16, 36, 53, 84, 110–111, 123, 148n47
Robbins, Lionel, 5, 12
Roemer, John, 15, 35
Rowbotham, Sheila, 85
Runciman, Walter Garrison (Garry), 127

Samurai class, 124
Schmitt, Carl, 3, 102, 134, 172n52
schools, 12, 66, 82
secularization, 113
Segal, Lynne, 85
Seldon, Arthur, 17–18
Sen, Amartya, 16, 60
'short twentieth century', 96, 100, 102, 115, 118–119, 122, 126, 130–133, 138, 171n35; and ideology, 134–136, 142
Smith, Adam, 17, 70, 103
social democracy. *See* socialism.
social liberalism, 21, 47, 117. *See also* liberalism, new